FEDERALISM, CITIZENSHIP, AND QUEBEC: DEBATING MULTINATIONALISM

The question of multinationalism has largely been treated as an issue that needs to be 'solved,' implying a negative but temporary situation that threatens the integrity of the political system. In *Federalism, Citizenship, and Quebec*, Alain-G. Gagnon and Raffaele Iacovino argue that multinationalism has been and continues to be the fundamental socio-political characteristic of the Canadian polity, and that it should guide and structure the negotiating principles and political processes upon which the institutions of federalism and citizenship are constructed.

The authors address future challenges for Quebec and for Canada, including the persistence of competing nationalisms, the federal compact in the global era, the impact of post-national citizenship on minority nations, and a reassessment of the relationship between citizenship and federalism. Drawing on historical accounts and contemporary critical theory, they provide an alternative picture of Quebec's contribution, presenting a conception of Canada's potential as an open, multinational federation committed to diverse conceptions of citizenship and a novel approach to constitutional association. In the final analysis, this study suggests a new model of federalism and citizenship that recognizes multinationalism as a cornerstone of belonging to Canada, for both citizens and governments of its respective political communities.

ALAIN-G. GAGNON is the director of the Centre de recherche interdisciplinaire sur la diversité au Québec (CRIDAQ) and holds the Canada Research Chair in Quebec and Canadian Studies in the Department of Political Science at l'Université du Québec à Montréal.

RAFFAELE IACOVINO is a PhD candidate in the Department of Political Science at McGill University and a research associate in the Department of Political Science at l'Université du Québec à Montréal.

D1260658

ALAIN-G. GAGNON AND RAFFAELE
IACOVINO

Federalism, Citizenship, and Quebec

Debating Multinationalism

UNIVERSITY OF TORONTO PRESS
Toronto Buffalo London

© University of Toronto Press Incorporated 2007
Toronto Buffalo London
Printed in Canada

ISBN-13: 978-0-8020-9216-8 (cloth)
ISBN-10: 0-8020-9216-0 (cloth)
ISBN-13: 978-0-8020-9448-3 (paper)
ISBN-10: 0-8020-9448-1 (paper)

Printed on acid-free paper

Library and Archives Canada Cataloguing in Publication

Gagnon, Alain-G. (Alain-Gustave), 1954–
    Federalism, citizenship, and Quebec : debating multinationalism / Alain-G.
    Gagnon and Raffaele Iacovino.

    Includes bibliographical references and index.
    ISBN-13: 978-0-8020-9216-8 (bound)
    ISBN-10: 0-8020-9216-0 (pbk.)
    ISBN-13: 978-0-8020-9448-3 (bound)
    ISBN-10: 0-8020-9448-1 (pbk.)

    1. Canada – Politics and government.   2. Citizenship – Canada.
    3. Multiculturalism – Canada.   4. Federal-provincial relations – Canada.
    5. Québec (Province) – History – Autonomy and independence movements.
    I. Iacovino, Raffaele   II. Title.

    FC105.M8G35 2006   971   C2006-903361-7

This book has been published with the help of a grant from the Canadian
Federation for the Humanities and Social Sciences, through the Aid to
Scholarly Publications Programme, using funds provided by the Social
Sciences and Humanities Research Council of Canada.

University of Toronto Press acknowledges the financial assistance to its
publishing program of the Canada Council for the Arts and the Ontario
Arts Council.

University of Toronto Press acknowledges the financial support for its
publishing activities of the Government of Canada through the Book
Publishing Industry Development Program (BPIDP).

To Louiselle and Vincent; Marie-Ève and Zoé

Contents

Acknowledgments

This book constitutes the synthesis of many years of exchange between the authors that began at McGill University within the activities of the Quebec Studies Program (PEQ), and continued without interruption at the Canada Research Chair in Quebec and Canadian Studies (CREQC) at l'Université du Québec à Montréal. This research was in large part inspired by the ideas of Charles Taylor, whose work has touched Quebec politics and society like no other, as well as the contributions, individually and collectively, of the members of the Research Group on Plurinational Societies (GRSP): André Lecours, Jocelyn Maclure, Geneviève Nootens, Pierre Noreau, François Rocher, James Tully, and José Woehrling.

Our ideas have been tested in front of a variety of scholarly conferences and have especially benefited from comments made by Frances Abele, James Bickerton, Roberto Breña, Michael Burgess, Alan C. Cairns, Linda Cardinal, Jan Erk, Joseph Garcea, Dimitrios Karmis, Michael Keating, Will Kymlicka, Guy Laforest, Sean Loughlin, Ramon Maiz, David McCrone, Kenneth McRoberts, Luis Moreno, Alain Noël, Bhikhu Parekh, and Alan Patten, as well as Ferran Requejo, Richard Simeon, and Luc Turgeon.

We would also like to acknowledge the helpful criticism and suggestions provided by the two anonymous reviewers as well as the assessors at the University of Toronto Press Manuscript Review Committee. For their financial support, we wish to thank the Aid to Scholarly Publications Programme (ASPP), the Fonds Québécois de la recherche sur la société et la culture (FQRSC) and the Social Sciences and Humanities Research Council of Canada (SSHRC). We also appreciate the professional efforts of those at the University of Toronto Press for bringing this project to fruition, particularly Virgil Duff (executive editor), Anne Laughlin (managing editor) and Diane Mew (copy editor). Luc Turgeon was extremely helpful in accepting to produce the index for this book, and we thank him.

Finally, the ideas explored in this book benefited significantly from the many informal and enjoyable exchanges with colleagues at the CREQC, including Fiona Barker, Olivier De Champlain, Jaime Lluch, Hugo Rangel, Charles-Antoine Sévigny, and Devrim Yavuz.

FEDERALISM, CITIZENSHIP, AND QUEBEC:
DEBATING MULTINATIONALISM

1 Introduction: Exploring Multinationalism

The 'Quebec question,' a familiar refrain to all Canadians, often elicits hostile reactions in the rest of Canada. It is seen as the catalyst of a seemingly endless political quagmire that is either taken seriously as a threat to the integrity of the country, or dismissed altogether as a cynical power grab by opportunistic interests – a consequence rather than a cause of a de-centralized polity. In such a light, Quebec is taken as anathema to our intuitions about liberal principles, at once undermining justice and stability by wilfully fragmenting the ties that bind Canadians together and undermining deeply held beliefs about equality. Why would anyone want to disrupt what is obviously a successful experiment in tolerance, diversity, liberty, and equality, based on shared values that representatives of this country openly tout as Canada's export to the world?

This book will provide an alternative picture of Quebec's contribution, presenting a conception of Canada's potential as an open, multinational federation committed to diverse conceptions of citizenship and a novel approach to constitutional association. Moreover, it will demonstrate that the Quebec case, in the process of persistent existential inquiry and an unwavering assertion of the right to self-determination, has been a significant rallying point for a burgeoning field of study centred on multinational federalism as a fruitful normative category in negotiating the constitutional possibilities of states composed of two or more nations. To be more specific, we believe that it provides a step forward in achieving Canada's promise – of eventually constituting itself based on principles that are unique and authentic to its history, its society, and its national and cultural diversity. Rather than instantly alienating Canadians as an irritant, in both English and

French Canada, the Quebec question ought to be embraced as an essential aspect of what it means to be Canadian in our ongoing self-examination and growth as a 'model' country. At a minimum, this book hopes to demonstrate that in exploring a history of self-determination in Quebec, in all its political manifestations, those both professionally and casually engaged in the 'Canadian conversation' will begin to listen.

No end of debates about unity and diversity in Canada have been produced. This discussion does not purport to provide a settled answer to the problem of the defining characteristics of the Canadian political community. Part of the reason for this is that conceptualizing Canada as a multinational democracy, along the lines that will be developed below, acknowledges the incomplete nature for the Canadian self-understanding as a constitutive feature of the polity. Canada can grapple all it wants with questions of national unity, but Quebec will always be there demanding the rightful accommodation of its status as a majoritarian democratic space within the larger federation. The problem, in a sense, lies with the use of the imperative of national unity as a structuring principle for the debate in the first place. Even the term 'diversity,' in many contexts, adds to the confusion in the Canadian debate, since diversity itself does little to address the multinational condition. All liberal democratic states are diverse, and they must all respond to questions about how they define themselves as political communities, and how to structure democratic institutions and citizenship accordingly. Moreover, the shortcomings of the Canadian debate with regards to its self-understanding can even be discerned in the language employed in addressing the Quebec question specifically. If this book can get only one point across, we sincerely hope that it alters our conceptions of Canada enough so that rather than asking 'What does Quebec want?' we will move on to structure the debate around the idea that 'This is what Quebec is.' While many constitutive elements of the Canadian political community are open to new conceptions and norms, to new power dynamics and identities, the existence of Quebec as a self-determining nation is simply not open to negotiation. Once this is recognized, then the Canadian debate can move forward. Until it is, we can continue to deny Quebec its rightful status while we discuss diversity, tolerance, multiculturalism, civic nationalism, symmetrical federalism, individual and collective rights, difference and equality, differentiated citizenship, and so on, but the conversation will take place for Quebec as opposed to with Quebec.

Again, the purpose here is not to have any pretence of speaking for Quebec. However, we hope to carry the debate forward by demonstrating that the project for self-determination in Quebec, in the areas of citizenship and federalism, is well advanced and is not going to retreat. The imperative of addressing Quebec's place in Canada stems from over one hundred years of democratic activity and nationalist contestation in Quebec; we hope that this book will allow interlocutors in the Canadian debate to take this fact seriously and not reduce the project to some phenomenon that is characterized simply as a 'problematique.'

Like any political community, the narrative of Quebec's self-definition is ongoing and characterized by contestation. With regards to its status as an internal nation within Canada, we can conclude that there is significant consensus across the political party spectrum. Perhaps one day in the near future Quebec and Canadian students of these matters may look back at this period and wonder why it took so long, through so much acrimony, bitterness and, in some instances, injustice, for the imperative of multinationalism to begin to structure our will to live together, our bases of solidarity, mutual trust and confidence. In short, simply referring to the debate itself and claiming that this is the essence of who 'we' are as Canadians is not enough if those that are supposed to be actively following, participating, and applying the agreed-upon conclusions of the debate fail to appreciate what Quebec *is* in the first place.

Finally, we would like to say a word about what many will perhaps argue is an obvious omission from this text. Upon embarking on this project, we decided to focus on Quebec, even though many of the conclusions about the multinational condition apply equally to Aboriginal peoples of Canada. This is not an omission that signals an implicit normative position; it was simply a decision to remain focused and to make the project more manageable. Indeed, redefining Canadian citizenship and federalism along multinational lines obviously applies to First Nations as well, yet their history in terms of challenges, relations with the central state, their place in the federal structure, and citizenship status is simply too large to include in a book of this size and focus.

The approach adopted in this study is both theoretical and historical. It follows what Joseph Carens has called 'a contextual approach to political theory.'[1] While abstract theorizing points to conceptual contradictions and generally allows for a framework for normative debate in various areas of interest, this approach permits the theorist to include the historical, political, and moral aspects of 'hard cases.' Without the historical part, we may fail to see some justifications that form part of the context. Without a consideration of politics, we may fail to see the element of power between competing claims that are, by themselves, morally defensible. For example, some competing rights claims, equally based on strong moral grounding, often come into conflict. Context allows the researcher to ground such claims in particular settings which may reveal justifications and legitimating factors that cannot be brought to light in the abstract. This approach has gained ground among theorists in Canada precisely because of its capacity to apply questions of abstract political theory to what many consider a 'theoretical anomaly.' There is no better case than Canada to discuss questions of identity, belonging, nation-building and, generally, federalism and citizenship, because sorting out its self-understanding seems to be Canada's intellectual contribution to the world. Indeed, as this book will demonstrate, the multination is particularly sensitive to context since abstract political theory, from both liberal and critical perspectives, in many ways serves to justify the status quo, since many basic assumptions of these approaches are simply not concerned with the boundaries of political communities and thus, implicitly, take political societies as fixed in time and place. Indeed, many perspectives that view minority nationalism as a retrograde phenomenon implicitly draw upon such theoretical approaches that assume political stability to be constant. A contextual turn in political theory has the virtue of attempting to attribute some consideration to the actions and thinking of those who legislate or make decisions on these matters. Abstract thought experiments based in counterfactual reasoning or 'what if' scenarios do have a place in this approach, since they still draw on real-world cases and the context surrounding them in developing theoretical formulations. What is avoided here, specifically, is the temptation to achieve 'grand theories' with universal application. In Canada, in particular, history has taught us that this is impossible in practice and in theory.

Towards the end of the 1970s, political theory witnessed a profound transformation in focus, with questions centred mainly on redistributive justice giving way to a closer examination of the relationship between various layers of identities and their impact on liberal theory and correlating institutional configurations. Due largely to conditions associated with transnational interdependence and globalization, as well as developments within liberal theory in which the concepts of individual and collective rights and related concerns about the confines of liberty and equality have been re-conceptualized to include broader social forces, the result has been to signal profound changes in the normative force of the Westphalian model of the nation-state. Generally, the model has been associated with various empirical indicators, including 1) political centrism and functional criteria for the evaluation of effective governance; 2) in 'national level' politics, a pluralism that implied the creation of majorities around coalitions of interests; 3) a uniformist conception of federalism that tended to disregard the claims of national minorities in favour of growing centralization as a progressive imperative; 4) the goal of assimilation or outright non-membership for migrants; and 5) a clear link between majority nations, sovereignty, and citizenship organized around fixed territorial boundaries.

This re/conceptualization of the Westphalian model opened up numerous avenues for exploration which touched on the role of national identity as a legitimate organizing principle for the state, its relationship to citizenship, the institutional role of federalism in addressing identity-based social cleavages, and the place of culture and other group identities that challenge monocultural and uninational conceptions of liberal-democratic political systems. The relatively linear and straightforward link that was assumed to exist between national identity, sovereignty, citizenship, and territory became a source of protracted contestation among theorists, including normative exercises in deconstruction and reconstruction of the bases of legitimate political and social orders that in many ways outpaced perceived empirical transformations of the state and the state system.[2]

Will Kymlicka has provided a useful overview of the changing currents in political theory with regards to these developments, identifying three clear stages.[3] First, in the 1980s, the liberal/communitarian debate revolved around criticism of liberal justice as formulated by John Rawls.[4] For Rawls, citizens were to enjoy various primary rights that trumped collective conceptions of the good. Communitarians initially questioned whether individual well-being and autonomy could be conceptualized outside of the experiences and context provided by particular communities. This led to debates about the extent to which the state should be concerned about collective goods that may signal a more authentic concern for individual autonomy, and a general attempt to situate the phenomenon of identity and culture in theorizing about liberal justice.

In a second stage, in the 1990s, the debate crystallized within the parameters of liberalism itself in an attempt to reconcile the idea that certain collective rights constitute a primary good, alongside individual rights. This discourse eventually culminated in theoretical frameworks which rested on the idea of particular cultures serving as contexts of choice and autonomy for individuals. Without such group identities, 'individuals are atomistic, not autonomous.'[5] No longer would liberalism be associated with strict conceptions of cultural neutrality. Indeed, many such approaches sought to rethink the idea of the neutral state, claiming in its place that all nation-states rest on an implicit foundation of a dominant culture and their active nation-building projects over time.[6] The main sticking points here centred on the extent to which the recognition of collective goods (for example, minority nations or ethnocultural groups) may entail limitations on individual members of such groups.

A school of thought of liberal nationalists[7] emerged to show how nationalism and liberalism are not incompatible doctrines – indeed, many of the dispositions required of liberal citizens are provided by national identity and communities organized around these sentiments of belonging as a basis for citizenship. The neutral liberal state in practice had been constructed around a dominant national culture, or at least this was the attempt of state policy. In this view, legitimate and effective democracy requires a well-defined *demos*, united around common values and symbols, and social consensus, without which there would be no durable measures of confidence and solidarity. As such, the traditional liberal response of nation-building through assimilation and uniform individual rights, undifferentiated citizenship, and neutrality in matters pertaining to cultural identity is not applicable in multinational settings, since the context of choice for autonomy and individual well-being for citizens of minority nations already exists as an established 'societal culture.'[8] Internal nations will always be politically dependent on the will of the dominant national majority if they are not recognized or accommodated as separate *demoi*. Moreover, certain socio-cultural ascriptive groups that cannot be qualified as 'nations' yet rely on culture or other collective identities as sources of experiential context can no longer be assimilated into the larger societies as individuals. This would deny the premise of culture serving as a primary good in the realization of individual autonomy and self-actualization. Liberal polities were thus forced to come to terms with established collective identities; they cannot be created and re-created and taken as interest groups, as a by-product of freedom of association. Indeed, Will Kymlicka even goes so far as to ask whether a 'liberal culturalist' consensus has taken hold in the field.[9]

At the same time, a more radical line of criticism that questioned the idea that liberal justice and equality entails strictly neutral individual rights looked specifically at the institutionalization of cultural pluralism. The most forceful defence of this approach was undertaken by Iris Marion Young, who introduced the idea of 'differentiated citizenship,' whereby different groups with distinct constituted identities ought to be treated differently, through actual institutional design, if the goal of citizenship is equality.[10] Liberalism and its application to the ends of just institutions could no longer avoid the thorny questions associated with constituted group identities.[11] Indeed, the idea that all groups in a liberal order are the result of freedom of association, and are constantly taking shape according to evolving interests in a 'free market' of belonging, had been convincingly dispelled; there were indeed some collective identities that could not be incorporated through an emphasis on individual rights as a basis for citizenship. While this group of critical theorists[12] reject basic liberal premises and institutions, theorists like Young did manage to speak to very similar concerns that were being questioned in the liberal framework. In particular, Young highlighted the unavoidable effects of power, domination, and historical oppression on the prospects for autonomy and meaningful participation for minority socio-cultural identities.

Others sought to retrieve the promise of liberalism by combining normative and empirical arguments in making the case for postnationalism, or cosmopolitanism, in which individual autonomy and equality is the goal but not necessarily 'fostered' by national boundaries. This tradition essentially builds on the cosmopolitanism of Immanuel Kant.[13] In this view, the rights and duties associated with citizenship are no longer confined to the nation-state. New forms of citizenship that transcend the particular markers of national identity such as language, culture or ethnicity may lead individuals to consider more seriously the imperatives of justice and moral obligations on a universal level, as being applicable to humanity as a whole. Many such arguments point directly to empirical developments associated with globalization and claim that the nation-state is no longer viable in providing for meaningful citizenship and democratic self-government. Moreover, identities themselves are being transformed by global integration; citizens are not assumed now to be bound by sentiments of belonging that are defined by territorially based national identity and citizenship. In short, mobilization, interests, and collective identities are no longer organized within the sovereign nation-state and are not viewed primarily in material terms. For David Held, perhaps the leading theorist of cosmopolitanism, democracy and citizenship are thus thrown wide open for re-conceptualization, including questions about the nature of primary political units, the role of representation, the form and strength of political participation, and the very relevance of the nation-state as a source of rights, duties, and general well-being of citizens.[14]

This 'multicultural' and 'postnational' turn in political theory thus came to reveal the difficulties associated with sorting out the boundaries, of both group identities that were to be subjects of group-differentiated rights within established citizenship regimes in the name of equality, and collective identities that were claiming separate citizenship regimes altogether, even in a limited and shared sense, within or outside of established nation-states, in which the rights and obligations of membership were subject to the democratic process. Thus a third stage was characterized by attempts to look more closely at legitimacy associated with processes of nation-building, the question of re-conceptualising citizenship in order that it fulfills its promise of inclusion in internally diverse and transnational societies, and generally, to question the limits and potential of multicultural and nationalist demands in light of democratic theory. This trajectory sought to ground theories of belonging away from a mere acceptance of the existence of pre-political cultures and has begun to expand the very sources of unity and diversity that are normatively defensible.[15]

As this brief overview suggests, the nation-state and its place in liberal theory has been under attack from below and from above. Recent debates have looked more closely at the actual processes whereby such relations are deemed to be legitimate. The normative element of questions of citizenship, democracy, representation, and sovereignty have moved to consider non-essentialist views of national and cultural identity and the processes through which such identities are articulated, institutionalized, and evolving. In other words, theorists have moved towards an attempt to gain a deeper understanding of some of the concepts that were assumed to be constant (such as culture, identity, and self-determination) and the relevance of these observations on multinational, federal, and multicultural institutions. Indeed, the prominent example of liberal democracies in which many of these questions continue to be debated is the multinational federation. Not only have these states' territorial divisions been called into question, but a whole array of issues related to national, social, and cultural pluralism began to be played out in this contested field of political theory, as though the empirical key to understanding the waning of the nation-state could be found here. Suddenly, the discourse surrounding political legitimacy turned from an emphasis on state stability, domestic order, and unitarist conceptions of sovereignty, citizenship, and national identity, to novel and revealing concepts such as diversity, multiculturalism, toleration, postnationalism, postsovereignty, and differentiated citizenship.

A multinational democracy as will be conceptualized here, while enshrining the principle of self-determination for its constituent nations, does not seek to replicate the nation-state's propensity to forge political and cultural homogenization as the basis for citizenship and its political institutions more broadly. This type of association is not indifferent to internal diversity. A multinational democracy is a specific type of political association that defines itself as democratic, yet is endowed with distinct layers of internal diversity; both national and socio-cultural pluralism must be negotiated in determining the right balance between individual and collective rights as a basis of citizenship. It is our contention that a radical postmodern turn that seeks to deconstruct identities, while valuable in demonstrating that questions of belonging to groups is generated through various social interactions over time and not a static and essentialist phenomenon, is nevertheless analogous to a neutrality-based liberalism in its failure to establish certain empirical boundaries within which democratic processes are played out. In concrete fashion, nations are where individuals flourish, enjoy rights, participate, share resources, debate in a common language, and so on. These acts of participation do occur on smaller scales, in cultural groups, within ascriptive identities related to gender and sexual orientation, and even in groups that form as a result of socio-economic interests, or more generally due to freedom of association – yet they have not been constructed to address fundamental 'political' issues, with the legitimacy and fundamental justice provided by the twin notions of accountability and representation that are reflected in the territorial nation-form.

Our focus will not specifically address the salience of identity politics and the role of ascriptive identities in new conceptions of citizenship and federalism. Democracy is indeed a key variable, but democracy functions best, at least for the time being, in the conditions provided by the nation form, and is understood to complement the principles of federalism, citizenship and self-determination in a larger picture concerned with the legitimacy of a democratic polity that is constituted by more than one national group. As such, we question the premise of this postmodern perspective that seeks to dilute understandings of the nation form, or culture, and rely on abstract theorizing to look for social processes behind the construction of identities. This book will make clear that the nation ought to persist as an organizational norm that contributes to democratic outcomes. It is not enough to turn to democracy as a catch-all and claim that an open-ended and abstract conception of collective identities ought to work out their relationships with one another in order to avoid the contentious issue of a hierarchy of belonging. This hierarchy is indeed established empirically – nations and territory allow us to configure institutions that best respect the principles of representation, accountability, and qualitative 'active' citizenship around which democracy is allowed to flourish. This is not to argue that identities, either cultural or social, in the broad sense, are not politically salient for individuals and should therefore be relegated to the private sphere in a traditional Kantian sense. Democracy ought to be the best avenue through which such identities negotiate their place in society, make a mark on the polity, acquire recognition as groups, make claims, and so on. However, postmodern deconstructionist attempts to extricate group identities from the confines of national politics suffer from the same hollowness as strict 'neutral' liberalism. They do not prescribe or provide a justification for particular contexts of choice that ground the boundaries of the polity. If we see the world as a wide spectrum of interlinked identities that resolve their conflicts through deliberation and democracy, then how do we legitimately delineate negotiating partners in the first place? How do we account for power relations between interlocutors? All groups emerge from somewhere. Assessing empirically-driven 'hard cases,' however, requires the researcher to avoid the lure of relativization of collective identities – this is obfuscating the political challenges associated with multinational democracies, federalism, and citizenship. This book will be about Canada, with a particular focus on Quebec: its perspective as an internal nation, within a multinational democracy.

What happened and how have such changes affected Canadian debates over citizenship and federalism? This book will wade into the perilous waters of Canadian identity, as an attempt to address questions related to citizenship, federalism, and sovereignty from a Quebec perspective. To imply a Quebec perspective may seem to some as sheer nonsense. Obviously, like any plural society, Quebec is endowed with a rich diversity of world views on these questions. However, in the larger Canadian debate about who we are and where we are going together, too many theorists continue to draw upon the Quebec case without a full appreciation of the overwhelming consensus in Quebec on certain constitutional (existential and institutional) positions. Indeed, Quebec nationalism is still interpreted by some observers as a reactionary movement, and others see the phenomenon as a new outcome of globalizing pressures. In the former case, there is a rich and lively debate in Quebec concerning the legitimate foundations of the nation, the role of citizenship, and the bases of belonging more generally, as there are in any open, liberal, democratic political community. With regards to the latter observation, the burgeoning literature on internal nationalist movements has indeed grown impressively, and policy-makers in majority nations can no longer ignore such pressures, but this is due in some degree to Quebec itself – its long-standing commitment to debating its place in Canadian federalism – as a model of democratic claims to self-determination. The movement in Quebec is not a product of novel external pressures; indeed, it has preceded the contemporary social, economic, and political order in which we assess multinational democracies. What is new is that in this emerging setting many of the questions played out in the arena of federalism have been moved to the realm of citizenship. Now, as political scientists, we seek new qualitative frameworks with which to evaluate citizenship, yet Quebec's debates concerning citizen obligations, entitlements, membership, and belonging is not a 'free pass' to reformulate the 'place' of Quebec in Canada. It is up to Quebec, as a political community, to address these aspects of citizenship. Moreover, as the concluding chapter will show, the multination may even be a case that promotes active citizenship as long as it is not stifled by strict forms.

Federalism is most often the preferred institutional configuration to address the challenges of multinationalism. A federal arrangement, in principle, can seek to guarantee autonomy for internal nations by specifying the sharing of sovereignty in a formal constitution. Empirically, however, the persistence of the dominant nation-state model has resulted in attempts by central states to deny the recognition of differences based on national diversity. Instead, it has opted for strict territorial divisions, the recognition of sociocultural diversity, and in some extreme cases, outright assimilation and a consolidated polity based solely of functional criteria for governance. Moreover, federalism is also characterized by divergent historical and theoretical rationales that come into conflict. Many accounts of the virtues of federal systems rely on legitimating principles related to the forming of factions to counter-act excessive intrusions by the state, or the notion that democratic life flourishes in smaller settings. Shaping a federal state along the lines dictated by national boundaries, to the extent that this may result in a concentration of power in the hands of one single member state, may actually contradict the purposes of federalism from these perspectives. Paradoxically, proponents of this view, self-proclaimed federalists, see the central state as somewhat of a caretaker of democracy and liberal rights in the face of 'illiberal' internal nations. Federalism is thus taken to act as a buffer against majoritarian tyranny, yet in what can only be interpreted as ironic, the fear is that this outcome is most likely to occur within a self-determining internal nation that is constantly striving to not be the victim of majority rule.

Canada is often presented abroad as a multinational federation and a multicultural state. It is neither.[16] It may be so rhetorically, perhaps even sociologically, and perhaps many Canadians believe this to be an apt description of the country, but its institutions of federalism and citizen-ship do not reflect these principles. If the notion of difference as the defining feature of the Canadian model is the subject of consensus in the hallways of academia in this country, it is not replicated in our political institutions. The defining aspect of Canadian political life, as it stands now, is an aggressive nation-building project that does little to address some of the underlying challenges associated with diversity and self-determination.[17] From the perspective of Quebec, two introductory points merit consideration. First, Quebec's predominant position with regards to its place in Canada is not the result of new circumstances, as though globalization and a greater awareness for the justice due to internal nations in liberal thought has somehow sparked an awakening. Many of the demands for some measure of self-determination in Que-bec have persisted since the country's founding, and have been sup-ported across partisan lines as a 'Quebec consensus' position. Second, while many attribute recent exogenous developments as inimical to the nation form as the focal point for political mobilization, representation, sovereignty, and generally, citizenship, the trend in Quebec and Canada contradicts such claims. The story of this country is one of competing nationalisms, and this remains the plot to this day, regardless of power-ful ideational trends that either revert back to the neutral liberal model or attempt to reconstruct the place of identity in the Canadian polity altogether.

This introductory chapter has laid out the main challenges associated with the Canadian multinational democracy, with regards to the institutions of federalism, citizenship, and multinationalism. The basic framework for understanding diversity in such a setting is a reciprocal and reinforcing relationship between sociological/ideological conditions and institutions. Institutions are seen to arise out of socio-political challenges and, once established, they define the contours or boundaries of identities and bases of belonging. In the Canadian case, diversity is multilayered, resulting in a complex interplay of political forces in which various political regimes must concurrently address multiple demands for recognition. The case of Canada cannot be grasped without assessing this persistent tension between the various layers of political and social identities. Canadian political and social cleavages, in terms of both formal representation and discursive and legal recognition, have long been defined along regional and linguistic lines. This study will demonstrate that political conflict and the management of diversity in Canada, expressed through the institutions of federalism, citizenship, as well as in the demands of Quebec, can best be assessed through the defining characteristic of multinationalism. This fundamental variable conditions actors' political and social interests and manifests itself persistently, structuring formal negotiation and the general contours of debate in Canada. Even in measures intended to undermine its legal standing such as the Charter of Rights and Freedoms, the policy of multiculturalism, and pan-Canadian bilingualism, the effects of multinationalism are clear in the political processes that informed, or in most cases failed to inform, such formal outcomes. Multinationalism, as a norm in its own right, serves as a conditioning variable in the fields of federalism, citizenship, and on conceptions of national diversity.

The question of multinationalism has largely been treated as an issue that needs to be solved, implying a negative connotation that threatens the integrity of the political system – as though central institutions can simply wish it away. We argue that it has and continues to constitute the fundamental socio-political characteristic of the Canadian polity, and that it should guide and structure the negotiating principles and political processes upon which the institutions of federalism and citizenship are constructed. As a starting point, this would go a long way in maintaining an acceptable balance between unity and diversity in Canada. Multinationalism reveals a political and social setting that is inimical to a teleological understanding of the defining questions of belonging to Canada; there may be no solution to what ails the Canadian political community besides a clear acknowledgment by all negotiating partners that it exists as a sociological fact, that it is a political question that requires mutual recognition, and that it guides and structures the Canadian debate. As it stands now, Canada makes no attempt to reconcile itself with a multinational reality.

Chapter 2 provides an historical overview of evolving attempts by state actors to settle Canada's constitutional impasse. It will begin with a brief theoretical assessment of the impact of multinationalism on our conception of a legitimate constitutional order, including some contemporary challenges associated with accommodating procedural, rights-based entitlements with the substantive provisions required by conceptions of differentiated liberal citizenship based on the recognition of national diversity. As such, both the processes associated with constitutionalism as well as substance will be discussed. In turning to the Canadian experience, the key aspect of multinationalism will be shown to drive the debates throughout the process, particularly from the perspective of Quebec. The idea of competing territorial notions of public space and the challenge of accommodating linguistic and minority groups, as well as Quebec's specificity as a societal culture and its own intentions with regards to constructing the boundaries of belonging for its political community, will be paramount here. The chapter will consist of highlighting successive constitutional orders in Canada since the country's founding, culminating in the particular political philosophy of Pierre Elliott Trudeau and the groundbreaking impact of the Charter of Rights and Freedoms on Canadian constitutional theory and practice.

Chapter 3 will assess the ebbs and flows of Canadian federalism over time, as a result of competing conceptions of representation since the original federal pact. It begins with a review of the conceptual and methodological study of the federal idea, including its institutional and sociological dimensions. In highlighting the salient 'visions' of Canada over the course of its history, federalism emerges conceptually as an ideological principle as opposed to merely an institutional device – as a defining aspect of the country. The chapter will show that the evolution of federalism has tended towards a greater reluctance to accept this fact as a moral imperative in structuring the federation. The country has witnessed an undermining of the federal idea as the common meeting ground for diverse political identities rather than its elevation as a guiding principle in navigating through the diversity of cleavages in

Canadian political life. As such, the chapter will highlight the selective use of particular political identities in the crafting of the contemporary prevailing vision of Canadian federalism, in which the imperative of national unity trumps the notion that federalism implies negotiation and dialogue between territorially based political communities. Essentially, this chapter will focus on the basic positions of the relevant political actors over time in the power relationships that fostered Canadian federalism, culminating in the victory of a conception of representation that does not respect the federal idea.

The national models' view of integration involves the distinct approaches undertaken by states in crafting the boundaries of citizenship with specific regards to immigrant incorporation. Most of the literature on national models takes it for granted that Canada consists of two host societies with two centres of allegiance. Chapter 4 will provide a comparative assessment of the Canadian model of multiculturalism and Quebec's own response to cultural pluralism, its model of interculturalism. Indeed, the case of immigrant integration in Canada is perhaps most revealing of the clash of national projects in Canada. This study contends that the contours of the models themselves stem in large part from this process of competition between two nation-building initiatives. In other words, the variable of multinationalism is ever-present, and the politics of integration involves more than mere linear responses to the challenges of polyethnicity in Canada. We contend that the Canadian model is implicitly aimed at negating a conception of Canadian citizenship based on national diversity, whereas the Quebec model is meant to clearly delineate a distinct political community for immigrants. Canada's self-understanding, through official, constitutionally-protected multiculturalism, does not concede that national identity in Quebec constitutes a centre for allegiance that supersedes other particular loyalties and identities that express themselves on a pan-Canadian level.

Chapter 5 will focus on the contemporary difficulty, both theoretically and in practice, of reconciling liberal citizenship with multinationalism in contemporary democracies. It will begin with a review of contemporary debates and challenges regarding liberal citizenship in contexts that diverge markedly from the ideal, homogeneous nation-state model. The main polemic is, on the one hand, between the traditional function of citizenship as a unifying identity which fosters certain liberal dispositions in the practice of democracy, as a preconceived social contract between individuals that is often taken for granted (a pre-existing and pre-defined political community in the abstract), and, on the other hand, horizontal conceptions of citizenship and their effects on the quality of democracy that must allow for the recognition of diverse polities and a plurality of citizenship spaces if liberal dispositions are to be taken seriously. Assuming or even actively creating political communities and simply 'plugging in' a liberal conception of citizenship in a given territory fails to generate the citizen dispositions required for substantive democratic practice. The chapter will introduce multinational democracies as a distinct field of study in the literature on citizenship, with unique theoretical implications. The bulk of the argument is for a differentiated citizenship which values the process of identity-formation itself, within distinct social and territorial contexts, as opposed to a strict centralized rights regime that is unsuitable for a multinational context, or a radically pluralist conception that makes no claim to circumscribe complete contexts of choice that ground the exercise of democracy. Federalism cannot be divorced from our understanding of citizenship in such a formulation, since our very conceptions of federal relationships, the legal status given to various representative institutions (territorial or otherwise), and the negotiating partners we choose to formally recognize, all serve to structure our understanding of political community in Canada. In such a setting, we contend that active citizenship in Quebec comes to be stifled, pan-Canadian homogenization prevails, and the very basis of the original compromise – the division of powers – is open to non-constitutional penetration by majority forces. Citizens in distinct political communities are witnessing a waning of their options for local mobilization, are conceptualized as exhibiting equal needs across Canada, and are conceived as clients of the central state, receiving both a bundle of rights and a packaged public policy agenda.

The concluding chapter will examine recent developments in Canadian federalism, emphasizing the trend towards non-constitutional renewal and the continuation of the pan-Canadian orthodoxy instilled in 1982. More specifically, it will highlight the increasing encroachment of the federal government in provincial jurisdictions, the Supreme Court's ruling on the Quebec secession reference, and the Clarity Act. Future challenges for the Canadian multination include the persistence of competing nationalisms, moving beyond the politics of recognition to a more activity-centred conception of citizenship affirmation, and a reassessment of the relationship between citizenship and federalism in Canada. Finally, we propose to sketch out a tentative plan through which Canada may build upon the Supreme Court's ruling and adopt an authentic federal system that is sensitive to its multinational character. In the final analysis, this study suggests a model of federalism, citizenship, and multinationalism as a constitutive feature of Canada that encourages and generates an ethos of engagement in Canada – one that recognizes multinationalism as a cornerstone of belonging in Canada, for both citizens and governments of respective political communities.

2 Historical Foundations and Evolving Constitutional Orders: The Politics of Contestation in Quebec

The relationship between democracy and federalism means, for example, that in Canada there may be different and equally legitimate majorities in different provinces and territories and at the federal level. No one majority is more or less 'legitimate' than the others as an expression of democratic opinion (...) A federal system of government enables different provinces to pursue policies responsive to the particular concerns and interests of people in that province.

– Supreme Court of Canada, *Reference re the Secession of Quebec*,
August 1998, section 66.

Multinationalism and Diversity

Seymour Martin Lipset, in *Political Man*, observed that political legitimacy 'involves the capacity of the system to engender and maintain the belief that existing political institutions are the most appropriate ones for the society.'[1] Regardless of the formal legality of political institutions, no political system can be deemed legitimate, at a fundamental level, if it does not represent the will of its members.[2] This implies, of course, that such members consider themselves a 'people,' a body through which consent over a given political structure is granted or withdrawn. Democratic institutions and liberal protections cannot be assumed to be legitimate simply because they follow certain abstract, universal rules – as though liberal democracy can simply be plugged in to an arbitrarily selected territorial space and the result is a legitimate political order. The boundaries of 'society' in Lipset's formulation thus cannot be taken for granted in multinational states.

In studying the foundations and historical evolution of Canadian constitutionalism, the one consistent strand that has survived the test of time is the fact that Quebeckers consider themselves a 'people': not a province like the others, with similar interests and demands on the central government, as though this was simply the result of institutional arrangements; not an ethno-cultural group among many; and not a language group in a bilingual state. Moreover, Quebec is not a mere administrative unit, subordinate to the central government. It is a political nation within a multinational state, a founding member state with its own legitimate representative institutions, legal traditions, and claims on framing citizenship status. This perspective is not the result of political opportunism, as though Quebec's institutions have allowed ambitious political elites in Quebec to seize a given opportunity.[3] Such a theoretical approach seriously undervalues Quebec's socio-historical contribution to Canadian federalism. Quebec does not represent a regional movement; it has always been a national project. For Quebec, Canada as a political unit is legitimate to the extent that it recognizes the principle of dualism as a structuring guide for representative institutions. The country was created as a compact between two founding peoples, and constitutionally, Quebec representatives across partisan lines have exhibited remarkable consistency in maintaining this position.

Multinational diversity in the contemporary era is the foremost constitutive tension at the heart of liberal democratic societies, since it goes beyond primary questions of justice in terms of relations between individual citizens and the state and addresses the appropriate 'people' that are to act as a unit of deliberation and decision. Indeed, questions of justice, when treated from a perspective of ethical individualism,[4] often assume a 'cooperative scheme in perpetuity.'[5] Certain liberal approaches to justice that rely on abstract conceptualizations of social cooperation, however, cannot be easily applied to the case of multinational democracies. Wayne Norman argues that, in multinational states, the language of justice as a first principle, at the expense of considerations of stability, is flawed due to three general concerns. First, justice renders compromise much more difficult. If public justifications for or against various constitutional arrangements are couched in the language of justice, each party will be less likely to stray from their initial positions. Second, neglecting the equally important consideration of stability in the name of justice, as though these goals are trade-offs, is irresponsible in the long term. In multination states, it is important that citizens support the given institutional structure, since constitutions by definition should be difficult to alter and, at a minimum, should not hinder attempts by political actors to work full-time on basic questions related to social cooperation. Unstable institutions may result in cease-less constitutional crises, reflecting a contested social contract, before the contract itself may be claimed to be just or unjust. Third, one group in a multination state is more likely to accept constitutional change seeking to accommodate another group if it can be assured that this will not result in a zero-sum scenario in which one group's gain is another's loss. This may require that negotiations go beyond looking at the inter-ests of the minority group and to simultaneously accept an approach which seeks to ensure that every group is secure in its interests. As such, this may require that stability, identity, and justice are all given equal standing as normative principles in constitutional discourse. In short, as Norman contends,

> It is noteworthy that when Rawls himself is claiming that justice is the first virtue of social institutions, such that it cannot be sacrificed for other goods, he is explicitly talking about a conception of justice based on indi-vidual rights. He is not claiming that whatever you end up calling a matter of justice, it is *ipso facto* the first virtue of social institutions! It is quite likely that many of the institutional changes that are debated in the constitu-tional politics of multination states are more or less neutral in terms of their impact on the basic civil and political rights of individual citizens ... It matters not just that one's state is *just*, but also that it is *one's* state, the state one can identify with.[6]

The question of simultaneously addressing social pluralism in con-stitutional discourse, on the other hand, may actually constrain the ability of institutional tools such as federation to permit a workable accommodation between peoples in multination states, particularly when the idea of 'managing diversity' fails to account for the layered quality of diversity. Federalism in multinational democracies is about recognizing the appropriate majorities for institutional accommodation and sovereignty; in multination states, such majorities cannot simply be invented or engineered – they are pre-existing and self-determining. It is then up to these majorities to address the challenges of social plu-ralism that all liberal democratic states are confronted with, including questions regarding minority rights and identity politics. These collec-tive 'national' groupings precede formal constitutional status.[7]

Indeed, one significant marker of a constituent nation is that attempts at 'refashioning community' (to use Cairns's depiction)[8] in the larger political context – the notion that constitutions serve to shape the boundaries of political communities – simply falls flat within the society of the national group which rejected the arrangement in the first place. Constitutions, in a more narrow sense, establish the parameters of factors generally described under the heading 'political culture' to describe politically meaningful boundaries and relations between citizens, civil society, and the state. In contrast, where the actual construction of the constitutive principles of a political system – the process and substance of this refashioning – does not 'take,' as is evident in Quebec, this may in itself indicate the qualitative distinction between 'peoples' and social actors as constitutive subjects. In other words, constitutions may play a meaningful role in shaping and reshaping communities, but the principles of sovereignty for national groups that seek majority status cannot be wished away through the creation of universal institutions. This is a process for negotiation, not for legal imposition.[9]

How best to represent French and English Canadians into constitutionally self-governing institutions? Until patriation of the Canadian constitution in 1982, this was the fundamental starting point of constitutional debates in Canada, and it remains largely so in Quebec today. Debates surrounding relevant majorities in certain areas of governance informed the initial distribution of powers in 1867. Subsequent constitutional negotiations and judicial decisions regarding sovereignty over given policy areas have all been guided by principles that have less to do with efficacy from a functional standpoint, and more about the legitimacy and recognition of territorial political communities. In this sense, Canada has always been a work in progress, lacking an essential founding myth that is shared by all citizens. Describing the outcome of 1982, Peter Russell observed that, 'patriation was complete but the patria had not defined itself.'[10] Indeed, if a country's amending formula represents the ultimate expression of where constitutional sovereignty is situated (citizens, social groups, provincial or federal governments, the judiciary, national constituents, and so on), then the mere fact that the Canada has never had a formal amendment procedure that is acceptable to Quebec reveals the unfinished nature of the Canadian federal project. Even the development of a rights consciousness, culminating in the entrenchment of a Charter of Rights and Freedoms in 1982 – seemingly concerned with the shielding of citizens from governments in a neutral, liberal tradition – in effect recognizes some groups and individuals to the detriment of others, giving it a marked 'national' quality on a pan-Canadian level by strengthening the ties of citizens to Canadian institutions.

As this overview of Canadian constitutionalism will show, Quebec's position with regards to its place in Canada has survived generational shifts, international political transformations, and mostly, domestic social currents both in the larger Canadian context and in Quebec, demonstrating remarkable consistency with regards to its existential standing. From both a socio-historical and historical-institutional perspectives, Quebec's place in Canada has rarely shifted, and when it has, it has been a matter of degree as opposed to a wholesale reconceptualization.

Constitution, Political Community, and Society: A Question of Sovereignty

Constitutionalism in multinational democracies, for purposes of legitimacy, must account not only for questions of justice, though it is a central aspect, but for identity and stability as well. These considerations must be addressed together in the management of diversity. In balancing between collective and individual rights, constitutions also recognize social categories, based on such characteristics as gender, sexual orientation, ethnicity, disabilities. As the previous section highlights, such challenges cannot be discussed from an approach that rests either on ethical individualism, radical cultural pluralism, or civic republicanism, if each is taken in isolation. This notion of recognizing constituent national minorities as but another social category – taken together as constitutional actors in a broad sense – confuses the purpose of constitutionalism in multinational settings on two fronts.

First, it fails to make explicit the distinction between the interests of social groups, who channel demands through state institutions, and the political identities of national minorities, who desire to form the basis of territorial representative institutions and a democratic polity in their own right – in other words, self-determination. By reducing collective demands to interests, and using the constitutional arena to accommodate them, proponents of a uniform conception of nationhood can frame the debate in terms of justice and claim that factors associated with social cooperation, unity, and functionality are the only criteria with which to judge the merits of constitutional outcomes, and in doing so they can neglect the process of arriving at such outcomes. Appropriate constitutional actors thus come to be formed not by political communities with mechanisms for democratic accountability, who had been party to the original compromise, but by any social group that can lay claim to sufficient resources for mobilization, with effective access to central government institutions, since this is the social and territorial space deemed essential in carving out a constitutional niche for themselves. The larger federation in this case ceases to be a multinational ensemble, since it is constituted by collective entities that are born out of political and social mobilization in *opposition* with the state, engaging in the normal business of politics yet in the constitutional arena. In a multinational democracy, a constitution cannot be neutral if it disregards its constitutive partners in the name of a 'higher procedural standard' from which to adjudicate political conflict. In multinational democracies, constitutions should privilege political communities and their legitimately elected governments.[11]

Second, and related to the first, it misconstrues the criteria with which to evaluate justice in constitutions. Constitutional accommodation comes to be determined by power as opposed to democracy, and getting into the constitutional game is like enjoying the privilege of entering some exclusive club that renders your particular cause invulnerable to the political process. A national minority must not only confront a centralist government at the federal level, with its own project for nation-building, but must also confront a set of social groups whose primary allegiance lies at the centre. This occurs because the constitution no longer represents a meeting ground for the country's founding constituents, with all of their historical legitimacy. Once constitutional talks are mentioned, citizens have a right to get involved, and political and social mobilization ensues, at a pan-Canadian level, as an act of citizenship itself. Constitutions in themselves are not democratic institutions; this would imply that referendums are the only legitimate institutions for amending them. They are not meant to compensate for failed representative institutions and a flawed federal structure, and they are just when they follow from procedures that privilege negotiations, deliberations and decisions by elected governments.

In Canada, the debate is taking place between those actors that believe the constitution is an appropriate tool with which to re-engineer society outside of its social bases, and those that believe the constitution represents a meeting ground in which the rules of association are to flow from sovereign constituents – in other words, as a reflection of communities recognized as nations by both international convention and by custom in the Canadian context, as the Supreme Court of Canada has maintained in 1998. Ironically, and counter-intuitive to basic liberal premises, constitutions in multinational states must overtly entrench principles of exclusion as well as inclusion with regards to representation. Social identities can be constantly made and remade, depending on a myriad of factors, including power dynamics, material conditions, and ideology. If constitutional actors are defined as such, then it is no wonder that Canadian constitutionalism is perceived to be an impossible game. Indeed, a limited constitution is not incompatible with multinational accommodation. By demanding constitutional affirmation as a founding member, with the full use of majoritarian democratic institutions in its jurisdictional fields, Quebec in effect wishes to limit the set of constitutional actors in Canada. The recognition of minority nations in multinational constitutions in this sense may be conceptualized as *substantive in process* and *procedural in application*. The constitutional game proceeds through negotiations about the substance of jurisdictional conflicts, but once settled and accepted by all, a dualist vision of Canada that may or may not imply asymmetry is not incompatible with a limited, procedural constitution.[12]

James Tully is the leading political theorist making the case that constitutionalism should embody a spirit of continuity as opposed to proceeding from abstract universal principles. In *Strange Multiplicity*,[13] he makes a forceful argument depicting how the modern age has shaped political discourse around the negation of identities, through the elevation of the independent self-governing nation-state and the equality of individual citizens. In his view, constitutional theory in the face of diversity ought to embody the idea of an open-ended series of contracts and agreements between adherents. Constitutions ought not to be imposed upon self-determining groups, as fixed and unchanging guides for social and political behaviour. Moreover, in response to fears that this approach may render the constitution susceptible to constantly changing political currents, Tully believes such processes can take place without hindering harmonious relations in daily sub-constitutional politics.

The normative backdrop employed by Tully rests upon the liberal ideal of being free from constraints, to be able to choose how to live one's life, yet he notes that contemporary liberals have also conceded the importance of belonging to a culture and a place – to be 'at home.' This is reminiscent of Kymlicka's reference to a liberal-culturalist consensus in the field. His concern is to show how constitutions in the face of this strange multiplicity may enhance the primary goods of liberty and equality. He thus develops three fundamental pillars of constitutionalism, conducive to the twin goals of liberalism while, at the same time, avoiding the imposition of extreme expressions of the universal and the particular: an abstract, uniform constitution, what he calls rootless cosmopolitanism, on one side, and purified nationalism on the other. For Tully, just constitutions must be based on the three fundamental principles of mutual recognition, consent, and continuity.

Let us further elaborate on the implications of these three principles for just constitutionalism. The common strand among these pillars is that while a modern constitution seeks to constitute, the traditions of an ancient constitution, as Tully advocates, builds upon what is already constituted. The basic polemic is between the imposition of a structure for individuals to be self-determining, where people are said to be free insofar as they forgo customs and historical associations, and custom-based recognition, which builds on long-held habits that have developed as binding principles by a free people, borne out of deliberation over time, and manifested as a consensually based association. Moreover, this view holds that constitutions need not be legally uniform. Rather, in reflecting a combination of freely formed associations, they are by nature multiform – in other words, an assemblage of jurisdictions.

The differential structure inherent in such an approach to diverse polities, however, is seen by most modern constitutionalist theorists as an affront to equality. Yet Tully notes that this view rests on the assumption that constitutions are a precondition to democracy, as opposed to his contention that constitutions ought to follow from democratic practices. Hence the emphasis on process in his three pillars. The example of Quebec is fundamental here. Quebec is not a mere cultural grouping that requires substantive protections in the Canadian constitution, as though the constitution is there to act as its guardian. Treating the question of Quebec's constitutional status as though it were a matter of cultural policy implicitly misconstrues the idea that Quebec is a partner in the determination of constitutional outcomes, not a target for policy. The question 'What does Quebec want?' in a zero-sum framework for distributing collective rights is in itself indicative of the modern conception of constitutionalism in Canada. In contrast, viewed through the prism of the three pillars, the approach would assume that Quebec exists as a historically self-determining entity, already constituted, and the constitution would be the result of an evolving set of agreements that are acceptable to all parties.[14]

We will recall Peter Russell's question about whether Canadians can be a sovereign people. As the exposition above illustrates, a constitution, by itself, cannot simply create sovereign institutions out of nothing. Linkages between the nation-state and sovereignty, however, are so inextricably tied together in the language of the modern age that it is inconceivable for some to make the case that Canada has simply never been founded upon the notion of popular sovereignty, even though it has attempted in vain to forge a constitution that implicitly embodies this principle. Canadians do not constitute a sovereign people, they are a plurality of sovereign peoples. This is a difficult assertion to make with our common understanding of nation-states, equality of individuals and constitutional supremacy, but constitutions precede legal imposition. Canada is an association of sovereign peoples, and Tully provides an extremely satisfying framework through which to build upon this reality, in conceiving a constitutional process that is not imperial or domineering.[15] It is not made up out of abstract universal principles. And it is not politically motivated, as a nation-building tool, meant to negate previously existing self-governing entities or peoples.

The First Constitutional Order

The philosophical underpinnings of the Canadian state are noteworthy because they are not interpreted with unanimity. Indeed, Canada was formed by imperial statute, and there was no watershed event, such as a war of independence, or a massive social experiment that ushered in a new era and new conceptions of sovereignty. The Canadian case is one of conservative beginnings. Indeed, perhaps the most noteworthy element of the country's foundation is that the project to create 'something out of abstract ideas' was never accepted by Quebec, while it has always been the intention of nation-builders in the rest of Canada. As interpreted in Quebec, and preceding actual Confederation in 1867, the Quebec Act of 1774 is perhaps the fundamental initiative defining relations between Canada's founding nations and its repercussions can still be felt today. The act in effect recognized the inherent dualism of the colony, establishing the idea of French Canada's autonomy. For French Canadians, Confederation is but a continuation of various turning points in the relationship between the founding peoples, while English Canadian history interprets the founding of Canada from 1867 onwards.[16] These distinct historiographies indeed reflect subsequent readings of community relations. Quebec views Canada as a compromise between existing nations, while for English Canada, Confederation represents the birth of a new nation, albeit with reference to the institutions and customs of Great Britain. For Quebec, emphasizing pre-Confederation legal accommodations for French Canada builds on a key tenet of constitutionalism – continuity – a principle that stresses nation-to-nation relations.

The practice of 'identifying communities and treating them differently' was first applied with the Quebec Act of 1774, which 'named, and provided for the continuation of, two institutions of the majority population – the Roman Catholic religion and French civil law, that distinguished it from the newly arrived minority.'[17] The act's importance cannot be understated, for it was the first imperial statute that recognized a colony's own formal constitution.[18] In the Constitutional Act of 1791, the British Parliament continued the process of entrenching dualism by virtually assuring that the two colonies would develop on their own. With the influx of Loyalists from the United States, Canada was divided into two separate provinces, each provided with an appointed upper house, the Legislative Council, and an elected Legislative Assembly. Taken together, these measures form the basis for continuity and the context for interpreting subsequent constitutional agreements for Quebec. Canada's constitution, in this view, cannot be conceptualized as a new beginning, as something to be created or engineered, and this position continues to this day in Quebec.

In 1840 Lord Durham simply dismissed this reality of dualism in what was to be the first attempt to employ the constitution as an instrument to (re-)engineer society.[19] The Act of Union in 1840, meant to reverse the recognition of difference inherent in the Quebec Act and the Constitutional Act, is most notable for its failure to achieve its desired goal of assimilation, and it marked the Quebec political psyche for generations to come. Upper and Lower Canada were merged in a single Legislative Assembly, without the institution of responsible government, which was to be implemented only in 1848. Colonial politicians, however, confounded these intentions by developing informal practices or conventions that reaffirmed existing community divisions, thwarting the assimilationist attempts of the legislative union. Indeed, in the Confederation Debates, John A. Macdonald observed that 'although we have nominally a legislative union in Canada ... we know, as a matter of fact, that since the Union in 1841, we have had a federal union; that in matters affecting Upper Canada solely, members from that section claimed and generally exercised the right of exclusive legislation, while members from Lower Canada legislated in matters affecting only their own section.'[20] Confederation was an experiment for a more sociologically based construction of the country, where French and English majorities would constitute the two main provinces, and was in part an explicit corrective to the Act of Union. While a liberal school among Quebec intellectuals was developing during this period, many French Canadians at the time turned to the Catholic Church for political shelter and as a marker of their distinct status, and the seeds of an incipient consociational formula were in the works.[21]

Indeed, Guy Laforest convincingly shows that Canada's constitutional founders were explicitly aware of a sort of special or distinct status for Quebec in the Resolutions adopted at the Quebec conference in 1864 and then reproduced in the British North America Act in 1867. Indeed, the tradition of asymmetry in Canada can be interpreted as a founding principle that came to be undone in the repatriated constitutional order of 1982. A particularly revealing quote by Brian Young is worth reproducing:

> Confederation and codification were bedfellows in the crucial juncture of the 1860's when the form of Canadian federalism was being negotiated. In the process by which Quebec became one province among others and in which French Canadians became a minority element in a federal state in which English would be the dominant language, codification institutionalized and reconfirmed Lower Canada's separate legal culture.[22]

Laforest provides powerful passages of founding debates that support this view, in particular, passage 29, subsection 33 of the Quebec Resolutions (which was reformulated slightly in section 94 of the Constitution Act, 1867): 'Rendering uniform all or any of the laws relative to property and civil rights in Upper Canada, Nova Scotia, New Brunswick, Newfoundland and Prince Edward Island, and rendering uniform the procedure of all or any of the courts in these provinces; but any statute for this purpose shall have no force or authority in any province until sanctioned by the legislature thereof.'[23] Laforest notes that the key principle at work here, even among those who interpret section 94 as a centralizing and standardizing provision, is the legislative supremacy of Quebec in the areas of property and civil rights. For Laforest, the founders clearly accounted for Quebec's distinct status by granting autonomy in local matters that are directly related to communitarian identity.

In 1867, Canada was born out of Confederation, where the key principles of a power-sharing formula were established. The main framework of this first constitutional order was maintained until repatriation in 1982. While distinct interpretations of the initial agreement have survived scrutiny in Canadian history, including its reduction as merely an imperial statute and as an agreement among provinces, Quebec has steadfastly regarded Confederation through the lens of dualism, as a pact between English Canadians and French Canadians. For an overwhelming majority of Quebec intellectuals, this is the legitimating constitutive aspect of the Canadian federal state and for Quebec-Canada relations. Indeed, a literal reading of the original agreement has led many scholars to maintain that its intentions were to establish a virtual legislative union with a dominant central government, in effect rendering it quasi-federal.[24] However, in over one hundred years of application, through the growth of state intervention, the development of the welfare state, increasing interdependence between the orders of government, and through judicial interpretations and adopted conventions, it has been consistently clear to most Quebec intellectuals and political actors that the first constitutional order was based on dualism, and this is affirmed by a rich literature on constitutional matters in Quebec.[25]

In 1956, the Royal Commission of Inquiry on Constitutional Problems (the Tremblay Commission) summarized this position succinctly, and was to form the backbone of subsequent events surrounding the Quiet Revolution – a period in which Quebec not only claimed it was a distinct national group in Canada, but behaved as one as well, through the wide use of statist instruments. The commission's report called for provincial autonomy for Quebec in fiscal and financial matters, full autonomy over its cultural development, and generally articulated a view that Quebec-Canada relations ought to return to the original principles underpinning Confederation. Indeed, an underlying theme of the report, as Donald Smiley has argued, is that constitutional history until that point can be summarized as the attempt of English-speaking Canada to subvert the original federal compact, with subsequent resistance by French Canadians.[26]

As Douglas Verney explains, for French Canadians, the compact theory of Confederation has always implied more than a strict provincial-rights doctrine. Many English Canadians who feared a strong central government have made explicit reference to the compact theory in federal-provincial conflicts over jurisdiction. For Quebec, an approach resting on provincial rights is not sufficient, since it implies that each province's needs are the same, and that the solution can be found in legal and political tinkering as opposed to a wholesale understanding of identity differences. In the eyes of French Canadians, and later Quebeckers, the compact expressed the sentiment that Canada represented a project in which two distinctive cultures came together, with the appropriate recognition of political status stemming from this premise. Philosophically, 'the compact theory made plausible the French-Canadian argument that they formed a special community, were a corporate entity, and had community rights,' which formed the very basis of the conclusions of the Tremblay Report.[27] Donald Smiley quotes a key passage of the Tremblay Commission:

> The powers [the Fathers of Confederation] entrusted to the federal government, in general, bore on subjects which did not divide the two [cultural] groups and in which they had a common interest ...
> ... The central government was entrusted with the main general, military, administrative and technical services but there was reserved to the provinces all – save the few exceptions mentioned above – that concerned social, civil, family, school and municipal organization; everything which touched the human side most nearly and which most influenced the Canadian citizen's manner of living.[28]

For Quebec, the very structure of the division of powers revealed a logic of dual majorities, and potential asymmetry. In the 1960s, Quebec would make full use of this vision as state interventionism became a lightning rod for its political, social, and economic development.

A Period of Transition: 1960s to 1982

The election of a Liberal government in Quebec in 1960 saw a reawakening, away from traditional expressions of nationalism centered around the Catholic faith and towards an openness that affirmed the value of state-led initiatives that broadened the scope of Quebec society on cultural, political, economic, and social matters. At the beginning of this period, the government of Quebec sought to align itself with the other provincial capitals to form a common front to combat unilateral actions by Ottawa that infringed on exclusive provincial jurisdictions.

Prime Minister Lester B. Pearson responded favourably with the launching of the Royal Commission on Bilingualism and Biculturalism (the Laurendeau-Dunton Commission), which acknowledged the existence and equality of two founding peoples. This period was characterized by great potential for a revised negotiated agreement, aimed at addressing Quebec's new assertiveness in returning to the spirit of federalism enshrined in 1867 and curtailing Ottawa's incursions into provincial matters. Moreover, an ethos began to develop around a de facto acceptance of asymmetry and bilateral agreements between Quebec and Ottawa, since Quebec often asserted its autonomy in areas that other provinces did not mind ceding to the federal government. Between 1964 and 1966, Paul Gérin-Lajoie, Quebec's education minister, went as far as to establish a doctrine in which Quebec could assert its right to act in the international arena in areas that stemmed exclusively from its jurisdiction, concluding several agreements related to education, youth, and cultural affairs.[29] The pressure for constitutional reform could not be put off any longer.

The main obstacle to finding an acceptable constitutional agreement was an amending formula that would satisfy all parties. During the Liberal tenure of Premier Jean Lesage between 1960 and 1966, two amending formulas were rejected by Quebec. First, in 1961, the federal minister of justice, Davey Fulton, presented a formula that was turned down because of its failure to curtail the powers of the central government in unilaterally amending the constitution in exclusive federal fields of jurisdiction and in reforms to central institutions such as the Senate, the Supreme Court, and the monarchy. In January 1966, the Fulton-Favreau formula also failed to garner the support of the Quebec government. This formula did include a provision requiring the approval of all eleven governments to amend the constitution in the division of powers, the use of both official languages, denominational rights in education, and representation in the House of Commons. Other measures related to the monarchy and Senate representation could be amended with the approval of two-thirds of the provinces comprising more than 50 per cent of the Canadian population. Having consolidated that it could deal in a bilateral relationship with the federal government, in a flexible and open-ended process that could account for changing circumstances, Quebec viewed unanimity as an undue constraint.

This set the stage for an approach by Quebec in which a constitutional overhaul was required, above and beyond mere tinkering with amending formulas. Lesage, faced with a growing nationalist electorate, viewed constitutional reform as a means towards a clear definition of Quebec's powers and responsibilities. The challenge for Canadian constitutionalism then moved from concerns about provincial autonomy to a special status for Quebec. This principle would eventually guide future Quebec governments in their relationship with the rest of the country. Daniel Johnson's election victory in 1966 took the nationalist discourse up a notch. Drawing on the Tremblay Commission, his Union Nationale government explicitly referred to the Quebec interpretation of the British North America Act as a pact between two founding peoples, demanding limits to the federal government's transfer payments to individuals through pan-Canadian social programs, and complete federal withdrawal if such programs were run on a shared-cost basis. In short, with the momentum provided by the Royal Commission on Bilingualism and Biculturalism, Johnson proposed a bi-national solution to Canada's constitutional impasse, in which Quebec would assume added responsibilities as the primary guarantor of the French-speaking community in Canada. With the federal government receptive to bilateral relations, several prominent agreements were concluded which paved the way for formal asymmetrical manifestations of federalism. Deals were made with Ottawa on tax revenues, an opting-out formula was implemented, Quebec assumed a larger role in *la fran-cophonie*, and Quebec expanded its small immigration bureau established during Lesage's tenure into a full-fledged department.

The arrival of Pierre Trudeau to the leadership of the federal Liberal government in 1968 brought an abrupt end to any attempts to consolidate special status for Quebec in a formal constitutional structure. While some bilateral deals were concluded, particularly in the areas of immigration and, to a lesser extent, in cultural and educational affairs, these were largely viewed as administrative deals and were easily reversible. The constitutional package offered at the Victoria conference in 1971, for example, was not ratified by Quebec Premier Robert Bourassa because he felt that it did not convincingly empower Quebec to legislate in areas of cultural and social policy, particularly article 94A, which was ambiguous with regards to pensions and other social programs. Moreover, the amending formula attributed veto power on a regional basis, and no mention was made of Quebec's particular status in Canada.

By 1975 Quebec explicitly sought to entrench its linguistic and cultural claims in the constitution. In exchange for patriation, Bourassa asked that the following provisions be included in a new constitution: a veto right on future amendments, full control of the policy areas of education and culture, the right to opt-out of federal programs with compensation, a more pronounced role in the selection and integration of immigrants, and limits on the federal government's declaratory and spending powers in areas of provincial jurisdiction. Ottawa's response was to threaten unilateral patriation, and an early election call by the

Quebec Liberal party resulted in a victory for the Parti Québécois led by René Lévesque, whose program included full sovereignty for Quebec with an economic association with the rest of Canada.

In 1978 Ottawa introduced Bill C-60, the Constitutional Amendment Bill, which was very similar in terms to the Victoria formula of 1971. The bill included intrastate modifications to the federation, aimed at strengthening provincial representation at the centre. It also proposed the entrenchment of a Charter of Rights and Freedoms, which was conceived initially as an 'opt-in' arrangement for the provinces. Yet in a reference decision, the Supreme Court of Canada ruled that the Parliament of Canada was not empowered to modify itself, since these changes would have affected the provinces. The Quebec government, in the meantime, showed no interest in such proposals, and developed its own white paper in 1979 titled *Quebec-Canada: A New Deal*, which reiterated the PQ platform of sovereignty-association. From the PQ perspective, this was the only way to ensure that the principle of duality was respected, since the notion of equality of the provinces was gaining momentum in the rest of the country.

In 1980 Quebec held a referendum on the option of sovereignty-association. The Trudeau Liberals campaigned against the program by promising a constitutional package that would respond to Quebec's long-held needs and interests, leading followers to understand that some sort of distinct society/special status recognition, with commensurate powers for Quebec, was in the making. Most federalists from Quebec thus rallied around Trudeau, believing that Quebec would finally be accommodated linguistically and culturally. The referendum was defeated by a margin of three to two.

On 2 October 1980 the federal government went forward with its project for repatriation by introducing a 'Proposed Resolution for Address to Her Majesty the Queen Respecting the Constitution of Canada.' Quebec and seven other provinces sought to block such actions by introducing reference cases that ultimately made their way to the Supreme Court of Canada, which reached a majority decision. Richard Simeon and Ian Robinson summarize the decision as follows:

> It would be legal for Parliament to act without provincial consent, but that this would still be unconstitutional since it would breach an established convention of substantial provincial consent ... Provinces had been warned that if they continue to delay action, Ottawa might move. The only way out was to return to the intergovernmental table. But now there was a

critical difference: the convention, said the Court, did not mean unanimity; it required only 'substantial consent.' Two provinces was clearly not 'substantial consent,' but one province could no longer stop the process. The groundwork for a settlement without Quebec had been laid.[30]

In a constitutional conference called for November 1981, Lévesque strategically relied on the principle of provincial equality to block the unilateral reform and repatriation of the constitution by the federal government, ensuring the support of other provinces. Apart from Ontario and New Brunswick, Lévesque had the support of seven other provinces. At the same time, he maintained the position that the constitution not be ratified in the absence of an agreed amending formula and a new division of powers that entailed the recognition of Quebec as a culturally and linguistically distinct society. The response by the federal government was to isolate Quebec. On 5 November the federal government and nine provinces agreed to repatriation with the entrenchment of a Charter of Rights and Freedoms, including a clause allowing for the right to opt-out of secondary provisions of the Charter (the notwithstanding clause). They also included their preferred amending formula[31] which was denounced outright across the political spectrum in Quebec. Lévesque responded by systematically making use of the notwithstanding clause, in a show of protestation, until the election of the Quebec Liberals in 1985. For Quebec, the Charter of Rights and Freedoms was a centralizing document that proved to be a major assault on Quebec's vision of federalism, particularly on the notion of dualism. This period of transition began in the 1960s with great optimism that the Canadian constitution could be patriated while ensuring that Quebec's particular status as a fundamental partner of the Canadian federation was to be formally recognized. Instead, the Canadian constitutional order took a new turn while isolating and excluding Quebec.

In short, the federal government patriated the constitution without the consent of Quebec. The new order in effect weakened Quebec, included no provisions for special recognition, and was denounced by both nationalists and federalists in Quebec, even those that sided with Trudeau during the referendum campaign of 1980.[32] The federal government had interpreted the results as an indication that Quebeckers rejected the option of secession, as opposed to a call for the renewal of the federation.

Indeed, between the early 1960s and 1982, all political actors in Canada operated on the assumption that the unanimity rule was absolute for both changes in the division of powers and in institutional changes touching federalism. Moreover, the idea of Quebec opting-out of federal programs, or striking bilateral deals with Ottawa, or assuming the prominent role as a distinct society both in law and in political practice, has been a characteristic of Canadian government since the country's inception. This approach to intergovernmental relations, as Richard Simeon argues, is simply 'what Canada has always been doing' in practice.[33] Entrenching this principle in the constitution is thus not revolutionary. It is, rather, following the path of continuity. The radical break would come instead with the patriation of the constitution in 1982.

A New Constitutional Order: Repatriation in 1982 and the Social Union Framework Agreement

The patriation of the Canadian constitution in 1982, without the consent of Quebec, represented a break with the continuity of Canada's constitutional order and a rejection of Quebec's vision of dualism as a defining element of the Canadian federation. The most fundamental break with continuity was the entrenchment of a Canadian Charter of Rights and Freedoms, which, as a central institution, directly undermines the principle of federalism in the eyes of Quebeckers. Quebec had lost its autonomous status as a member state on two basic levels. First, other provinces and the federal government had imposed an amendment without Quebec's consent. Second, the amending formula renders it virtually impossible to reform the constitution so that Quebec will have the status as a nation.[34] Quebeckers were thus thrust into a Canadian self-understanding that promptly shifted – with the salient cleavages in Canadian politics and society moving from traditional territorial conflicts to socially-based rights claims – from dualism to a pan-Canadian pluralism.[35] Charter federalism soon took hold with Canadians, and dualism formally took a back seat to multiculturalism, institutional bilingualism, and the primacy of individual rights as the defining features of the country from coast to coast.

Richard Simeon has argued that the constitution should not be about defining the 'essence' of Canada from a liberal, proceduralist perspective.[36] However, along with political philosopher James Tully, we are of the view that it should be about an open-ended process where identities emerge from the political process.[37] Many observers, most notably Pierre Trudeau, believe this essential and defining function to be the very virtue of a charter. To the extent that the constitution stymies the political process as it has been understood in Quebec throughout the country's history, these concerns are warranted from the perspective of Quebec. The constitution defines relevant political interlocutors, which in Canada have traditionally been represented along federal lines (by provincial representatives and the federal legislature) and in Quebec through the notion that a nation is being represented. When constitutional ends negate this fundamental feature, then a wholesale renegotiation of the 'essence' of Canada is inevitable. Again, this perspective presents the Charter as a neutral, uniform document. It is clearly not neutral from Quebec's viewpoint, as it values some modes of belonging and participating to the Canadian polity at the expense of others.

Indeed, the entrenchment of the Charter of Rights and Freedoms in the repatriation package is perhaps the most overtly nationalizing act undertaken by the federal government. The Charter broke with Canadian constitutional and legal traditions[38] and severely undermined the supremacy of legislatures in both federal and provincial jurisdictions. Moreover, the fact that Quebec never consented to the entrenchment of the Charter moves the act beyond a simple reformulation of power-sharing in the Canadian political system to a fundamental redefinition of federal practice. In effect, the institutions through which Quebec exercises its sovereignty were severely weakened without any input from the elected representatives from Quebec's National Assembly.

The Charter of Rights and Freedoms was the brainchild of Trudeau and, along with multiculturalism and bilingualism, it represented the added piece of the puzzle in instilling universal bases of identity across Canada. It was practically a lesson in how to proceed with a nation-building project while publicly and rhetorically decrying the nation form as a basis for citizenship. For Trudeau, the juridical nation, in which each citizen enjoys a measure of individual rights, represented the institutional expression of a 'just society' – that is, one based on reason in contrast to the parochial and emotive particular collective identities upon which Canada was supposedly constructed.[39] This was a blatant attack on the policy-making capacity of the Quebec legislature, as the individual rights regime created by the Charter does not comply with Quebec's interpretation of federalism. James Tully aptly describes the effects of dominant nationalism implicit in the adoption of the Charter:

When the National Assembly seeks to preserve and enhance Quebec's character as a modern, predominantly French-speaking society, it finds that its traditional sovereignty in this area is capped by a Charter in terms of which all its legislation must be phrased and justified, but from which any recognition of Quebec's distinct character has been completely excluded. The effect of the Charter is thus to assimilate Quebec to a pan-Canadian national culture, exactly what the 1867 constitution, according to Lord Watson, was designed to prevent. Hence, from this perspective, the Charter is 'imperial' in the precise sense of the term that has always been used to justify independence.[40]

Rights are pre-political goods, and the government charged with defining them is the winner in any political dispute in a federal system. According to Guy Laforest, the federalist shortcoming of a nation built on a Charter of Rights lies to some extent in the fact that, contrary to the Quebec nation, whose expression was bolstered and modernized by the provincial government during the Quiet Revolution, the English-Canadian nation was very much a creation of the central state, dating back to confederation.[41] The central state in this view has always represented the Canadian nation: Canadian identity, or the expression of majority nationalism, runs through the federal government.[42] The Charter can thus be interpreted as a direct response to the growing influence of the Quebec state in defining and promoting the Quebec nation. Through a rights regime, the federal government defined what level of allegiance would be accepted by citizens in Canada. Alan Cairns states this intention clearly:

> The Charter, as it emerged from the epic constitutional struggle of 1980 to 1982, was clearly intended to be a nation-building tool, a purpose that was understood much sooner and more fully by political scientists than by academic lawyers. Although it is rarely so described, the Charter, as, of course, is generally true of written constitutions, is a future-oriented act of imperialism, designed to reinforce the regime by distributing regime-supporting identities to the citizenry.[43]

For Peter Russell, writing soon after the entrenchment of the Charter, its unifying and nation-building aspects are threefold.[44] First, the Charter is a unifying symbol in that its audience, through a set of rights and a discourse of shared values, are Canadians from coast to coast. This symbolic function is fundamental in defining Canadian citizenship and identity. Second, in a similar argument to Tully's, the Charter promotes national standards: as such, it homogenizes policies to conform to a set of rights that cannot be touched by the National Assembly in Quebec.

Language policy is an obvious example. Finally, the judicialisation of the Canadian political system meant that issues ceased to be regionally defined and addressed by provincial representatives and instead took on a non-territorial and 'national' character. This contention is reinforced by the fact that the Canadian judicial system is hierarchical, and the Supreme Court's jurisprudence is binding on all other courts. Laforest supports this last point in arguing that 'the 1982 Charter shifted the ground of conflict, drawing it out of provincial confines and inserting it in a pan-Canadian legal and political arena, where the Supreme Court, which is under the jurisdiction of the central state, is the court of final appeal.'[45] Moreover, Laforest adds that while standardizing certain social practices, the Charter also contributes to the convergence of common law and Quebec's civil code, a central tenet of Quebec's distinct status in Canada.

As a corollary to its nation-building functions, the Charter's impact is also felt in its capacity to undermine federalism as a legitimating principle of the country. Again, federalism is built upon regional or territorial demarcations, and the Charter shifts the arena of political conflict towards minority groups with no territorial bases – in effect demarcating the forms of political and social pluralism that define the polity away from the federal principle. The principle of 'two majorities,' which has been supported by most political and social actors in Quebec as a minimal condition of membership in the federation, was diluted to include non-territorial groups and individuals operating within the Canadian national community. Quebec, now formally a province like the others in this new constitutional order, is constrained in terms of the extent to which it can promote a set of community values and priorities that are distinct from other jurisdictions.

Janet Hiebert undertook the task of empirically examining whether the Charter's interpretation and application has indeed undermined the territorial pluralism of Canadian federalism or whether it has allowed for provincial diversity in policy-making.[46] Without detailing the particular court cases she highlights, she concludes that Charter decisions have, for the most part, been interpreted in a manner consistent with federal diversity. In this sense, the Supreme Court's sensitivity to provincial concerns is claimed to serve as a buffer against the centralizing tendencies of the Charter. While not going so far as to argue that the Charter has had no impact on diversity in policy-making among provinces, Hiebert does contend that there are no empirical reasons to support the idea that Charter jurisprudence has resulted in a uniform interpretation of rights that disregards regional differences. However, one key qualification is offered:

> The Charter poses the greatest constraint on provincial autonomy when legislation is in direct conflict with a protected right that is specific in its definition ... However, the majority of protected rights are stated in vague and abstract terms. Therefore the constraint on Quebec's capacity to determine school language instruction policy should not serve as the basis for a general proposition that the pursuit of cultural objectives or community values by provinces will inevitably be vetoed by the Charter.[47]

The basis of such decisions is that the 'reasonableness' clause provided by section 1 of the Charter is interpreted specifically in a federalism context. Limits on a rights regime, in other words, are precisely what make the Charter compatible with federalism. In this view, a particular policy initiative is given sufficient leverage to trump individual rights if the values to be promoted are consistent with a free and democratic society. The onus is on governments to justify their objectives, and this is wholly compatible with the principle of provincial diversity. While section 33, the override clause, would more explicitly allow for provincial diversity, its perceived illegitimacy in an increasingly 'Chartered' political culture has meant that provincial governments are unlikely to employ it.

Hiebert's study, while important for its empirical contributions to the debate surrounding the Charter's compatibility with federalism, does not fundamentally challenge the contention that the Charter is a non-federal document and that it represents a rupture with Canadian constitutional practice. First, as Hiebert concedes, the jurisprudence with regards to provincial diversity is rather limited. This is not simply a statistical question. It may very well be the case that the Charter's impact is felt prior to such matters going to the courts, as state managers succeed in complying with the Charter at the stage of policy formulation. The homogenizing effects of the Charter cannot, in this sense, be determined by looking at jurisprudence alone. Stated differently, the process of homogenization may take place ahead of litigation, and a more accurate measure of such effects of the Charter might emerge by looking at the policy process itself. As such, by merely looking at a minimum body of jurisprudence, Hiebert can make the claim that the Charter is not biased in favour of the central government's agenda, when all along the strongest homogenizing/centralizing effects of the Charter are occurring as policy-makers attempt to avoid litigation in the first place. Hiebert's analysis rests on a methodological approach that serves to obscure the effects of the Charter rather than to clarify them.

Second, even if we accept that provinces enjoy leverage through section 1 of the Charter, they are still required to demonstrate their intentions and to justify their actions to a central institution. The effects of Canadian nation-building and majority nationalism may be subtle, but a central institution is still acting as an arbitrator in areas of exclusive provincial jurisdiction. The logic here is similar to the one that nourishes the popularity of the Clarity Act among English Canadians. Do what you please but we (a central, pan-Canadian institution) have the final say!

Third, as Rainer Knopff and Fred Morton argue, the federal government is in a win-win situation. If provinces lose an appeal, the result is the loss of provincial diversity and the maintenance of uniform boundaries for provincial policy initiatives. If the federal government loses an appeal, the result is that a central institution won – a central judiciary interpreting a central Charter of Rights – and the policy-making forum remains country-wide. For the federal government, a lost appeal is nothing more than a lost appeal, while for provinces, it severely limits their ability to experiment and adapt policies to the particular needs of their populations in their areas of jurisdiction. Moreover, every time the Supreme Court is called upon to rule on a Charter case it reinforces the sentiment that Canadians are bearers of non-territorial rights, and the federal government adds to its arsenal of resources in future conflicts with the provinces.[48] This point cannot be understated, since federalism presupposes regional diversity and experimentation. Again, the Charter is a non-federal document and the costs of losing an appeal are significantly greater for the provinces relative to the federal government.

Finally, the Charter may be redundant if the claim is that section 1 promotes federal diversity. As Knopff and Morton state, if diversity itself is enough of a test for reasonableness, this renders the Charter a practical nullity. If rights are vague and represent 'targets' whose limits are open to interpretations that vary from state to state, then why shouldn't provinces be allowed to differ in their interpretations of fundamental rights? Indeed, Quebec enacted its own Charter of Human Rights and Freedoms as early as 1975. It has demonstrated a commitment, in line with most liberal democracies, to fundamental human rights. Why, then, should its own legislature not be responsible for upholding the rights of its citizens in its fields of jurisdiction? The answer points directly to the nation-building efforts of the federal government, acting as the care-taker not only of citizens across the country but of the perceived vagar-ies of provincial governments, and Quebec in particular.

The Progressive Conservative government of Brian Mulroney, elected in September 1984, sought to gain Quebec's constitutional approval, with 'honour and enthusiasm,' and the Meech Lake Accord and ratifi-cation process (1987–90) was the next mega-constitutional episode in what was viewed by most parties as a corrective to the hasty result of 1982. Quebec Premier Robert Bourassa had whittled down the twenty-two demands presented earlier by René Lévesque to five minimal con-ditions to settle the constitutional crisis: the explicit recognition of Que-bec as a distinct society; increased power to Quebec in immigration, including the recruitment, administration and integration of new arriv-als; the appointment of three Supreme Court judges out of nine with expertise in Quebec civil law; limits on the federal spending power; and a full veto to Quebec for any additional amendments to the Canadian constitution.

In June 1990, two provinces failed to ratify the agreement and the Meech Lake Accord failed. The end of this particular round of constitu-tional negotiations signalled the consolidation of a vision for Canada that did not recognize Quebec as a founding partner, with the constitu-tional arena defined not merely as a meeting point for representatives of the founding 'peoples,' accommodating traditional cleavages in Canadian federalism, but as a zero-sum game between and among tra-ditional constitutional partners and social interests. The prominent dis-course following Meech Lake was that a new Canadian constitution would no longer be negotiated by governments, as though this was somehow inimical to social interests and Canadian citizenship. Richard Simeon and Daniel-Patrick Conway summarize the general aftertaste left by the Meech Lake process: 'This episode demonstrated a profound difference in perceptions of the nature and purpose of the Canadian federation. For most Quebecers it is seen as a partnership of two equal peoples, for most non-Quebecers, it is seen as a partnership of 30 mil-lion individual citizens, and of ten equal provinces.'[49] The pan-Cana-dian vision of Trudeau had taken hold in the rest of Canada. Any special status was now deemed to be a threat to Charter federalism, as though the two were inherently mutually exclusive.

Following the defeat of Meech, the Quebec Liberal party tabled the Allaire Report, a new policy platform that spelled out twenty-two pow-ers that ought to be transferred to the provinces. This was preceded by the bipartisan Commission on the Political and Constitutional future of Quebec (the Bélanger-Campeau Commission), in the summer of 1990, whose mandate was to outline a new definition of the political and constitutional arrangements that determined the status of Quebec and its relations with other member states of the federation. This constituted a watershed moment in Canadian history. Like the unanimity that prevailed following unilateral patriation in 1982, a provincial government, with the full backing of the opposition, decided to ponder the appropriateness of its association with the country of which it was a founding member.

After the tabling of the Bélanger-Campeau report, Bill-150 was enacted in June 1991 to set up two special National Assembly committees. This served to put constant pressure on the other governments (federal and provincial), by making questions of renewed federalism and sovereignty visible on a daily basis and providing a valuable platform for commissioners, and also key sovereignists such as Lucien Bouchard, Jacques Parizeau, and Mario Dumont, respective leaders of the Bloc Québécois, the Parti Québécois, and the Action Démocratique du Québec. The commission also recommended that a referendum on the future of Quebec in Canada be held no later than 26 October 1992.

The federal government responded with a parliamentary commission (the Castonguay-Dobbie and later Dobbie-Beaudoin commission) to study Quebec's relations with the rest of Canada. On 7 July 1992, the federal government and the nine other provinces reached an agreement, confirmed on 28 August 1992 as the Consensus Report on the Constitution, or the Charlottetown Accord. A reversal from the spirit of Meech Lake, the report emphasized an enhancement of the federal spending power and a greater emphasis on reforming and strengthening central institutions. Rather than devolving powers, the report sought to augment provincial representation in the Senate and to increase Ottawa's intervention in spheres of exclusive provincial jurisdiction. The accord also replaced the distinct society clause with the Canada clause, which accorded equal standing to the distinct society clause, the equality of provinces principle, and the recognition to promote Quebec's anglophone minority. In a Canada-wide referendum, the accord was soundly defeated, with 60 per cent of Quebeckers voting against it. As an omnibus package that attempted to include a wide audience in its process, while appeasing all segments of Canadian society in substance, it was not difficult to predict the accord's failure, as Peter Russell speculated in 1991:

Reflect, for a moment, on the arguments which were so telling in turning public opinion outside of Quebec against the Meech Lake Accord: rejection of English-French dualism as a fundamental feature of Canadian society; recognition of provincial equality as *the* principle of federal justice; insistence that the Québécois' collective right to cultural security be subordinated to the individual rights of the Charter; support for uniform national standards of social policy in areas of provincial jurisdiction. It is difficult to conceive how a large majority of Quebeckers could be induced to join a constitutional covenant based on these precepts. By the same token, it would seem equally unlikely that a majority of Canadians could be persuaded to support constitutional changes designed to accommodate the extreme nationalist demands which have issued thus far from the constitutional discussions within Quebec [the Allaire Report].[50]

The failed accord constituted a major defeat for Bourassa and the Quebec Liberal party, whose tacit acceptance of the accord was criticized as a failure to defend Quebec's traditional demands and political *acquis*. Indeed, Bourassa had not even secured the five minimal conditions of the Meech Lake proposals required for Quebec to consider reopening constitutional talks. Moreover, Quebec had made no gains in the sharing of powers, while centralization was being further ensconced, since the federal government could negotiate five-year reversible deals with individual provinces. The accord also placed virtually no limits on Ottawa's capacity to intervene in areas of exclusive provincial jurisdiction. Throughout the country, the accord was interpreted as the 'last straw,' with many arguing that no longer would governments negotiate the defining principles of the country behind closed doors and without significant citizen input.

In September 1994, the PQ, led by Jacques Parizeau, won the Quebec election on a platform that called for a referendum on sovereignty. At the federal level, the Liberal government of Jean Chrétien proceeded as though the national question in Quebec was of interest to no one, and focused instead on a major reform initiative in the area of social programs, beginning in February 1995 with Bill C-76, which cut transfers to the provinces by a third – $6 billion over two years – in the area of health.[51] The PQ called a referendum in October 1995, calling for 'sovereignty with partnership,' with the implication that a yes vote would trigger the process of Quebec secession, with or without agreement from the rest of Canada.[52] This time, the sovereignty option was defeated by a margin of less than 1 per cent, with 52,000 votes separating the two camps. The Canadian experiment with federalism had been clearly called into question. The country found itself at a crossroads, with faith in the original compromise seriously eroded in Quebec, and the possibility for a new relationship virtually closed off – both formally and at a strictly political level.

Rather than take a cue from the close referendum results, Chrétien responded by claiming citizens were fed up with constitutional matters and decided to turn instead to what he considered to be more pressing matters, such as unemployment and the economy, in order to justify the government's inaction. Moreover, in a show of support, the Chrétien government affirmed the distinct character of Quebec society in a simple statutory initiative, on 11 December 1995 – a feeble attempt to appease Quebec since it did not have constitutional legitimacy.

In the same vein, Ottawa and the provinces tabled the Calgary Declaration on 14 September 1997, without Quebec Premier Lucien Bouchard's assent, in order to outline the basic principles on which Canada would be based without invoking constitutional fanfare. The statement rendered a qualified recognition of the unique character of Quebec society, with so many stipulations and counter principles as to render it meaningless, particularly the stipulation that if any future constitutional amendment confers powers to one province, it must be available to other provinces as well. At the same time, the signatories rejected all forms of asymmetrical federalism and agreed to prioritize, on a pan-Canadian basis, the delivery of social programs, which was under exclusive provincial jurisdiction. The Calgary Declaration is striking in its attempt to specify the unique character of Quebec – thus avoiding the term 'distinct,' which caused so much acrimony in Canada throughout the constitutional negotiations – while also affirming an equality of provinces doctrine, multiculturalism, and bilingualism. It is, in short, Trudeau's dream declaration with a mention of Quebec's uniqueness, hardly affirming its status as a constituted internal nation or possible implications for an asymmetrical formula for coexistence. The document is worth quoting in full:

   i. All Canadians are equal and have rights protected by law.
   ii. All provinces, while diverse in their characteristics, have equality of status.
   iii. Canada is graced by a diversity, tolerance, compassion and an equality of opportunity that is without rival in the world.
   iv. Canada's gift of diversity includes Aboriginal peoples and cultures,

the vitality of the English and French languages and a multicultural citizenry drawn from all parts of the world.

v. In Canada's federal system, where respect for diversity and equality underlies unity, the unique character of Quebec society, including its French-speaking majority, its culture and its tradition of civil law, is fundamental to the well-being of Canada. Consequently, the legislature and Government of Quebec have a role to protect and develop the unique character of Quebec society within Canada.

vi. If any future constitutional amendment confers powers on one province, these powers must be available to all provinces.

vii. Canada is a federal system where federal, provincial and territorial governments work in partnership while respecting each other's jurisdictions. Canadians want their governments to work cooperatively and with flexibility to ensure the efficiency and effectiveness of the federation. Canadians want their governments to work together particularly in the delivery of their social programs. Provinces and territories renew their commitment to work in partnership with the Government of Canada to best serve the needs of Canadians.[53]

For purposes of analysis, the Calgary Declaration is an extremely useful document in that it captures well the mood in which the debate of unity and diversity is allowed to proceed in Canada. In other words, Quebec is unique, but not unique enough to alter a basic federal structure to which they never consented, not unique enough to be allowed to question the premise of social policy based on functional criteria for effectiveness. Moreover, its unique character is derived by the fact that the province *includes* a French-speaking majority, as though this has no historical significance whatsoever. This is as far as it gets to affirming that Quebec is a constituted political community within Canada and a founding member. Also, the Quebec legislature and government have a *role* to play in protecting and developing the French language. This is left so vague as to be rendered virtually without meaning. What other body could legitimately claim to legislate in this area, whose limits are conveniently left open to interpretation? Like many of the rhetorical devices upon which Canadian diversity is built, we can say that Quebec is unique as long as our institutions do not affirm this principle. In Canada, the overwhelming basis for unity is to claim that there exists a 'gift' of diversity, and that it is 'graced' with tolerance while ensuring that a strict uniformity in status of citizens and provinces remains intact.

The Calgary Declaration paved the way for an agreement on social policy that was directed by Ottawa. Indeed, the pattern was set, Ottawa would dictate the terms of agreement, and if provinces disagreed, their transfers would be cut. This approach was ironically labelled 'collaborative federalism,' and it culminated in the signing, again without Quebec's approval, of the Social Union Framework Agreement (SUFA) in February 1999. This agreement merits a more profound assessment. While it has been generally regarded as insignificant outside Quebec, at least in terms of its role in constitutive matters, in Quebec it is fundamental in signalling the shortcomings of federal practice, and all Quebec political parties lined up against it.[54] Indeed, the SUFA formally recognized the federal spending power in areas of exclusive provincial jurisdiction, and this was Quebec's main objection.

It is our contention that social policy involves more than considerations surrounding spending, the delivery of programs, and bickering. Social policy represents an appropriate field of study with which we can assess the salience of political power in institutionalizing the values and preferences deemed important to a political community. In a multinational federation, it is thus a constitutional question in the large sense of the term, since it delineates certain boundaries between sovereign actors. The particular question of interest is why nine provinces and the federal government signed the agreement although the governments involved exhibited divergent ideologies in terms of the state's role in the delivery of social policy? How do we explain the fact that Ontario and Alberta, for example, went along with the agreement with fiscally conservative governments in power – governments that have shown an interest in scaling down Canada's traditional social safety net? The contention here is that SUFA is not merely a document that acts as a blueprint for social policy delivery in Canada. It is the equivalent of a constitutional document that defines the contours of Canada's political communities – a new national policy.

The idea of a social union came about soon after the failure of the Charlottetown Accord, and emerged largely as an alternative to the constant constitutional struggles which were rejected outright by Canadians. The Liberal government that took power in 1993 adopted an incrementalist approach to intergovernmental relations, sidestepping constitutional negotiations in favour of issue specific agreements. In this light, why was the social union hailed as necessary for Canada? Was it to address the growing perception of dissatisfaction towards federalism by Canadians, or was it aimed at resolving the persistent existential question forced by Quebec? Why has Quebec refused to consent to an arrangement that on the surface resolves the arbitrary nature of the incrementalist approach and serves to clearly delineate responsibilities between orders of government? Why was Quebec's refusal to sign regarded as insignificant?

The SUFA represents the continuation of a political project for the construction of a pan-Canadian political community, which aims to forge universal bases of citizenship across the country in the name of unity. As such, at issue here is not to assess the SUFA as though it was merely a centralizing effort by the federal government, and thus to employ the usual language associated with the merits of decentralization versus centralization in federal systems. Instead, it is a question of divergent *federal visions* for the country. The identity-building aspects of past constitutional arrangements had now moved to the realm of social policy delivery as though defining constitutional questions, which are political, had been solved. As a result, the logic of individual rights as a defining feature of Canadian citizenship, to the detriment of collective/territorial expressions of entitlement and obligation, has been transferred to the delivery of social policy. Statecraft remains and will continue to be inextricably linked to the struggle to legitimate sovereignty over a given bounded territory. The territorial feature of federalism lies at the core of debates concerning the construction of political communities and the subsequent configuration of policy space between federated entities. The inclusion of the mobility principle in the SUFA is a clear example of the blurring of distinct policy spaces in Canada. Article 2 of the SUFA reads as such: 'All governments believe that the freedom of movement of Canadians to pursue opportunities anywhere in Canada is an essential element of Canadian citizenship.'[55] By enshrining this principle, the central government manages to impose its presence in a field of jurisdiction exclusive to the provinces while at the same time consolidating its hold on the institution of citizenship – defined from coast to coast. Indeed, the mobility principle is of significant interest in a world characterized by mass migration, and it poses problems for those who perceive Canada from the perspective of two 'host societies,' each endowed with the capacity to offer comparable life chances to their citizens in distinct contexts of choice. Each community, in this sense, ought to be allowed to constitute a 'space' in which citizens' political expectations, their cultural traits, and their collective interests are allowed to flourish. The mobility principle thus undermines one host society by forging a larger one.

The realm of social policy can thus be conceptualized as an instrument of statecraft since the use of public power contributes to shaping communities. The choices that state actors make in the area of social policy are not merely administrative or functional; rather, they serve to define the way citizens relate to one another and to structure the territorial state. In this light, social policy can be conceptualized as a key aspect of citizenship: how do social policy choices orient citizens in terms of forging a framework for 'belonging' to a political community? This question is particularly salient in federal states because of the omnipresent potential for dual, compounding and, at times, competing loyalties towards the different orders of government – towards the different 'shapers of allegiance,' to formulate it more precisely.

For instance, the SUFA cannot be interpreted merely as a functional, non-constitutional solution to the ambiguities involved in the configuration of social policy delivery between the central government and the provinces. Rather, the SUFA represents a particular ideological vision for federalism, a political strategy forged by the central government with the aim of asserting its predominance in the face of regional and provincial pressures for constitutional reform and decentralization. Donald V. Smiley, a foremost student of federalism, had this to say about the federal government's intentions with regards to economic and social policy, the 'Third National Policy,' in the wake of patriation in 1982:

> These interventionist measures were aimed at enhancing federal visibility by procedures in which federal authorities would deal directly with individuals, businesses and other social groups rather than by channelling federal support through the provincial governments ... The common impulse behind the various elements of the Third National Policy was that of countering the provincialist influences in the Canadian polity and economy by making the federal government more pervasive and visible in the lives of individual citizens and thus to reinforce the allegiance of citizens to the national political community.[56]

Smiley's observation points to this underlying ideological impulse that was maintained with the SUFA.

Alan Cairns has captured this vision effectively, depicting Canada as an expression of 'territorial federalism,' in the sense that it is defined around a large expanse of land rather than along community lines, similarly to the cases of Australia, Germany, and the United States – that is, a federal state that is insensitive to its social bases. Assessing the impact of the Charter of Rights and Freedoms on the construction of a single Canadian community, Cairns argues that it is 'strengthening the national community, diminishing the salience of provincial cleavages, and supplementing the discourse focused on federalist definition of issues with a counter-discourse relatively indifferent to territorialism and organized around rights.'[57] If SUFA can be taken as a continuation of this form of federal 'ideology,' one may argue that it, in effect, undermines the social bases of citizen allegiance to specific territorial communities by casting (and clouding) the discourse surrounding social policy in functional terms. In short, the fact that it is said to be non-constitutional and functional should not weaken the contention that it is indeed an ideological vision for federalism.

Alain Noël picks up on these issues in challenging the argument that decentralization in a federal state actually restricts the policy preferences of political communities. He disputes the idea that each constituent unit's isolated insertion into a competitive market causes a neoliberal 'race to the bottom,' where each unit limits its range of government intervention to attract investment. In this view, being 'closer to the people' does not provide for innovative choice in social policy measures; rather, it isolates communities in the face of systemic imperatives. Central governments are said to be in a better position to implement social programs because they can manage the diverse political economies and thus promote more redistributive policies if they so choose. Noël, however, questions, as do we, the empirical validity of such arguments and claims that there is no sound evidence indicating that such developments actually occur in the event of decentralization. He invites us to be prudent and instead to put the emphasis on federal principles: 'Centralization and decentralization remain, in the end, choices made by political communities, and these choices reflect various viewpoints about the community, about its political organization and about its social orientations. No specific solution ever becomes obviously preferable.'[58]

Let us further assess Noël's treatment of systemic arguments about the supposedly conservative bias of decentralization. Such arguments need not be limited to federal states; rather, they are based on an economic determinism that acts as a conservative argument against the welfare state more generally. In other words, federalism is not a determinant factor in this equation, as the argument can be applied to international market competition. The idea that good social programs could contribute to a society's prosperity and competitiveness is precluded in such assessments. Such systemic determinism can thus be viewed as a methodological bias that circumvents the value of welfare provisions altogether, limiting the potential richness of citizenship by contributing to undermining social rights.

The analytical lens with which to view decentralization – and, more generally, the impact of federalism on options related to social policy – is to conceptualize Canada as not one but many Canadian welfare states.[59] Rather than treat Canada as a single political community and proclaim that it is involved in a structurally determined struggle to adapt to certain market imperatives, which empty social relations and politics of any content, we should, first, examine the political processes of federal relations themselves and, second, evaluate the social policy regimes available based on the idea that actors make a difference – in other words, that political agency matters.

In full agreement with this position, Michael Keating claims that the new discourse surrounding the de-territorialization of governance is short-sighted and fails to appreciate the continued salience of territory as a basis for social and political action. Function cannot be divorced from territory in any assessment of modern government. Territory remains an essential base for social solidarity. In Keating's words, 'Despite all the pressures of globalization, of markets and of social individualism, politics always seems to come back to a territorial basis.'[60] Territory continues to provide a solid basis for political representation and accountability in liberal democracies.

Keating alludes to new features of territorial politics that have come out of social policy discourses that are directly relevant to our assessment of SUFA. Under the conceptual label of 'governance,' the link from territory to function, identity, and institutions is taken as complex and variable, unable to be captured by simple territorial models based on the federal division of powers. Such complexity refers to the phenomenon that public policy is taken out of government control and given to a network of agencies answering to multiple constituencies. 'In this complexity the federal division of powers, in which a territorial government exercises determinate competences over a specific area and is answerable to a territorial constituency, can easily get lost.'[61]

We assert that political communities cannot be continually redesigned to reflect new functional needs without undermining democratic debate and participation. The new discourse surrounding governance conflicts with the federal principle, meant to bring government closer to the people and to allow more variations in policy choices. Yet this obsession for governance is precisely the direction taken by the central government in its SUFA vision. Policy options previously available to constituent communities are severely constrained in the current reorganization of social policy delivery. What was once territorially grounded is now fashioned within a myriad of non-territorial agencies in the name of better functional management, at the expense of member states. Consider, for instance, the central government's management of student loans and bursaries, granted directly to citizens through agencies that are not accountable to provincial representatives even though the policy area lies within provincial jurisdictions. This blatant encroachment barely raises an eye, since through this logic, it no longer matters who meets a certain policy objective as long as it meets 'citizens' needs.'

Gilles Bourque, Jules Duchastel, and Éric Pineault contend that we have entered a phase of techno-bureaucratic regulation which will have deleterious effect on the nature of democracy: 'Governance thus appears as government that transcends politics. It participates in the development of consensus, directly produced between the actors, within the extra-parliamentary institutional framework where the rules of social practice are henceforth defined, either prior to legislative assemblies or outside the legislative process (for example, at a global level, large international organisations).'[62] The political communities comprising the federation are indeed being redesigned and this process has been justified in the name of systemic pressures and imperatives. As the approach adopted here makes clear, options and preferences do exist. This insistence on the non-territorial basis of the delivery of social policy is indeed a choice by the central government – an element of statecraft – and stems directly from the same impulses that nourished its vision for patriation in 1982.

The limits of appeals to functional requirements in evaluating social policy delivery in federal states are summarized by Keating in the following manner:

> Governing institutions can never be determined entirely by functional requirements, since they reflect identity and loyalty, and must serve the needs of democratic deliberation and decision. Yet if they get too far out of line, new problems of accountability and democracy arise. So constitutional arrangements do matter and need to be addressed.[63]

Under the rubric of collaboration, the SUFA purports to act as a blueprint for the management of social policy delivery that serves to circumvent many of the perceived pitfalls of competition between governments. Intergovernmental relations in all areas of social policy are to be structured by this agreement. The key centralizing aspects of the agreement are its establishment of national standards in social programs, as well as the forced recognition of the federal spending power in areas of provincial jurisdiction. Moreover, the SUFA allows the federal government to impose a nationally-defined program in areas of provincial competence if the majority of provinces agree. Questions that were once deemed fundamental to federal legitimacy in Canada are now treated as mere administrative matters. Several authors stress that this approach mitigates federal practice and comes closer to a hegemonic rather than collaborative attempt by the federal government to resolve constant 'sticking points' in social policy delivery.[64] First, for collaboration to be genuine and non-hierarchical, it must produce cooperative solutions when there are significant differences in interests and perceptions. Second, social policy through this agreement is defined more around 'persons and through income taxes' than around places and through services.[65]

Stressing outcome rather than process, the social union does imply the absence of a clear chain of command, yet it falls short in terms of providing partners with an equal say. Indeed, Alan B. Simmons and Kieran Keohane argue that a principal motivation for the central government, regardless of the policy field, is to assert its hegemony (and authority) in the context of globalization.[66] It proceeds by claiming that policies are a product of consultations with a wide array of actors, ranging from provinces to local and international non-governmental organizations. The latent effect of such an approach, however, is to regulate the forces which may potentially come in the way of the central government's role in a changing global context. Social policy delivery, rather than resting with territorial communities, has been optioned out to third sectors in the name of 'citizen engagement' and greater effectiveness by the central government. An effective metaphor is employed by Noël: the central government 'steers but it does not row,' it sets objectives and outcomes and leaves others to implement them.[67] In short, democratically accountable provincial governments are lumped with private and voluntary sector providers.

This severely undermines the logic of federalism. As a result, the division of powers is presented as having less importance than concrete results, and policies can best be judged by outcomes. Canada as an area of study for social policy becomes unipolar with a myriad of centers of delivery. For example, social assistance will take the form of direct cheques from the central government to individuals. However, in the event that the financial situation deteriorates, it will rest on provincial responsibility through their constitutional obligations. A case in point is provided by the need for job-training programs without any federal money. Services will no longer be the result of community-based choices; rather, choices are now conceptualized as mostly technical and presented as best defined by the central government.

Setting the Scene

More recent developments occurring within the present constitutional order will be assessed in the final chapter. The purpose of this chapter is to provide a broad overview of the process of constitutionalism in Canada in light of some normative criteria for legitimacy and Quebec's historical understanding of its place in the country. We contend that the present constitutional order, in both process and substance, and the increasing presence of the central government in shaping social policy, represents the imposition of a majority nationalist agenda on Quebec. This state of affairs is characterized by a dismissal of the fact that Quebec has not consented, it breaks with the continuity of constitutional tradition, and refuses to accept Quebec as a negotiating partner in an act of mutual recognition. Moreover, Quebec is denied any legal recourse for constitutional reform short of secession.

The Canadian federal system is a liberal democratic polity that is more suited to unitary conceptions of the country and it lacks legitimacy with regards to its commitment to federalism. Its institutions are geared towards the attainment of stability, in the name of a domineering conception of national unity that emphasizes an equality of provinces doctrine, defines membership along the lines of equal individual rights from coast to coast, and portrays social policy as a functional challenge rather than a reflection of community preferences. Moreover, constitutionalism itself has come to a standstill. It is deemed to be damaging to the country's psyche on the one hand, and representing a pandora's box of actors and interests that view the process as a democratic act of participation, akin to the normal politics of a pluralistic polity with cross-cutting social cleavages, on the other.

This historical overview of Canadian constitutionalism does not dispute the validity and legitimacy of claims made by a diverse array of social interests and identities. Indeed, this reflects healthy democratic practice and active citizenship. However, in a multinational democracy such as Canada, certain cleavages based on national identity and territory ought to enjoy prominence as constitutional actors, as a matter of justice. Once a power-sharing constitution is in place, reflecting the demands of elected and accountable representatives from the country's constituent peoples, then questions on how to manage pluralism and diversity can be addressed, as is the case in all liberal democratic societies, *within* such units. This is the fundamental basis of legitimacy which representatives from Quebec have always understood to be the pre-condition for association in the Canadian federation, and it is based on inviolable sovereignty and self-determination in matters related to communitarian identity. The idea that the Canadian constitution ought to reflect the complex and diverse social composition of the country, but which fails to distinguish between groups in civil society and representatives of elected and accountable governments, has the latent effect of minimizing the importance of distinct internal nations. This is because the constitution, in this view, becomes a centralizing instrument; groups target their demands to the centre, and see this as an appropriate avenue for the voicing of their preferences. The community of reference for citizens is delineated – it is Canada – and Quebec becomes one of many such voices vying for recognition. Such a situation bodes ill for the future of the country, since this state of affairs is rejected in Quebec, as it always has been.

Canadian federalism is complex, in large part caused by prevailing disputes about the visions that ought to sustain it. The following chapter will look more closely at the various conceptions of the federal idea in Canada, demonstrating once again that at different points in history and under varying circumstances, there has been very little unanimity across the country as to how federalism ought to structure legitimate and acceptable representation.

3 The Federal Principle in Canada: Multifaceted Conceptions of Representation

Understanding the Federal Idea

The British victory in the Seven Years' War resulted in a British colony that inherited 65,000 non-English speaking subjects and housed two distinct nationalities. In what is a remarkable story of coexistence and identity survival, much of Canada's political history can be traced back to this socio-historical factor. Multinationality in Canada is not driven by opportunistic and self-serving political elites in an endless stream of disagreement over the (re)definition of constituent groups and the means as opposed to the ends of governance. Rather, multinationalism is the defining variable that conditions the manner in which distinct collectivities identify with this country, their subsequent visions of coexistence and, more specifically, with a federal arrangement.

The condition of Canadian federalism is thus one of competing visions for the accommodation of territorially based diversity, and more recently with the constitutional entrenchment of a Charter of Rights and Freedoms, for the formal recognition of non-territorial identities as well. Indeed, the one certainty of Canadian federalism is that any one conception of political community is accompanied by a chorus of dissent, by competing visions about the principles upon which the federal system should be constructed – what Daniel Elazar has termed 'a prismatic view of federalism.'[1] For Elazar, the distinction between systematic thought – characterized by fixed and uniform boundaries in the relationship between the state and civil society – and prismatic perspectives, in which the very foundation of the whole is interpreted differently by specific constituent actors, is an important conceptual starting point for assessing the distinctions between American and Canadian federalism. Jane Jenson describes the breadth of clashes over the construction of political community in Canada as follows:

> In Canada, three sets of collective identities have contended: individuals in a pan-Canadian community; regional and linguistic communities defined by territory; and a variety of other collectivities defined on bases other than territory – class, gender, ethnicity and so on. In addition, given these collectivities, a second debate has been about where and how they will be represented: in the institutions of the federal government and party system, in provincial institutions, or in the institutions of federalism itself – the Senate, Supreme Court, and the machinery of intergovernmental relations.[2]

As such, as Alan Cairns has noted, the process of finding a working balance between unity and diversity in Canada has been characterized by 'blunt and brutal compromises.'[3] Traditionally, the most distinctive features of Canadian politics are that its primary cleavages have centred on regional and linguistic divisions and its political clashes have been fought between federal and provincial governments. Since the repatriation of the constitution in 1982, governance in Canada has been characterized by an assortment of socio-political issues, ranging from questions of territorial national sovereignty, recognition and group-protection of various non-territorial identities, and fundamental individual rights on a pan-Canadian level. While many historical accounts of Canadian federalism have centred on classifications of relative power relations between the orders of government,[4] including constitutional positions and non-constitutional federal-provincial relations, François Rocher and Miriam Smith aptly point out that, taken alone, this approach is inadequate for grasping modern developments in federal practice, particularly since 1982. For these students of federalism, the very rules of the game have been fundamentally called into question due to increasingly diverging political identities,[5] and, simultaneously, a greater reluctance to accept this fact as a moral imperative in structuring the federation. In short, Canadian federalism – the challenges it faces and the conflicts that surface – stem more from existential questions relating to the status of particular collective actors within the structure of the Canadian federation than from actual policy outcomes, where there may or may not be disagreement about substantive matters related strictly to governance issues and functional considerations.

On the face of it, Canada follows the basic institutional and legal configuration of all federations.[6] As Ronald Watts has illustrated in a comparative study, federations express self-rule and shared-rule through the distribution of powers as provided for by a constitution. Central governments are charged with addressing issues common to all constituents while member states govern for the purposes of local autonomy with particular identities, interests, and policy preferences. Federal systems across the board must consist of at least two orders of government, each with an independent base of political legitimacy in the electorate and independent sources of revenue. There is a written constitution that is endowed with stringent amendment procedures and some form of judicial review for the resolution of conflict in matters relating to the division of powers.[7] This legalistic approach, however, tells very little about how federations actually function, particularly in their omission of political processes and social composition. As Edwin Black has noted, in a poignant reminder of the ideological aspects of federalism, 'Much political debate in Canada has revolved around the real meaning of federalism, a generally fruitless enterprise, because what most disputants have in mind is the ideal structure of the Canadian state; the "real meaning" of federalism or Confederation has been of interest only to the extent to which it justifies or discredits particular policy preferences.'[8]

In the Canadian case, Black points to various factors which have prevented a general agreement on the nature and purpose of a federal system, including the phenomenon of cultural dualism and its normative implications, the lack of a unifying national identity, and the tensions of representation and sovereignty associated with the combination of two divergent theories on constitutional authority (parliamentary democracy and federalism). Indeed, on this final point, Douglas Verney illustrates how the philosophical bases of Canadian federalism did not flow out of a precise 'logic of federalism,' in which judicial review and constitutional supremacy is understood to act as a mediating force between orders of government to ensure that each remain within their assigned spheres, as was developed early on in the American federal system. The British North America Act was a statute of the British Parliament like any other, and its legitimacy emanated from the imperial prerogative. Verney summarizes:

> [W]e need to remind ourselves that the Judicial Committee of the Privy Council did not play a role comparable to that of the American Supreme Court. It did not engage in judicial review of the Constitution. It did not enjoy the legitimacy of a written Constitution emanating from the people,

but depended on the prerogative power. Its status was not even that of ordinary English Courts: it was part of the executive branch. Its function was not that of broad review but of careful interpretation in conformity with the doctrine of parliamentary supremacy, the supremacy of the British Parliament. Finally, the Judicial Committee did not really interpret a Constitution but an Act of the British Parliament which by English law had to be treated as an ordinary statute.[9]

Although Verney and others note that Canadian federalism eventually evolved to include a de facto appellate court and later a Charter of Rights and Freedoms, the patchwork fashion in which federalism and parliamentary supremacy were reconciled has resulted in lingering questions about legitimate representation in the country's political institutions. In the United States, the will of the people is expressed through a constitution, which includes a Bill of Rights whose normative force is not questioned. In Canada, the document that was supposed to settle this ambiguity – the so-called 'peoples' package' – was patriated without the consent of the National Assembly of Quebec, a body that claimed, under the doctrine of parliamentary supremacy in the Westminster system, to represent the will of the citizens of Quebec. Pierre Trudeau's response to such an assertion was that Quebec was represented in the federal Parliament, and in matters outside the strict guidelines provided by the division of powers, even the basis of legitimate democratic representation is a matter for federal-provincial politicking.

Federal systems differ markedly in their mechanisms for resolving federal-provincial disputes in shared and overlapping jurisdictions, particularly in Canada, where formal institutions provide only a partial picture of the evolution of federal-provincial relations. While Canada can be classified as a federation by the general indicators highlighted above, two key features of federal-provincial conflict management must be highlighted. First, since its inception, Canadian federal institutions have been consistently influenced by the twin processes of state-building and national integration. This has resulted in a push and pull of institutional centralization and subsequent resistance by various socio-political forces, both territorial and non-territorial. Consequently, any portrait of Canadian federal practices cannot be provided without a full appreciation for both process and substance of policy outcomes. As a result, much political squabbling on the condition of federalism has been centred around division of power considerations: who delivers public policy, who represents constituents, how are political communities formally demarcated, along with 'normal' political questions based functional criteria and policy substance. Second, centralizing tendencies from both constitutional and non-constitutional sources have done more to destabilize the country than demands placed by the various layers of social diversity in Canadian political life. From the very founding debates on the institutional arrangements between the orders of government, the central state has been unable to cement a vision for the federation that would legitimate a concentration of power in Ottawa.[10] While constitutionalism has been set aside since the Liberals came to power in Ottawa in 1993, the only remaining certainty in Canada is that its defining constitution remains unfinished business. However, central institutions cannot wipe away federal societies: politics will continue to be defined by the condition of federalism in the Canadian context.

Assessments of mechanisms for conflict management within federations cannot be focused exclusively on formal constitutional arrangements and power-sharing configurations. Federal structures inform the relative salience of political issues. This study adopts an approach consistent with Preston King's[11] conceptual differentiation between federalism and federation in assessing federal-provincial disputes in federal states. The key contribution of this perspective is that 'federalism' is understood not only in its institutional arrangements but encompasses a sociological/ideological dimension and need not necessarily take concrete form in strict federation. As such, we can speak of 'federal societies'[12] and evaluate inter-community political dynamics without focusing on institutions as though they have been 'settled.' Federalism in this sense is conceptualized as a political device for establishing viable institutions and flexible relationships capable of facilitating inter-state relations (for example, the division of powers between orders of government), intra-state linkages (such as states' representation at the central level), and inter-community cooperation (nation-to-nation treaties, intergovernmental relations, and so on). Through an emphasis on process, institutions are taken to arise out of political conflicts and power struggles between economic, social, and political actors. This approach thus moves principally between two planes of analysis – institutional and sociological. The institutional level focuses on arrangements that structure community or regional relations between orders of government. The sociological level stresses issues of homogeneity and diversity, as witnessed in several federal practices that address questions of territorial sovereignty and political identity and the reaction of groups or communities that feel threatened or see greater potential in alternative arrangements that give broader expression to community or regional interests.

The conceptual difference between 'federalism' and 'federation,' which refers to the institutional sharing of sovereignty between various orders of government, bears relevance, since federal traditions and their impact on public policy systems do not stop short at a cursory reading of constitutional arrangements as a generic conceptual tool. This understanding allows for the conceptualization of 'federal entities' as sociological units of study, and as 'spatio-temporal' constructions that take form across relationships of power and are constantly evolving. If state actors employ the instruments of public policy towards the forging of communities of allegiance, then we must be aware of the legitimate representation of particular collective identities in the delivery of public policy, which is in the realm of politics, prior to delving into issues concerning which government can get better results. The latter approach is outcome-oriented, functional, implies that politics have been solved, and finally, assumes a pre-existing community of allegiance as a target for public policy. Such a focus in and of itself represents a methodological bias towards a single polity and disregards the variable of federalism as it is understood here. Issues relating to sovereign prerogatives between territorially-delimited communities are real – they are political – and they reflect potentially divergent preferences or choices for society and distinct views on the boundaries of political community. The challenge for federalism, and public policy systems within it, is to factor politics in, not to wish it away.[13]

Federal institutions do play a significant role in determining the actual contours of debate and relative bargaining positions of relevant actors, and this legalistic political configuration structures politics in a manner that is unique to federal states. We do not contend that legalistic interpretations of federal practice are altogether irrelevant. The state's relationship to actors in civil society, for example, cannot be conceptualized as though federal institutions, as defined by the constitution, are simply epiphenomenal. Again, it is this interplay between social forces and existing structures that forms a complete picture. Ed Black highlights five common characteristics of federal regimes, which may serve as a yardstick:

1. A written constitutional document which distributes significant powers between two sets of territorial governments, co-equal in the exercise of their exclusive jurisdictions.
2. A method of authoritative interpretation of the constitutional division of powers.

3. Dual citizenship, which implies that both sets of government have dealings with the people in respect of some important areas of life.
4. Some representation of the provinces as provinces in the central legislature.
5. A federalized executive, either in composition or appointment.[14]

Taken together, these characteristics provide a useful starting point for identifying key defining variables of federal states. Although the fourth point does not apply to Canada, the system has evolved to incorporate quasi-institutionalized negotiating platforms between executives from the various orders of government.[15] Our contention, however, is that such institutions are in part a response to sociological forces at work in Canada. Each one of these indicators, for example, while characterizing the Canadian federation, has been largely contested and open to varying interpretations in the course of Canadian history. Studying the various attempts to consolidate and settle the actual configuration of these pillars of federation are more reliable in determining the various challenges confronting Canada as a federal state, both in their implications for a political philosophy associated with Canadian federalism, and in terms of pragmatic considerations relating to ongoing political conflicts.

Will Kymlicka's conceptual distinction between multinational and territorial federations merits attention here.[16] Territorial federations are essentially characterized by a common sense of nationality that underpins the federal state, such as the United States, Australia, or Germany. Multinational federations include more than one linguistic or cultural grouping, with distinct institutions that are territorially based, and with legitimate claims to recognition as a national community. Examples include Canada, Belgium, and Spain. This typology makes room for a more sociological/ideological understanding of federal-provincial relations and the power dynamics at work between federated entities, as it sidesteps the analytical temptation to treat all federations as a generic category, where federal sub-units are taken as mere administrative units.[17] Without such a conceptual distinction, analyses of policy jurisdictions in federal states may be prone to a bias towards the centre, as territorial federations are more likely to be centralized. Watts has also observed this tendency: 'the more degree of homogeneity within a society the greater the powers that have been allocated to the federal government, and the more degree of diversity the greater the powers that have been assigned to the constituent units of government.'[18] Federation exists to meet the need to structure and institutionalize difference and diversity. With so many regular interests, socio-economic and cultural, territorial demands sometimes get lost in the shuffle. With federal societies, political elites are in a position to draw upon the very raison d'être of the polity to make demands for constitutional change, since the purpose of the polity is based on the idea of shared and separate sovereign spaces. Groups also organize, and the polity can sometimes move away from normal political disagreements to fundamental, constitutional, defining struggles over political community in which the stakes are much higher. Changing a constitution in a federal society is particularly difficult and could tear the country apart, while inaction may also lead to the same result.[19] Both substance and process become daunting issues. In Canada, constitutional wrangling was followed by much criticized non-constitutional renewal partly because of misgivings with regards to process. Jennifer Smith, for example, claims that informal constitutional change is not only an expedient process that in part serves to subvert the difficulties associated with constitutional change, but an anti-federal one that undermines the very founding of the federal system.[20] In short, subverting the rule of law negates the idea that unequal partners are to be treated equally, it affords less protection for traditional views in Quebec that will not change, and finally, it allows state actors to forego clear accountability by tangling governments in a complex web of interdependent initiatives.

The remainder of this chapter assesses the ebbs and flows of Canadian conceptions of federalism over time. It provides a historical backdrop for a subsequent discussion about the distinct conceptions of Canadian federalism and its capacity to accommodate identity claims. In turn, it highlights the selective use of particular political identities in the crafting of the prevailing vision of Canadian federalism. Essentially, this chapter presents the basic positions of the relevant actors over time in the power relationships that fostered Canadian federalism, from pre-Confederation arrangements, the original compromise, and competing constitutional visions. The history of distinct approaches to addressing multinationality in Canada shows that regardless of shifting historical circumstances, relative power bases of various government elites, or a convergence of values, the country has always been marked by diverging socio-political and competing national identities.

Pre-Confederation: The Seeds of a Federal State

The British conquest of New France coincided with the Treaty of Paris, ending the Seven Years' War and severing France's association with its

American colonies. This culminated in the Royal Proclamation of 1763, which gave the French-speaking inhabitants of Quebec their first civil constitution under the British crown. In this early post-conquest period, inhabitants were not consciously aware of their rights as a collective unit – indeed, their identity was largely predicated on their ties to absolutist France – and they were expected to assimilate as but another trading unit in the British Empire. Their fate was largely dictated by external events over which they had little control: the American Revolution and the persistence of Anglo-French international conflict constituted the main concerns of London. While most accounts of Canadian federalism begin with Confederation, or in some cases, with the Act of Union in 1840, this period is nevertheless pertinent to the extent that the British authorities were faced with inhabitants who, collectively, were not loyal to the crown, had to face the knowledge that they were formally cut off from France, and were made aware of public declarations by British governors that assimilation was the preferred policy course. Although the Conquest did not result in an indigenous nationalist movement, the early French-speaking *Canadiens* nevertheless feared the loss of their culture and traditions (perhaps most importantly, at the time, their Catholic faith), their institutions, and their laws. The early foundation of a distinct cultural collective sense of belonging was paradoxically the result of a conquest by a foreign military power. Perhaps of utmost importance is that the British authorities themselves defined the new subjects as a 'separate race' and tailored the royal proclamation to address this particular sociological reality.

The Royal Proclamation formally instituted British law. The *Canadiens* had no political rights – indeed, they could not hold official positions or be publicly employed unless they denounced Catholicism – and the English made it clear that a bishop would no longer be appointed by the pope. A House of Assembly was proposed, yet it was exclusive to English merchants. The proclamation also sought to replace civil law with English common law and to disband the seigneurial system. The intentions of the British authorities were to assimilate these adopted inhabitants as soon as possible. Yet the reality on the ground was interpreted much differently by the colony's first governor, General Murray, who learned soon after the Royal Proclamation came into effect in August 1764 that this group of subjects would not be easily assimilated, and did not enforce many of the act's provisions. He allowed the *Canadiens* to serve on the King's Bench and as lawyers in the lower courts. Moreover, he believed that a House of Assembly with no representation for the overwhelming majority of inhabitants would be an unworkable arrangement, so it was never actually adopted. Murray also reinstituted the seigneurial system and allowed the *Canadiens* to continue practising the Catholic faith, going as far as to endorse the first bishop under British rule, Jean-Olivier Briand.[21]

In 1774, the Quebec Act was adopted to redress the failed policy of assimilation of the Royal Proclamation. Indeed, many of the provisions in this policy shift by the British authorities simply formalized what Governor Murray had already practised. Murray's disdain for the crumbling of the *ancien régime* in the American colonies is well documented, and his vision of a distinct social and political order for the *Canadiens* was inherently conservative, preferring to restore the quasi-feudal privileges of the church and seigneurs. The Quebec Act thus opted for a legislative council, to be appointed by London, as opposed to a House of Assembly. According to A. L. Burt, the seigneurial system had already been re-established as early as 1771, and the act simply formalized this fact in law.[22] The act also acknowledged the legitimacy of the Catholic Church, yet Bishop Briand had been installed as early as 1766, along with the tithe. Moreover, Murray had already allowed for the application of French laws in lower courts, the use of French when litigants were French-speaking, and permitted *Canadien* lawyers and juries. The act essentially affirmed the pre-eminent status of aristocracy and clergy, denied popular government, and restored the body of civil law that had been in use prior to the Royal Proclamation, although clear demarcation lines between the application of common and civil law remains a debate among historians.[23]

For Alain-G. Gagnon and Luc Turgeon, the primary significance of the act is that it constituted the first imperial statute to establish a constitution for a British colony,[24] which institutionalized Quebec's distinctiveness and responded to the demands of the French elite regardless of whether it was motivated by events surrounding the American Revolution or by altruistic considerations.[25] Even under the force of imperial dictates, sociological variables could not be undone in the colony. Whether or not one ascribes the birth of a national consciousness to this event is not the salient issue. Civil society was allowed some continuity; the customs and habits of a minority group were permitted to persist. Historian Maurice Séguin explains:

> Whether they were seigneurs or men of the legal profession, the repeal of the Royal Proclamation and later the Quebec Act of 1774 provided Canadian leaders with a Constitutional text, a 'grand charter' that they later

exploited to the benefit of the French-Canadian collectivity. The Quebec Act legalized survival. It encouraged those Canadians to continue to consider themselves as a people of the colony.[26]

Indeed, James Tully contends that this nascent constitution was part of a broader normative philosophy of the Whigs that rested on the continuity associated with the ancient constitution, in which fundamental laws that were custom-based could not simply be wiped away by a conquering force without negating the liberty of the people.[27]

Brian Young disputes the tendency of historians to view the act as the founding moment of a French-Canadian national identity: its recognition, affirmation, and legitimacy. Indeed, Young notes that mainstream history in Canada has tended to appropriate the act as an early indication of a tolerant pan-Canadian nation. For Young, the Quebec Act institutionalized an early variant of pluralism which sanctioned the co-existence of distinct social and legal traditions, not the reimposition of an organic order that can be somehow conceptualized by employing secular Jacobin conceptions about national belonging and equality.[28] Indeed, according to Jean-Pierre Wallot, the Quebec Act did not constitute a radical shift in approaches by Great Britain.[29] Rather, it stemmed from aristocratic conceptions that were well anchored in British tradition. Wallot even claims that the British would have probably preferred to institute such constitutions in its other North American colonies if it was possible. For this historian, the contemporary idea that the act was the first to recognize the distinct status of Quebec is misleading, since it was not based on recognition of distinct status as though it was an earned moral imperative. Rather, Quebec was distinct because it was the only colony where circumstances allowed the British to reimpose the much preferred order of the *ancien régime*. Wallot gives the final word to Hilda Neatby:

> If ... the Act is to be taken with all its accompanying instructions, it cannot possibly be called 'liberal' from any modern viewpoint. If the instructions are forgotten and the Act stands alone, it is a Charter for French-Canadians ... If the instructions are emphasized, then the concessions to Canadians become a simple protection to property and custom, and in no sense a recognition of ... 'nation' ... In short, if the Act and all the instructions are read together and thought of as equally expressing the policy of the ministry, that policy can be seen only as one of gentle but steady and determined Anglicization.[30]

Whatever dualism existed after 1774 was purely cultural and inherently conservative, and without significant political repercussions that can be appropriated for proof of early signs of contemporary notions of national political recognition. This was not a national movement but a rejection of the burgeoning idea of the nation altogether.

It was the Constitution Act of 1791 that formally connected the cultural duality of the colony with territorially-based quasi-representative institutions. At the request of some 10,000 British colonists who sought to separate from 150,000 *Canadiens*, as well as Liberal professionals who had begun to assert themselves as leaders among the *Canadiens*, London divided the colony into Upper and Lower Canada, consisting of two parliaments but one appointed governor. The implication of the act, according to historian George Stanley, was 'to give renewed vigour to the idea of French Canadian separateness. It provided the French fact with a geographical as well as a political buttress.'[31] By the early 1800s a full-fledged nationalist movement developed among French Canadians. Many liberal professionals demanded an end to the political pre-eminence of Anglo-dominated executive bodies. This movement sought a shift of power to Lower Canada's representative institutions and, generally, greater autonomy from London. Similar uprisings in Upper Canada were quite distinct,[32] and by the time armed rebellion erupted in 1837, they functioned separately, under two different leaders, Louis-Joseph Papineau and William Lyon Mackenzie. Cultural dualism, coupled with distinct territory and institutions, was beginning to take shape in the colony.

The defeat of the rebellions resulted in a concession that, a decade later, granted responsible government, along with the recommendation that the two colonies be merged into a United Canada. Lord Durham, asked to provide an assessment of the unrest in the colonies, believed the ultimate resolution to the conflict was to rid the colony of cultural dualism and to assimilate French Canadians. Flowing from liberal traditions at the time, Durham believed that 'undoing the backwardness' of the French Canadians was necessary for their own good. In order to accomplish this, he argued that a legislative union with an ever-increasing majority of English colonists, loyal to the crown, would eventually coerce French Canadians into abandoning any notion of a separate nationality.[33] The Act of Union of 1840 united Upper and Lower Canada, renaming the territories Canada West and Canada East. The language of the new legislature was to be exclusively English, and both provinces were allotted an equal number of seats, ensuring that the English majority would prevail. While the intention was to assimilate the French, the new arrangement paradoxically allowed French blocs in the legislature to protect their interests in the face of the split English majority, with English Reformers[34] from Canada West often aligned with the bloc from Canada East. Conventions thus began to develop around a 'double majority,' in which any proposal that affected one language group could not be adopted without the majority consent of that bloc. Other conventions included parallel administrative structures, the maintenance of French services, the Church and civil law in Canada East, alternating capital cities, and even two prime ministers. Kenneth McRoberts notes that, given the intentions of the Act of Union, it is remarkable how far dualism progressed out of a legislative union, leading John A. Macdonald to proclaim, during the Confederation Debates, 'we have had a Federal Union in fact, though a Legislative Union in name.'[35] When the Reformers from Canada West began to call for 'rep by pop' due to disproportionate growth in the West, they split with the French bloc in the legislature, and while the Tories resumed the alliance for a short period, pressures for a new regime mounted. The French, however, had understood that dualism was the only acceptable formula for coexistence, and any new arrangement would have to include some legislative sovereignty for Canada East in a spirit of equality with English Canada.

The Confederation Debates thus unfolded under the legacy of United Canada. Proponents of Confederation from Canada West were firmly convinced of the need to abandon dualism in favour of a strong central government with a clear national (or pan-Canadian) integration strategy, and to escape stalemate and the perceived deference to French-Canadian interests in the legislature. Indeed, John A. Macdonald, while conceding that the particular situation of the French in Quebec and the desire for individuality by the Maritime provinces warranted a federal system, nevertheless believed privately that the provinces would eventually be absorbed by the central state.[36] On the other hand, the lessons learned by the French convinced them of the need to employ federalism as a means by which to institutionalize the double majority and other dualist conventions that arose in United Canada. The theme that united the federalists and centralizers was the need to secure their external commercial relationships, particularly following the abrogation of the Reciprocity Treaty by the United States in 1866, and the need for common colonial defence against the prospect of American absorption.[37]

In many respects, ambiguities about the intentions surrounding the adoption of a federal system have provided a point of origin for the diverging conceptions of Canadian federalism that continue to exist to this day. Ed Black has argued that Canada lacks a charter myth, and as such, in its absence, it is in the perceptions and actions of those responsible for framing the direction of federalism and national identity that we find the best evidence of Canada's political philosophies.[38] Unlike the American federal system, which constantly looks for guidance in the words of the Founding Fathers, Canada relies as much on interpretations of intentions and partisan clarifications of conventions surrounding the original pact, or in its 'spirit.'[39] Indeed, it must be recalled that the founding provisions of Canada's federal system did not aim to spell out clear founding principles, since it was not a document for independence: Canada was essentially strengthening its bonds and loyalty to the British system, not finding a new way that would appease all parties and constitute a national covenant. In the course of its history, the Canadian federal system has been portrayed both as among the most decentralized and also the most quasi-federal. This paradox lies at the heart of the continuous strains produced by competing visions of federalism[40] that have coincided with the dual challenges of Canadian nation-building and expressions of multinationality. It is this inherent tension that has underscored much of the enduring strains associated with constitutionalism, federal-provincial relations, and identity claims. In the remaining portion of this chapter, we will discuss the main visions for Canadian federalism in the century and a half that followed the original compromise.

Competing Federal Visions

The founding moments of the Canadian federal system have not been interpreted with unanimity. Beyond the rough guide provided by the division of powers, the intentions of the framers continue to inform debates about the principles upon which federalism was adopted. Moreover, subsequent developments have continued to exhibit an uneasy sense of ambiguity about the grand ideas that legitimate Canadian federalism, as evident in the ongoing tensions between identity claimants. In the end, federalism is impossible to evaluate outside of specific political contexts. In the United States and Germany, for example, federalism was adopted to limit the excesses of executive power, as a device that was to promote the liberty of citizens, not as a means by which to accommodate diversity. Franz Neumann went as far as to conclude that evaluating federal systems in general is futile: federalism could be good, bad or indifferent depending on particular circumstances and the positions of key participants.[41] Several interpretations of federalism have emerged in the course of Canada's history.[42] The following sections offer a cursory review of the main conflicting visions.

Visions of Decentralization I: The Compact Theory

This view flows from a classical theory of federalism and in its basic formulation establishes that Canada is a creation of the provinces. Theoretically, it implied that each member state was sovereign in its area of jurisdiction. The very existence of a federal regime was deemed to be the result of a contract between pre-existing states. This conception of federalism defines allegiance along provincial lines – that is, the first order of representation for citizens are provincial governments. An early interpretation of this conception was provided by Justice Thomas-Jean-Jacques Loranger[43] soon after Confederation in 1867. Judge Loranger's views were summarized in the preliminary report of the Royal Commission on Aboriginal Peoples in 1993. Its main premises are as follows:

1. The confederation of the British Provinces was the result of a compact entered into by the provinces and the United Kingdom.
2. The provinces entered into the federal Union with their corporate identity, former constitutions, and all their legislative powers intact. A portion of these powers was ceded to the federal Parliament, to exercise them in common interest of the provinces. The powers not ceded were retained by the provincial legislatures, which continued to act within their own spheres according to their former constitutions, under certain modifications of form established by the federal compact.
3. Far from having been conferred upon them by the federal government, the powers of the provinces are the residue of their former colonial powers. The federal government is the creation of the provinces, the result of their association and of their compact.[44]

In reference to Justice Loranger's position, James Tully prefers to call this perspective 'diverse federalism,' due to its underlying capacity to accommodate heterogeneous societies and polities. Tully highlights some implications of this form of constitution for countries such as Canada:

Since the pre-existing forms of provincial governments are bound to be various, and since the citizens will amend them from time to time, the

resulting federation is an irregular and multiform assemblage. The equality it embodies is not the identity of political and legal institutions, but the
equal recognition and autonomy of the diverse forms of provincial self-
government ... Since the consent of each province is required for confederation and any subsequent amendment that touches their legal and political culture, some provinces may agree to delegate powers to the federal
government that others choose to retain until they see how economically
the federal government exercises them, or perhaps to experiment with a
different model themselves.[45]

In examining the period from Confederation to 1921, Ramsay Cook
has argued that the compact theory, in its earliest and most lasting formulation, has always consisted of a variation between two versions: a
compact between two cultural groups and a compact between provinces.[46] For Quebec, the importance of the distinction would surface
much later, since it was clear soon after the birth of Confederation that
it was an original party to the agreement, whether or not it was defined
as a province or as a distinct national grouping. By implication, this
approach assumed that no substantive changes could be effected to federal-provincial jurisdictional lines without the consent of the provinces.
According to George Stanley, a prominent historian of Confederation,
the compact is not a legally binding notion in the conventional sense,
with enforceable provisions and a certain clarity of language. In his
words,

> If we attempt to look upon this pact or entente as a legal contract, freely
> entered into by two parties and intended by them to be legally enforceable
> in a court of law, our vision will be so limited as to be distorted; for a pact
> or compact is not a contract in the legal sense. It is a gentlemen's agree-
> ment, an understanding based on mutual consent, with a moral rather
> than a juridical sanction.[47]

It is clear that the idea of the compact in itself contains a moral imperative that cannot be neglected in any assessment of Canadian federalism,
and this constitutes a glaring weakness of legal interpretations of Confederation.

For early French-Canadian nationalist intellectuals, the notions of
provincial autonomy and clearly-defined cultural groupings were
already beginning to take shape as the driving forces behind federalism. The idea of federalism was legitimate insofar as it respected pro-

vincial – and by extension cultural – autonomy. This would be a near-universal theme from Quebec representatives up to today. Differences of opinions among Quebec elites stemmed only from the degree of autonomous action vis-à-vis the central government, but not with the issue of full jurisdictional integrity itself. Quebec governments from all parties have always held the original division of powers as a minimal condition of membership. Proponents of provincial autonomy were given much credence from the Judicial Committee of the Privy Council (JCPC) in the United Kingdom, which interpreted the general 'Law for the peace, order and good government of Canada' (POGG) provision of the BNA Act merely as an emergency power of the central government; the committee interpreted property and civil rights generously in favour of the provinces, and by implication, offered a limited definition of the federal government's ability to expand its competency over trade and commerce. However, an English-Canadian school of political scientists, including Garth Stevenson, contends that the JCPC:

> ... fundamentally altered the whole nature of Canada's federal constitution. It appeared to lend credence to the argument that the purpose of Confederation had been to protect and promote provincial interests, rather than to create a new nation, and it did so just as the generation that had direct memories of the Confederation negotiations and debates was passing from the scene. Henceforth, the ideological weight of Imperial authority was placed on the side of those who espoused provincial autonomy.[48]

Nonetheless, several English-Canadian provincial leaders also embraced the compact theory in its strict formulation: that is, one of provincial rights and watertight orders of government. Although Oliver Mowat, the premier of Ontario, joined forces with the Quebec premier, Honoré Mercier, in convening the first interprovincial conference in 1887, cracks in the interpretation of the compact were beginning to emerge. While in Quebec the compact meant that the federation would be built upon the notion of two founding peoples which happened to coincide with the territorial demarcation of the provinces, events in Manitoba and Ontario demonstrated that the theory was being invoked to justify the province's rights to limit cultural dualism on their own territories – by restricting access to minority French-language education, for example. It soon became clear to Quebec that the spirit of the original compromise would not be reflected in the acceptance of dualism by the other partners of Confederation, and Quebec was the only province where French Canadians could secure their standing as a majority in representative institutions. Henri Bourassa, a leading French-Canadian nationalist at the turn of the twentieth century, reformulated the theory and referred to a 'double compact' – a theory that was to resonate in Quebec for much of its subsequent history. For Bourassa, dualism constituted a moral premise of Confederation, even though it was not clearly outlined in its formal text, the compact could not refer simply to institutional demarcations. The original delineation between colonies represents one aspect of the contract, the other being the notion that the country was meant to serve the interests of two founding peoples, stemming directly from the experience of the United Canadas. According to Bourassa, 'The imperial statute which the current government has given us is only the force of a double contract. One was concluded between the French and the English of the old province of Canada, while the aim of the other was to bring together the scattered colonies of British North America. We are thus party to two contracts – one national and one political. We must keep a careful eye on the integrity of these treaties.'[49]

The depression in the 1930s led to greater calls for central economic management and new-deal style intervention across Canada by the federal government, deemed by many as the only plausible saviour. Presentations to the Royal Commission on Dominion-Provincial relations (the Rowell-Sirois Commission) signalled widespread support for centralized Keynesian policies that would significantly expand the powers of the federal government relative to the provinces. After the Second World War, proponents of decentralization in Canada began to diverge in their understanding of the founding pact. With the postwar economic boom under way and the increasing revenues allotted to the central government, English Canada gradually accepted a stronger central presence in policy areas that had previously been deemed strictly provincial. Indeed, Keynesian practices were well established in Ottawa, cementing a 'national' economic role for federal policy-makers in public investment. The expansion of the welfare state severely challenged the compact theory in Canada.

Quebec, however, remained steadfast in its conception of federal principles. A key document was the provincial Royal Commission of Inquiry on Constitutional Problems (the Tremblay Commission), published in 1956 as a long overdue response to the Rowell-Sirois Commission. The Tremblay Commission argued for the continuation of strict adherence to the division of powers because of the distinctive 'cultural' communities upon which Canadian federalism receives its mandate. For these proponents of decentralization, Ottawa did not represent a national government: the primary centre of allegiance for French Canadians was Quebec. This report would lay the groundwork for what was to become conventional wisdom in Quebec – and would shape the compact theory along the lines of two founding peoples as opposed to a strict doctrine of provincial rights. Indeed, by the time the Quiet Revolution took hold in Quebec, the provincial compact theory was somewhat rejected, since this would allow other provinces to veto Quebec initiatives to deal directly with Ottawa for more autonomy in an era where the scope of state intervention was growing rapidly. In the rest of Canada, the compact theory was waning in relevance by the time the Tremblay Commission was released. However, this did not stop Lester B. Pearson during his tenure as prime minister from insisting on its political relevance to find a solution to Quebec's growing uneasiness with English Canada. In 1963 he set up the Royal Commission on Bilingualism and Biculturalism (the Laurendeau-Dunton Commission), yet many of its recommendations were subsequently discredited and scrapped upon the arrival of Pierre Trudeau as Pearson's successor in 1968. This vision would re-emerge later, in a somewhat different formulation, on the one hand as a result of Quebec's vision for Canadian federalism and on the other because of the perception that Canadian federalism did not accommodate the interests of the Western provinces.

According to François Rocher and Miriam Smith, the compact theory evolved to incorporate more than the principle of provincial sovereignty and a 'watertight compartments' conception of the federal system. To the extent that this vision is employed outside of Quebec, it continues to accommodate some federal presence in shared fields of jurisdiction. Yet in federal-provincial dynamics, it views all provinces as diverse sovereign entities, each with a 'distinct' nature, that are equal in their relationship to the federal government. In this formulation, federal-provincial relations come to represent a zero-sum game: if one province is recognized as having special sovereign status, or more jurisdictional latitude vis-à-vis the federal government, then this implies a loss for the remaining provinces. In the final analysis, this view maintains that federalism must be symmetrical, and particular status for one province is said to be contrary to the original pact in which provinces are equally responsible for determining the relative levers of power in their relationship with the central government and with each other. Any changes to the federal-provincial balance must be assumed equally by all provinces. For Rocher and Smith, the 'equality of provinces' doctrine is salient to the extent that it constitutes a formidable vision of the Canadian political community that is deeply engrained among citizens: provinces must possess the same powers as the others in order to guarantee that they can act within their areas of competence. In other words, each province is equal as a constituent unit of Canadian federalism.[50]

Visions of Decentralization II: Intrastate Federalism

Those seeking to accommodate the diversity of provincial interests without defining Canadian federalism as a compact between two founding peoples, or as a political community marked by intergovernmental bargaining espoused a vision that would reform central institutions. In effect, calls for intrastate federalism, particularly in force in the 1970s, were meant to represent more adequately provincial concerns at the federal level without conceiving of the polity as a loose confederation of provincial governments at the expense of a national community. Constant federal-provincial conflict, in this view, would be resolved if provincial governments were equally represented at the centre, in a permanent institutional framework that would allow provincial concerns to be expressed without recourse to executive-level bargaining between the orders of government. Territorial interests would not have to be invested solely in provincial governments. Alan Cairns summarizes the thrust of this vision for Canadian federalism:

> Given the hypothesized inability of the federal government effectively to incorporate and represent the primary sociological realities of Canada ... that government was considered to be rootless. Accordingly, the provinces were viewed as having more legitimacy than jurisdiction, and the federal government as having more jurisdiction than legitimacy ... Since [Ottawa's] attenuated legitimacy was attributed to its inadequate contact and empathy with provincial values and concerns, the solution was to incorporate provincial perspectives into its workings, a process often described as federalizing central-government institutions.[51]

Cairns notes that this vision can be further divided into distinct provincialist and centralist variations. In the former version, the main institutional reform would be a revamped Senate, whose members were to be appointed and accountable to provincial governments, and could veto federal legislation deemed incompatible with the interests of provincial communities. The Senate's traditional role of reviewing and revising legislation from the Commons, which in a British system of responsible parliamentary government is in practice ineffective from the perspective of reformers,[52] would be replaced by a permanent body charged with managing the complexity of interdependent relations between governments. The centralist vision, by contrast, sought to restructure central government institutions in order to insulate the federal government from the active input of provincial delegates. Briefly, the main idea behind this approach was that the federal government could govern in its own areas of jurisdiction, on a pan-Canadian level, with the credentials that its institutions are adequately representative of provincial concerns. For Cairns, in a speculative exercise, the shortcomings of intrastate reforms are that they do not address the fundamental problem of providing an institutional framework that would at once balance the requirements of both unity and diversity upon which the original federal compromise was based. In other words, each version falls into the trap of prioritizing one level of allegiance over the other. Intrastate federalism, in the final analysis, is decentralizing to the extent that it represents a tacit admission that a national community in Canada does not exist. All provinces are equal and legitimacy at the federal level stems directly from provincial identities and communities. Federal governments have for the most part rejected such proposals, claiming that Canada is more than an aggregation of provincial communities.

Nation-to-Nation Relations: From Binationalism to Multinationalism

> The tension between Quebec's struggle to strengthen and reinforce its particularities and the federal government's efforts to act as a national government has determined much of Canadian history.[53]

While Quebec was an ardent supporter of a provincial rights doctrine from the period following Confederation to the mid-1950s, there emerged after the Quiet Revolution a view that its status within the federation was more than a province like the others; Quebec's government represented a constituent national unit in Canadian federalism – one of two founding peoples. Kenneth McRoberts contends that the implication of such an approach to federal legitimacy is that asymmetrical arrangements would permit each nation to develop according to its particular needs.[54] Quebec gradually viewed the federation as a compact between nations, with one nation represented by the Quebec government and the other covering the rest of Canada. The status of the Quebec state was thus that it constituted a distinct society, which, in more moderate versions, strictly adhered to the division of powers granted by the original compromise and consistently rejected federal government encroachment into its jurisdictions. In its more forceful manifestations, in particular under Parti Québécois governments, such a vision sought to recast the compact to recognize two sovereign nations whose relations would be conducted as equals in a sort of confederal arrangement. In this view, Quebeckers would govern themselves as a majority territorial community as opposed to being a perpetual minority as a component of a larger Canadian political community. René Lévesque aptly described this sentiment in proclaiming that Canada is composed of two distinct nations 'concealed behind the fiction of ten provinces.'[55]

The various visions for Canada stemming from Quebec nationalist forces, as well as the evolution of the boundaries of Quebec nationalism itself, are too diverse and complex for full treatment here.[56] However, several prominent themes about the federal system have been almost universally accepted by successive Quebec governments. For Quebec, federalism as an organizing principle is not equivalent to a single political community; thus there is an inherent rejection of the federal government's tendency to forge a national identity across the country. Quebec's insistence on dualism as a fundamental characteristic of federalism can be traced back to the Confederation Debates. Initially Macdonald proposed a legislative union similar to that of the United Kingdom. He conceded, however, that federalism was the more satisfactory option and proposed a more sociologically sensitive solution to the persistence of national consciousness among French Canadians:

> [We] found that such a system [legislative union] was impracticable. In the
> first place, it would not meet the assent of the people of Lower Canada,
> because they felt that in their particular position – being in a minority, with
> a different language, nationality and religion from the majority – in case of
> a junction with the other provinces, their institutions and their laws might
> be assailed, and their ancestral associations, on which they prided them-
> selves, attacked and prejudiced.[57]

George-Étienne Cartier, the principal voice of French Canada during the debates, was more forceful in his vision of duality: 'Such is ... the significance that we must attach to this constitution, which recognizes the French-Canadian nationality. As a distinct, separate nationality, we form a State within the State with the full use of our rights and the formal recognition of our national independence.'[58] Of particular salience in the initial agreement, at least with regards to Quebec's specificity, are provisions that recognized Quebec's distinct legal tradition (civil law, in contrast to common law elsewhere in Canada), and provincial autonomy in education and most 'social' matters, including linguistic provisions respecting the use of French in Quebec.

During the 1960s, the Royal Commission on Bilingualism and Biculturalism (B&B Commission) received a mandate from the central government to review the federal system with specific regards to the principle of equality between the two founding peoples – a tacit acknowledgment of this vision. Following the Tremblay Commission in Quebec, the B&B Commission marked the emergence of an era that would revisit the pillars of Canadian federalism and the original compromise. These initiatives were in large part a reaction to events related to the Quiet Revolution, which came to see Quebec autonomy less as a defensive provincial-rights issue and more as a political, economic, and social project aimed towards greater state intervention in affirming national specificity. Daniel Johnson, the Quebec premier in 1966, expressed this more affirmative sentiment when stating:

> At the base of operations as a nation, it wants to be the master of the decisions which deal with the human growth of its citizens (that is to say education, social security and health in all its forms), with their economic affirmation (that is to say the power to establish the economic and financial levers they believe necessary), with their cultural flourishing (that is to say not only arts and literature, but also language) and with the extension of the Québécois community (that is to say relations with some countries and international organizations).[59]

Again, the reasoning stems from the basic premise: the Quebec government is the only institution in North America in which francophones constitute a majority. The accommodation of Québécois identity is the first principle of federalism in this view.

Two dominant visions emerged in Quebec, which, in many respects, constitutes the mainstream divide among nationalists to this day. The first sees asymmetrical federalism[60] as an option that would adequately satisfy the requirements of stability and unity in Canada without subsuming its national diversity. For proponents of this vision, asymmetry would be a more accurate reflection of social and historical realities. Moreover, it would exhibit a degree of flexibility that might put an end to Quebec's perception of federalism as a rigid, centralizing, and instrumental structure; in other words, it reflects a certain willingness to 'adopt' Canada as a legitimate political community in its own right, able to address fundamental diversities that acquire political salience. The minimal conditions put forth by the leader of the Quebec Liberal party, Robert Bourassa, in the lead up to the Meech Lake negotiations for constitutional renewal in the latter half of the 1980s, serve as somewhat of a culmination of this vision. More specifically, these conditions were:

   i. The explicit recognition of Quebec (in the preamble of the Constitution) as a distinct society;
   ii. Increased power to Quebec in immigration regarding recruitment, administration, and integration of new arrivals;
   iii. Quebec's participation in the appointment of three Supreme Court justices with expertise in Quebec civil law;
   iv. Limitations on the federal spending power;
   v. The recognition of Quebec's right to veto any constitutional amendment that affects it.

Taken together, such demands reflect the view that Quebec's political future in Canada can best be accommodated by affirmative measures that go beyond the original compromise. For proponents of asymmetrical federalism, such affirmations were necessary to redress the increased presence of the federal government in provincial matters as a result of a blurring of the division of powers over time. Definitions of the Canadian political community could no longer operate along symmetrical lines, since the perceived sentiment from this perspective was that citizens and governments of the other provinces looked to the federal government as their national government and their principal instrument of growth, while this was not the case in Quebec.

The second vision among nationalists is that the federal experiment has failed – that no mutually satisfying compromise is possible. The 1979 White Book of the PQ government aptly captures this sentiment. In this view, Quebec could only achieve what it desired through a clear break from Canada, in which a new Quebec-Canada agreement would be negotiated outside the confines of the federal framework. The main thrust behind this vision was stated clearly in *Quebec-Canada: A New Deal*: 'The fact that it is impossible, in the present federal framework, for Quebec to become a nation, constitutes the very basis of the Canada-Quebec political problem.'[61] The solution was to be found in the notion of sovereignty-association, which promoted a new political partnership based on two separate, sovereign entities while maintaining formal economic links. A decade later, following the demise of the Meech Lake Accord which would have entrenched asymmetry, the Commission on the Political and Constitutional Future of Quebec (the Bélanger-Campeau Commission) arrived at a similar conclusion.[62] The report, however, added the adoption of the Constitution Act, 1982 to its justifications for a rupture, since Quebec had not been a signatory to the agreement. It was noted that the principles upon which the Canadian political community was constructed could not accommodate Québécois identity for several reasons, as summarized by Rocher and Smith:

> Three dimensions of this new Canadian identity were given: the equality of all citizens, which does not allow special constitutional recognition for the Québécois collectivity; the equality of cultures and of cultural origins in Canada, which would undermine Québécois aspirations for the French language and the cultural origins of francophones; and the equality of the provinces, which would forestall the granting of special status for Quebec.[63]

The dualist vision of Canada has largely been driven by Quebec. Aboriginals, however, have made the basic claim that binationalism in Canada is sociologically inaccurate and has detracted attention away from the notion that they possess an inherent right to self-government. In what would constitute a third order of government in Canada, the asymmetry sought by Aboriginals challenges the very conception that Canadian federalism is based solely on a division of powers between the federal Parliament and the provincial legislatures. As such, the discourse of federalism that has provided the framework for conceptions of binationalism must be revisited to accommodate new institutions, a new sharing of powers, and a corresponding fiscal formula. Although the details of future relations remain unclear, since the present constitution merely makes reference to the inherent right of self-government for First Nations, the salient starting point for Aboriginal groups is clear: the federal government must terminate its paternalistic relationship with Aboriginal peoples and begin the long road to accommodation on a nation-to-nation basis. Such groups seek a partnership that would, at a minimum, recognize that they possess sovereignty over the territories and resources upon which they depend.[64] Indeed, Kiera Ladner notes that 'treaty federalism' should be considered as a founding principle of Canadian federalism, as opposed to the more conventional view that Aboriginal peoples' official status in Canada's federal configuration began with their explicit recognition in the Charter of Rights and Freedoms.[65] The Royal Commission on Aboriginal Peoples provides a cogent summary of this emerging vision of Canadian federalism as it applies to Aboriginal peoples:

> Over time and by a variety of methods, Aboriginal people became part of the emerging federation of Canada while retaining their rights to their laws, lands, political structures and internal autonomy as a matter of Canadian common law ... the current constitution in Canada has evolved in part from the original treaties and other relations that First Peoples held with the Crown and the rights that flow from those relations. The treaties form a fundamental part of the constitution and for many Aboriginal peoples, play a role similar to that played by the Constitution Act, 1867 in relation to the provinces. The terms of the Canadian federation are found not only in formal constitutional documents covering relations between the federal and provincial governments but also in treaties and other instruments establishing the basic links between Aboriginal peoples and the crown.[66]

Although Aboriginal visions remain on the margins of discourses relating to Canadian federalism, the justification of their claims is garnering increased attention and will constitute a fundamental challenge for the flexibility of the federal system to adapt to distinct visions and circumstances.

James Tully notes that the challenge brought about by a just accommodation of First Nations requires that we examine two confederal arrangements in Canada. The first refers to the treaty confederation of the First Nations with the crown, and later with federal and provincial governments. The second is the more familiar legal framework – the constitutional confederation between the federal government and the provinces. Tully contends that incorporating Aboriginal peoples into the second framework misrepresents their historical rights to self-government and is ill-equipped to accommodate the notion of treaty relations, since they had no part in its formation. As such, subjecting

Aboriginal peoples to the legal framework established by Canadian federalism – either as individuals, minorities, or even quasi-autonomous governing units – simply perpetuates a colonial relationship. For example, Aboriginal peoples have been steadfast in proclaiming an inherent right to self-government, rejecting 'pragmatic' approaches that would simply state this as a right within Canadian law and approach negotiations as a minority rights issue. For Tully, the basic challenge – indeed, the paradigm shift in terms of Aboriginal self-government – requires the acknowledgment of a political association of two confederations.[67] This essay will not venture into the difficulties and opportunities associated with such a radical break from federal practice, although it recognizes it as a challenge that the Canadian federal system, if it indeed is a living tree, will have to accommodate.

Centralizing Visions I : The Nationalizing Conception of the Founders

> The Dominion was to be a deliberate creation which could be established, in the perspectives of the Fathers of Confederation, only through the instrumentality of a strong and vigorous central government. This meant both that the federal authorities would assume the decisive leadership in the task and that the dominant loyalties of the people, insofar as they were those of a political allegiance, would be focused on the Dominion rather than its constituent parts.[68]

According to Roger Gibbins, the recurring theme in the construction of Canada's founding principles as seen from the perspective of the central government is articulating the need for a single political community, one that is more than instrumental, through the institution of federalism. Institutionalist scholars fail to see the paradox of such an approach – and indeed, the centralizing visions of Canadian federalism have in many ways reflected a desire for national integration as opposed to federalism in its classic sense. For Gibbins, the compact theory of premiers and the dualist approach of Quebec make it difficult to even talk of a Canadian community or nation, much less base the country's self-understanding on such principles.[69] The common element of the decentralized visions for Canadian federalism outlined above is, in many respects, that they are reactions to a competing vision of federalism that seeks to craft a larger political identity in a nationalizing project. Interpretations of such intentions for the future of the Canadian political community also date back to its founding debates.

As noted above, John A. Macdonald, the principal author of the Quebec Resolutions that had served as the basis of the BNA Act, favoured a legislative union, and when he opted for federalism, it was to be a strong centralized federation in order to avoid what he perceived to be shortcomings of the American constitution:

> a conflict may ... arise between the Dominion and the 'States' Rights' people. We must meet it, however, as best we may. By a firm yet patient course, I think the Dominion must win in the long-run. The powers of the General Government are so much greater than those of the United States, in its relations with the local governments, that the central power must win.[70]

In early federal practice, the BNA Act gave the central government unlimited powers to tax and spend, while provinces were restricted to direct taxation. Moreover, the federal government appointed lieutenant-governors in each province with the capacity to reserve provincial legislation for a period of a year, which could be subsequently disallowed by the federal government, and all residual powers were to be granted to the federal government. In the context of an emerging state, it is not altogether surprising that the central state would undertake a nation-building project. In terms of actual substance, the federal government was given crucial powers over defence and external relations, development and economic integration, trade and commerce – all areas that were deemed necessary to pursue a national integration strategy. This culminated in Canada's First National Policy in 1879 which entailed a three-pronged strategy: the construction of a trans-Canadian railway system, the promotion of immigration policy, and the adoption of a protective tariff in order to forge an integrated and self-sufficient national economy.[71]

Other centralizing provisions included a uniform system of criminal law, with a general court of appeal, and the right to take unilateral action in bringing provincial responsibilities under federal control. According to Donald Smiley, some of the Fathers of Confederation probably anticipated that the political party system would contribute to Dominion supremacy over the provinces; envisioning that close partisan working relationships with provincial legislators might allow for great authority and influence given the relative position of power of the federal parliament, and in some cases with prominent leaders holding membership in both bodies.[72] Peter Waite has pointed out that many of the centralizers may have believed that cabinet government itself would undermine 'local' powers, since this would weaken the capacity of the Senate to effectively represent regional interests.[73]

Indeed, while the Judicial Committee continued to frustrate the realization of this conception of Canada by insisting on the integrity of provincial jurisdictions, the nationalizing project would come to the fore in a different version with the great depression of the 1930s. Attempts to concentrate more power in the central government was thus a direct response to the perceived need to craft Canada's very own 'new deal,' which would place the federal government at the forefront of state intervention for the purposes of economic recovery. While Macdonald's centralizing vision implied an interventionist federal presence in order to develop a national economy adequately, in a strategy meant to foster national integration, these new centralizers viewed the promise of the central state in terms of its potential for increased social and economic planning – areas that were more strictly embedded in provincial jurisdiction.[74] Supported mostly by left-leaning intellectuals, this vision thus considered federalism as an unnecessary impediment to the construction of a modern welfare state. The most pronounced centralists of this era formed the Cooperative Commonwealth Federation in 1933, and their founding document, the *Regina Manifesto*,[75] called for greater capacities for central planning at the federal level. The document argued for a more flexible constitution that would allow for a national labour code, a pan-Canadian system of public health care, and the abolishment of the Senate, which was seen as a failed experiment in provincial representation within central institutions. However, federal conditional grants were deemed illegitimate because the order of government with the full capacities to raise revenue should be responsible for spending it. To the extent that provincial diversity was desirable, this could be planned from the centre as well, with tailored regional policies. Institutionally, the role of cabinet as a representative body was limited in favour of functional criteria, based on those members of Parliament with greater capacities in specific portfolios. Clearly, provinces and regional/community differences constituted a fundamental problem of Canadian federalism, not its essential character and raison d'être.

By limiting the levers of intervention of the central state, federalism contributed to undermining the role that a 'positive state' could play in equalizing conditions for citizens across Canada. In this sense, Canadian federalism was deemed to be inherently conservative; it impeded

attempts to build a cohesive political community based on the equal-
ization of socio-economic conditions, and a new distribution of powers
was necessary for progressive policies to take hold. Federalism simply
frustrated the actions of governments by imposing legal restraints on
their authority. By the 1960s, the country would be thrust into an all-out
re-examination of its self-understanding, and the variable of federalism
would once again take centre stage in its debates.

*Centralizing Visions II: The Trudeau Era, Individual Rights, and National
Unity*

Upon assuming leadership of the Liberal party in 1968, Pierre Elliott
Trudeau sought to settle the question of splintered loyalties in Canada
once and for all by introducing a model of national integration that
sought to transcend local allegiances as the basis for citizenship.
Trudeau's vision of federalism stemmed in part from his political philosophy, which rejected what he perceived as a closed and inward-look-
ing nationalism in Quebec in favour of a uniform liberal conception of
the state resting on his notion of a 'just society,' where citizenship
implied equal rights across Canada, provincial equality and institutional bilingualism. Indeed, Trudeau's ascendance in Ottawa reflected a
desire to settle the mounting state-led nationalism in Quebec, which
culminated in the election of the secessionist Parti Québécois in 1976.
By far the most powerful centralist vision ever articulated in Canada,
Trudeau's mark on federalism remains embedded to this day. While
Trudeau's political philosophy favoured universalism over particular-
ism and reason over what he termed 'emotive' sentiments of belonging,
he nevertheless recognized the power of state-led pan-Canadian
nationalism in offsetting what he considered to be backward and retrograde nationalist movement for secession in Quebec:

> One way of offsetting the appeal of separatism is by investing tremendous
> amounts of time, energy and money in nationalism, *at the federal level*. A
> national image must be created that will have such an appeal as to make
> any image of a separatist group unattractive. Resources must be devoted
> into such things as national flags, anthems, education, arts councils,
> broadcasting corporations, film boards; the territory must be bound
> together by a network of railways, highways, airlines; the national culture
> and the national economy must be protected by taxes and tariffs; owner-
> ship of resources and industry by nationals must be made a matter of pol-
> icy. In short, the whole of the citizenry must be made to feel that it is only

within the framework of the federal state that their language, culture, institutions, sacred traditions, and standard of living can be protected from external attack and internal strife.

It is, of course, obvious that a national consensus will be developed in this way only if the nationalism is emotionally acceptable to all important groups within the nation.[76]

Trudeau's main contribution was to strengthen national unity by entrenching a constitutional Charter of Rights and Freedoms that would define Canadians as a rights-bearing citizenry regardless of regional or cultural distinctions. Moreover, and contrary to the dualist thrust of the Laurendeau-Dunton Commission, Trudeau defined Canada as a 'multicultural country in a bilingual framework'; no one state in Canada would be recognized as representing the interests of a particular ethnic or cultural group. While he acknowledged that Canada was a dualistic polity in a sociological sense, he did not equate this with the need to devolve powers to the provinces, or to accommodate Quebec with asymmetrical institutions. Indeed, the federal government's dualism is summarized in this statement by the Report of the Task Force on Canadian Unity:

> Canada, seen from the federal government's perspective, is a linguistically dual federal state composed of two societies – one French-speaking and one English-speaking, which extend geographically beyond the borders of any one province. Thus the federal government believes that it is necessary that this linguistic duality be more fully reflected in Canada's central political institutions and in federal policies and programs.[77]

The task force went much further, however, in recommending the recognition of both regionalism and Quebec's distinct status in their conception of Canada. Trudeau, however, quickly shelved such recommendations and instead opted for a minimal definition of dualism. In essence, by espousing a view of federalism based on the primacy of individual rights, multiculturalism, and pan-Canadian bilingualism (in terms of access to federal government services and minority language education rights), Trudeau sought to strengthen the civic component of Canadian identity by limiting the capacity of federalism to promote a diverse treatment of citizens as demarcated by provincial boundaries. The principles upon which federalism in Canada would be conceived were based on the universality of liberal-individualism. As Kenneth Carty and Peter Ward explain:

At one time or another most provinces have represented the nation as the sum of its provincial components or, at least, of its regions ... But all such claims, whether based on the assumption that the nation is composed of cultures, regions or provinces, deny a fundamental principle of liberal democracy: that citizens are individually and equally incorporated into the political community.[78]

By formally recognizing non-territorial groups such as women, multi-cultural groups, and disadvantaged groups in the Charter of Rights, this vision made it clear that the political community of reference for all Canadians would be Canada, as defined by a central institution that would be the guarantor of equality for individuals and disadvantaged groups. The compromise that conceived Canada as a pact between territorial groupings was broken: citizenship in Canada was meant to override such sentiments of belonging. Even in the process leading up to repatriation, Trudeau threatened to proceed with unilateral constitutional renewal without the consent of the provinces, by appealing directly to the people in a referendum. Moreover, in defence of this approach, and in response to Quebec's claim that the central government was foregoing long-standing conventions of provincial assent in constitutional change, Trudeau reiterated the symbolic national role of the federal government by claiming that federal members of Parliament adequately represented the interests of Quebec. For critics of this approach, particularly in Quebec, a pan-Canadian charter is inconsistent with the diversity of treatment that is at the core of federalism. Quebec would be limited in defining its own language policy, a core aspect of its national aspirations. Renewing federalism in this direction meant rejecting basic federal premises about the integrity of member states' capacity to act in their areas of jurisdiction. Indeed, Quebec rejected Trudeau's vision and to this day has not given its consent to the constitution of 1982.[79] Quebec's demands to reconfigure the division of powers, maintain its traditional veto in any amending formula, and the formal recognition of Quebec as a distinct society were all summarily dismissed in favour of a constitution that defined the country as a centralized, homogeneous pan-Canadian nation composed of individuals and certain social groups that were afforded constitutional protection *as a counterweight to* provincial autonomy.[80]

Trudeau's vision has been somewhat consolidated in a view of Canada that emphasizes the primacy of individual rights. Canadian federalism today contains elements of non-territorial political identity that is the direct result of Trudeau's centralizing initiatives. This represents a watershed in Canadian federalism, with the polity increasingly characterized by groups and individuals making rights-claims to a central institution, in direct contrast to the traditional dualist and provincialist visions outlined above and seen to constitute the basic foundations of the original compromise. The legacy of the Charter is that the future reshaping of Canadian federalism must contend with the entrenched notion that any provision threatening 'equal rights' across Canada is an affront to its self-understanding as a political community. An amending formula that alienates Quebec, the failure of the Meech Lake and Charlottetown accords because of perceived injustices associated with special status for Quebec, the drafting of the Calgary Declaration which emphasized an equality of provinces doctrine, the signing of the SUFA without blinking an eye at Quebec's refusal to consent, and the popular imposition of the Clarity Act among Canadians outside Quebec, all indicate the continuing force of Trudeau's vision in Canada.

Conclusion

In discussing the relationship between diversity and federalism, Daniel Elazar has noted that federal unity 'is not only comfortable with the political expression of diversity but is from its roots a means to accommodate diversity as a legitimate element in the polity.'[81] Federalism, as such, precedes institutional forms – it is a value concept that involves certain assumptions, values and beliefs about the political salience of difference. In many ways, the federal idea is inimical to a nationalizing project, since this process tends to subsume differences, or at least relativize them in status in their relationship to the 'national' state. Federalism is thus inherently in a state of flux. While adopting a strategy of actively promoting unity has been tempting in an age of nation-states, in the long term it actually contributes to greater and more permanent instability, since it assumes that partners in the federal project can be made to shed the very bases of consent to 'living together' that prompted federation as an institutional accommodation in the first place. In other words, there is no federalism if the institutions of the federation do not recognise what Charles Taylor called 'deep diversity.'[82] The very values, beliefs, and assumptions that constitute the raison d'être of the federation are broken, politically salient social cleavages are disregarded, and federalism ceases to exist. In this scenario, it is only a matter of time until the federation follows suit. Michael Burgess outlines the normative basis of the federal idea: 'The federal polity is founded upon certain shared assumptions, values, beliefs and interests that together presuppose the politics of recognition, cooperation, compromise and accommodation. This is because the polity is rooted in notions of human dignity, toleration, respect, reciprocity and consent.'[83]

Like most federal societies, Canada will always experience conflicts and tensions, and, perhaps most importantly, ambiguity with regards to legal arrangements, regardless of the form the federation takes. Many observers take this fact to conclude that a federal state is a 'soft' state that needs to be strengthened at the centre, rather than let the various political identities negotiate the parameters of representation and sovereignty in a spirit of mutual trust and accommodation. The various conceptions of federalism that have conflicted over time reveal inherent disagreement over how Canadians of a myriad number of interests and identities ought to be represented in the polity. This chapter does not purport to reveal a magical solution. Indeed, federalism relies on faith and trust as much as it does on a written legal text, and faith and trust cannot be so easily assessed empirically. One conclusion that cannot be avoided, however, is that no dominant political identity ought to impose a particular vision of representation unilaterally in order to keep the country together, much less so if this involves forging a national project to achieve such ends.

From the proposed legislative union of some of the founders, the mid-century welfare-state centralism, Trudeau's conception of a patriated constitution based on a Charter of Rights and Freedoms, the rejection of the Meech Lake Accord (which represented a minimal condition of Quebec's assent), and the populist Calgary Declaration and Clarity Act inspired sentiments that now prevail in Canada as majoritarian 'winners' in the debate, we are left with an internal nation – Quebec – that has refused to consent to the country's defining document, has been validated in its quest to assert its right to self-determination by the Supreme Court of Canada, has elected a majority of sovereignist representatives to the federal Parliament for nearly fifteen years, and is constantly begging Ottawa for its fair share of revenues. Such diverging visions will not go away: they are federal cleavages, requiring federal solutions. They are not special interests that can be processed by majoritarian liberal institutions that operate on a pan-Canadian basis. Quebec, and the promise of Canadian federalism, will always be left behind if this non-federal vision is allowed to prevail.

4 Distinct 'National Models' of Integration: Establishing Contexts of Choice

This chapter addresses the impact of polyethnicity on political communities by focusing specifically on the symbolic aspect of citizenship – the markers of a country's self-identification through which citizens are said to exhibit a sense of social cohesion and allegiance for effective democratic participation in a given polity.[1] What are the symbolic 'anchors' that frame and define sentiments of belonging in a democratic polity? How do we evaluate such criteria in light of the challenge of polyethnicity? Such questions will be explored through a comparative conceptual assessment of the Canadian policy of multiculturalism and Quebec's model of interculturalism. Both of these liberal political communities have responded to the challenge of polyethnicity by formulating models of integration that go beyond the idea of benign neglect in cultural matters. A comparison of two distinct approaches may serve to elucidate some of the issues and challenges confronting culturally heterogeneous liberal democracies more generally, as well as indicating the inherently political nature of such activities.

The idea of a 'revival of citizenship' coincides with an unravelling of the linear relationship between national identity, territory, and citizenship in the contemporary era. The notion of 'society,' in classic liberal perspectives on citizenship, is conceived as a bounded, functional whole that is structured by a state rather than a diverse mosaic of distinct collective identities which must be accommodated through specific state policy in the area of integration. Caused by massive population movement through migration, as well as declining birthrates, contemporary liberal democracies have been forced to be more explicit about the kinds of entitlements and obligations of membership, since outright assimilation into an established national culture no longer dominates liberal thinking as an approach for incorporation of immigrants or minority cultures. Theories of liberal citizenship have come to be concerned with the question of accommodating a plurality of identities rather than simply assuming the existence of a national culture into which immigrants and ethnic minorities are expected to assimilate. As such, 'national models' of integration, in conceptual terms, reveal much about the bases of citizenship in distinct political contexts – an important empirical development that has forced theorists of citizenship to look more closely at particular hard cases in which states must explicitly define the normative criteria in establishing bases of belonging.

Citizenship, however, extends further into the realms of formal representation (electoral systems, governing bodies) and issues related to social entitlements (the relationship between the state, market, and society). Indeed, citizenship involves multiple mechanisms, practical and symbolic, of social and political inclusion. This chapter does not intend to cover the issue of citizenship exhaustively. It merely attempts to address an increasingly salient aspect of citizenship that has gained prominence in the political communities of liberal democratic states. This may be caused in part by migration and the subsequent growth of identity politics, by incomplete nation-building projects or, in the case of internal nations such as Quebec, by the quest for recognition as a host society in its own right – its affirmation as a global society. In short, the aspect of citizenship discussed here relates to sentiments of belonging and solidarity. This chapter will proceed, in the first section, to unpack the concept of multiculturalism as a theoretical paradigm, and attempt to develop normative criteria with which to evaluate current models of cultural pluralism in Canada and Quebec. The second section will offer a conceptualization of Quebec's model of interculturalism. Third, a brief overview of the Canadian policy of multiculturalism will be exposed. Fourth, the chapter will proceed with an assessment of the models in terms of their normative contribution to cultural pluralism and their place in Quebec-Canada relations. We conclude by exposing the main debates on the place of identity in Quebec in light of its growing role as a framer of citizenship in its own right. Regardless of strict definitions, multiculturalism constitutes a response to the late-twentieth-century phenomenon that has been called the 'age of migration,' inviting countries to redefine the rules of political life.[2]

Multiculturalism versus Homogeneous Citizenship

According to Christian Joppke, multiculturalism is an intellectual movement premised around the concepts of equality and emancipation. Its appeal lies in the defence of particularistic, mostly ascriptively defined group identities that reject Western universalism as the basis for allegiance to a given collectivity. Western universalism in this view is seen as 'falsely homogenizing and a smokescreen for power.'[3] As such, multiculturalism implies the salience of multiple cultures coexisting within a limited state-bounded territory, rejecting the modern Jacobin view of the nation-state and the homogenization of identities. The key issue is that historically rooted cultures are said to regulate not only specific aspects, but the entire life conduct and sources of meaning of the individual.[4] Joppke summarizes:

> Defenders of multiculturalism have argued that the exercise of individual rights and liberties depends on full and unimpeded membership in a respected and flourishing cultural group. But the tension between liberalism and multiculturalism is real, as the latter is based on the ontological primacy of the group over the individual and, if necessary, takes into the bargain the suppression of individual claims.[5]

This approach views assimilation or acculturation as a violation of the integrity or dignity of the individual, whose cultural habits should be recognized fully as an integral element of a person's identity. Any stifling of particular cultural expressions by way of the symbolic construction of a larger socio-cultural identity limits the individual's capacity for self-realization, thus negating the liberal democratic ideal that individuals, as members of the larger society, be given the means by which to explore their own life chances and directions. Ascriptive aspects of identity – particular cultural sources of meaning – are said to act as prerequisites to self-realization. Stripping such sources of meaning in the name of universal markers of identity, in the construction of a mononational (Jacobin) identity that is meant to provide common purpose, denies the individual the empowerment to determine the direction of his/her life through participation in the affairs of society. Iris Marion Young argues that if one conceptualizes such cultural differences as 'relationally constituted structural differentiations', then the supposed link between citizenship and the common good is upheld, because it 'becomes clear that socially situated interests, proposals, claims and expressions of experience are often an important resource for democratic discussion and decision making. Such situated knowledges can both pluralize and relativize hegemonic discourses, and offer otherwise unspoken knowledge to contribute to wise decisions.'[6]

The polemic between universal and particular bases of allegiance thus demarcates the contours of the debate. The idea of multicultural- ism can be embedded in a wider area of postmodern consciousness – or 'identity politics' – as an attack on the assimilation implied by nation- states with the aim of attaching a sense of common purpose to citizen- ship status.[7] Multiculturalism has also made inroads in liberal theory. Perhaps the most polished defence of the role that cultures play in pro- viding a context for individual autonomy remains Will Kymlicka's groundbreaking work *Multicultural Citizenship*. In a difficult endeavour of applied liberal thinking, Kymlicka qualified some established liberal premises by looking at specific cases. While emphasizing the normative primacy of individual autonomy as a basis for justice, Kymlicka moved the subject matter of multiculturalism into the liberal framework by realizing that ethical individualism is atomistic if it is accompanied by a disregard for the sociological contention that individuals need histori- cal communities and cultures in order to flourish.[8] Indeed, as a testa- ment to that seemingly ontological status of multiculturalism, radical cultural pluralists and liberal nationalists have converged around the notion that cultures matter and states need to accommodate them if they are serious about just citizenship.

The sentiments associated with equal citizenship status have long been regarded by liberal theorists as integral to democratic political communities: for fostering the civic spiritedness, mutual trust, and alle- giance required for meaningful self-government, self-realization and political stability. Kymlicka notes that the classic liberal response to polyethnicity has been to develop common (undifferentiated) bases of citizenship in a universal vein. In this view, the integrative function of citizenship requires that cultural differences be treated with benign neglect, in order that a shared civic identity is forged regardless of col- lective or group-based identity differences. Young notes that propo- nents of such arguments view any particular demands based on sociological differences as detrimental to the functioning of democracy, since citizens concern themselves less with the common good and more with their own group-based, or special interests.[9] Kymlicka summa- rizes this view:

Citizenship is by definition a matter of treating people as individuals with equal rights under the law ... [If it is group differentiated], nothing will bind the various groups in society together, and prevent the spread of mutual mistrust or conflict. If citizenship is differentiated, it no longer provides a shared experience or common status. Citizenship would yet be another force for disunity, rather than a way of cultivating unity in the face of increasing social diversity. Citizenship should be a force where people transcend their differences, and think about the common good of all citizens.[10]

In short, culture, like religion, should be left to the private sphere and ought not to concern the state. The only way for democracy to flourish is for the political community to be predicated on universal bases of belonging which are civic and amenable to identification across cultures.

For defenders of multiculturalism, however, the notion of benign neglect is in itself infused with cultural meaning. It simply represents a preservation of the status quo in many consolidated nation-states. State inactivity thus reflects a failure to adapt to dynamic polyethnic realities in society. Minority cultures are rendered unequal participants and second-class citizens if their sources of meaning are neglected in the public realm. As such, the ideal of equality cannot be achieved if citizens are forced to conform to a civic denial of identity, a renewed self-definition for individual citizens. Wsevolod Isajiw notes that the force of multiculturalism arises out of a particular sentiment in which citizen dignity is tied to the collective dignity of one's ethnic community. Multiculturalism represents a set of values whereby the recognition of identity needs is linked to the instrumental power of members of ethnic communities.[11] Charles Taylor explains:

The demand for recognition in [the politics of multiculturalism] is given urgency by the supposed links between recognition and identity ... The thesis is that our identity is partly shaped by recognition or its absence, often by misrecognition of others, and so a person or group of people can suffer real damage, real distortion, if the people or society around them mirror back to them a confining or demeaning or contemptible picture of themselves. Nonrecognition or misrecognition can be a form of oppression, imprisoning someone in a false, distorted or reduced mode of being.[12]

The recognition of cultural pluralism by the state is thus a call for increased citizen empowerment. How are citizens in a polyethnic society to be equally empowered to share and participate in the affairs of the polity, without sacrificing self-fulfilling 'modes of being'? How have states adapted to such challenges?

The theoretical contours outlined above reveal that normative evaluations of integration rest on two broad considerations. The first is that full citizenship status requires that all cultural identities be allowed to participate in democratic life equally, without the necessity of reducing conceptions of identity to the level of the individual. This applies for cultural pluralists as well as liberal nationalists. Empowerment implies that citizens are permitted to maintain their cultural differences when affecting the affairs of the polity through democratic participation. The second concerns the salience of unity in any society. Here the key element is a sense of common purpose in public matters in order that deliberation is not confined to pockets of self-contained, fragmented collectivities in juxtaposition. These two broad poles are at issue in any model of integration and subsequent conceptualizations of citizenship status. In short, a balance must be struck between the *equal empowerment of group identities* as active constituents of the larger community and the need for a *common ground for dialogue*, for the purposes of unity – a *centre* which also serves as a marker of identity in the larger society and denotes in itself a pole of allegiance for all citizens.

'Interculturalism': Quebec's Model of Cultural Pluralism

Quebec's persistent attempts to establish itself as a 'host society' can be traced back to the Quiet Revolution, the increased activity of the state in many aspects of the lives of Quebeckers, and can be qualified as a project to gradually construct Quebec citizenship. In other words, the idea of Quebec citizenship cannot be divorced from the larger issue of Quebec's national affirmation in the face of pan-Canadian attempts at nation-building. In this sense, the idea of two founding peoples is not merely symbolic. In constructing its own model for integration, Quebec has in effect formulated a response to the Canadian policy of multiculturalism, one that affirms the primacy of the Quebec state in the areas of politics and communitarian identity and challenges the reductionist notion that Quebec is a monolithic ethnic group. The treatment of diversity, when placed in a larger historical context, can be seen as but one of the many areas of contention between opposing visions regarding Canada's constituent political communities, or national groupings. Kymlicka highlights this progression towards a formal Quebec citizenship:

> The notion of a distinctly Québécois citizenship has seen a spectacular progression. In the space of a lifetime, the dominant identification of Que-

beckers has been profoundly transformed. From Canadians, they became French-Canadians, then Franco-Québécois, and finally, Québécois ... These transformations cannot be interpreted as a simple evolution of a sort of sentiment of belonging to the tribe. Rather, they represent a continuing progression of Québécois identity, in which its foundations have passed from non-citizenship to citizenship.[13]

Historically, the main impetus for the increasing importance of the discourse on Quebec citizenship has been language: the idea of the French language as the primary vehicle for the preservation and flourishing of Québécois identity. Language was indeed the precursor to concerns over immigration and integration. Compounded by an alarming decline of the birthrate in Quebec, state actors became concerned with the tendency of allophones to gravitate linguistically towards the anglophone community. Immigration and integration thus became inextricably tied to the fate of the Quebec nation. With a Ministry of Immigration in place since 1968, the Quebec government was very active in almost all aspects of immigration except recruitment and reception.[14] Some of its activities included an employment search service for newly arrived immigrants, support for community groups with the aim of adaptation, and the funding of cultural and linguistic heritage programs, including the translation of literature into French, with the hope of building bridges between the allophone and francophone communities. From 1969 to 1979–80, the ministry's budget grew from $2.8 million to $20 million. The Quebec government took a wide range of measures in the areas of language acquisition and cultural adaptation, the initial steps towards a more fully articulated model of integration. Indeed, as a response to critics who view the legal imposition of French on individuals as an affront to liberal principles of individual rights over society, Joseph Carens turns to this participatory aspect of the model to defend the liberal democratic merits of the Quebec model: 'The duty to learn French is intimately connected to the duty to contribute and to participate in society, which is connected, on this account, to fundamental democratic principles. Learning French is, among other things, a necessary means to participation in society so that if one can defend the duty to participate, and I think one can, one can defend the duty to learn French.'[15]

As Michael Behiels argues, however, many such positive measures were overshadowed by more controversial language legislation, as perceived by anglophones and allophones,[16] which began with the Quebec

Liberal government's Official Language Law (Bill 22) in 1974, in which Quebec was formally declared a unilingual French society, and later culminated in the Charter of the French Language (Bill 101) in 1977 under Rene Lévesque's PQ government. Indeed, during this period, the Quebec consensus was very much reflected in language legislation, as such attempts to entrench the use of the French language in Quebec extended across partisan lines. The Charter was seen by many as a hardline approach, out of line with the bridge-building measures in progress, and was generally rejected by allophones and anglophones.[17] With the adoption of the Charter, the PQ government established the vision of a linguistically unilingual and ethnically pluralistic political community in Quebec, a vision that has nourished subsequent models of integration to this day. As early as 1981, the Quebec model began taking shape, with a policy statement entitled *Autant de façons d'être Québécois.*[18] The essence of the policy was that, unlike Canadian multiculturalism, Quebec integration would stress the idea of convergence. This will be elaborated below. Of significance here is that the Quebec model explicitly challenged the Canadian variant as a primary basis for citizenship. The jurisdictional battles of the Quiet Revolution and the linguistic conflicts of the 1970s culminated in a fully articulated discourse centred on citizenship in Quebec. As such, it can no longer be disputed that Quebec constitutes a host society whose model of integration can potentially be a subject of emulation by other liberal democracies.

Quebec has formally adopted a model of interculturalism to address its polyethnic social composition. This view contends that the incorporation of immigrants or minority cultures into the larger political community is a reciprocal endeavour – a 'moral contract'[19] – between the host society and the particular cultural group, in the aim of establishing a forum for the empowerment of all citizens – a 'common public culture.'[20]

The moral contract is summed up as follows: a society in which French is the common language of public life; a democratic society where participation and the contribution of everyone is expected and encouraged; and a pluralist society open to multiple contributions within the limits imposed by the respect for fundamental democratic values, and the necessity of intercommunity exchange.[21]

The government of Quebec describes the general thrust of this model:

The 'moral contract' affirms that, in its options for society, it follows that rights and responsibilities apply as much to immigrants, on the one hand, as the receiving society itself (including Québécois of cultural communities already integrated or on their way to being integrated) and its institutions, on the other hand. Being a Québécois means being engaged in fact in Quebec's choices for society. For the immigrant established in Quebec, having chosen Quebec as an adopted land, there requires an engagement like all other citizens, and to respect these very choices of society. It is the simultaneous existence of complementary rights and obligations attributed to all parties – and to engage in solidarity in relationships of reciprocal obligation – which justifies the vocabulary of 'moral contract' to designate the general environment governing such relations with the aim of fully integrating immigrants.[22]

The common public culture in this view does not consist solely in the juridical sphere: it is not a procedural model based on formal individual rights. Instead, the basic tenets of the moral contract are such that established 'modes of being' in economic, political, and sociocultural realms are to be respected as markers of identification and citizenship status, with the institutions of democratic participation acting as a point of convergence for groups of specific collective identities in order that all may share equally in democratic life. Carens highlights this key feature of the model:

> Immigrants can be full members of Quebec's society even if they look and act differently from the substantial segment of the population whose ancestors inhabited Quebec and even if they do not in any way alter their own customs and cultural patterns with respect to work and play, diet and dress, sleep and sex, celebration and mourning, so long as they act within the confines of the law.[23]

In establishing a model based on convergence of collective identity, the French language is to serve as the common language of public life. This is seen as an essential condition for the cohesion of Quebec society. Indeed, the French language constitutes the basis for Quebec's self-definition as a distinct political community. In this view, language is not conceptualized as an individual right. Rocher et al. elaborate: 'In Quebec, ... the French language is presented as a centre of convergence for diverse groups which can nevertheless maintain and let flourish their specificity. While the Canadian policy privileges an individualist approach to culture, Quebec's policy states clearly the need to recognise French as a collective good that requires protection and encouragement.'[24]

The contours of public life are somewhat ambiguous. Indeed, what constitutes a public exchange is often unclear and contingent. As a general rule, the confines of public space are not relegated solely to the activities of the state, but encompass the 'public space of social interaction' as well. For example, students may, as a matter of individual right, communicate in any language they wish on the playground of a francophone school. However, language use in the classroom is considered public space. More examples of what constitutes private interaction are relations with family members, friends, colleagues, or anyone involved in the social circle of the individual in question in which the choice of language use is of a consensual nature. Again, in the words of Rocher et al.:

> It must be emphasized that valuing French as the common language does not imply in itself the abandonment of a language of origin, for two reasons. The first is related to the democratic nature of society that must respect individual choices. The second is a question of utility: the development of languages of origin is considered an economic, social and cultural asset. It must be stressed that there exists a fundamental distinction between the status of French as a common language of public life and that of the other languages.[25]

Thus an emphasis on the proficient use of the French language is taken as a minimal condition of the exercise of common citizenship – as an instrument of democracy. To quote France Giroux: 'It is of importance that the French language is taken first and foremost as a condition of the exercise of citizen rights, the modern nation cannot claim to be a forum for discussion and decision-making without the existence of a community of language.'[26]

Moreover, the host society expects, as a matter of obligation, that members of minority groups fully integrate into the larger community, with the expectation that all citizens are to contribute and participate in the social fabric of the common public culture. As a democratic community, this implies that once citizenship is attained, all members are equally encouraged to 'participate in defining the general direction of our society ... at all stages and in all sectors where the judgement of citizens can be manifested and heard.'[27]

With regards to the eventuality of conflict between individuals or groups, the method of resolution must correspond to democratic norms. This point is important because it highlights a fundamentally different perspective from an emphasis on procedural legal channels.

The Quebec model stresses that in the initial manifestation of conflict, deliberative measures such as mediation, compromise and direct negotiation are preferred, leaving as much initiative and autonomy to the parties in question. Legalistic measures and the recourse to specified rights are to be an option of last resort. In other words, this model values deliberation, mutual understanding, and dialogue as fundamental characteristics of democratic life in the realm of civil society, and is instrumental in the aim of fostering a cohesive and participatory conception of citizenship.

The treatment of difference in this model does not imply a society built on the juxtaposition of a mosaic of ethnic groupings, nor does it reduce citizenship status simply to procedural safeguards from state intrusion through the codification of fundamental individual rights, and the assimilation of particular identities to universal principles. The idea is that cultural contact constitutes a new synthesis and a new dynamic for the community as a whole.[28] The Quebec model of cultural pluralism operates in the tradition of parliamentary democracy, with an emphasis of deliberation and representation. Michel Pagé summarizes:

> In conceptualizing a common civic space, it is common civic norms that constitute the basis for social cohesion. The norms are situated above particular ethnic cultures and have a scope general enough to govern the actions of a society consisting of individuals belonging to a plurality of ethnic groups. *These norms are established by democratic institutions, which are capable of accounting for pluralism in seeking always, through decisions arrived at by democratic voting, as large as possible a consensual base, which does not limit itself only to the majority ethnic group or an ensemble of minority groups.*[29]

Within the framework of basic principles – a commitment to the peaceful resolution of conflict, a Charter of Rights and Freedoms in order to provide legal recourse for the protection of individual and group rights, equality between the sexes, a secular state, equality and universality of citizen access to social provisions[30] – interculturalism attempts to strike a balance between individual rights and cultural relativism by emphasizing a 'fusion of horizons' through dialogue and consensual agreement. Through the participation and discourse of all groups in the public sphere, the goal of this approach is to achieve the largest possible consensus regarding the limits and possibilities of the expression of collective differences based on identity, weighed against the requirements of social cohesion and individual rights in a common public context. The recognition of cultural differences is assumed in such a view – the sources of meaning accrued from cultural identity are acknowledged as an explicit feature of citizen empowerment – yet an obligation is placed on all parties to contribute to the basic tenets of a common public culture.

For example, with the goal of promoting the contribution of immigrants in society, the government of Quebec, since 1978, has directed the Programme d'Enseignement des Langues d'Origine (PELO). This initiative has contributed to a valorization of immigrants' heritage. According to the data supplied by the Mouvement pour une école moderne et ouverte (MEMO) before the Commission of the Estates General on the Situation and Future of the French Language in September 2000 in Quebec, no less than 1,847 students of the Montreal school board participated in these classes. Moreover, for 15 per cent of these students, it consists of a third spoken language, contributing to making Montreal one of the most trilingual cities in the world.[31] Another important instrument has been a targeted hiring policy to permit members of recent communities of immigration to attain available positions within the public service. In 2000, the government of Quebec adopted an Act Respecting Equal Access to Employment in Public Bodies as an amendment to chapter A-2.01 of the Quebec Charter of Rights and Freedoms. The act has been in force since 1 April 2001 and obliges public authorities to develop equal access in employment programs for women, Aboriginals, visible minorities, and people whose mother tongue is neither French nor English. In order to ensure that the policy is effectively enforced, the government also set up the Commission des droits de la personne et des droits de la jeunesse (CDPDJ), a body mandated to assess availability in the labour force and oversee the substance of various employment equality access programs.

In the final analysis, the recognition of minority cultures is built into the model; the moral contract is an integrative principle whereby ethno-cultural groups are provided with the means to contribute, in a common language, and to make their mark on the basic principles of the common public culture. Difference is recognized within the limits of societal cohesion and political community, not as an *essential starting point* for common identification and unity.

Canada's Policy of Multiculturalism

Multiculturalism as a political force in Canada came into play largely as a result of the negative response to the recommendations of the Royal

Commission on Biculturalism and Bilingualism[32] in the 1960s by a 'third force' – that is, groups which represented immigrants and ethnocultural communities. The commission itself was spearheaded by Prime Minister Pearson as a response to the rise of a reinvigorated Quebec nationalism through the Quiet Revolution, and the subsequent questioning of Quebec's collective place in a federation dominated largely by Anglo-Canadians in economic, cultural and political affairs.[33] To quote Raymond Breton: 'The immediate motive ... was the rise of the independence movement [in Quebec] and the government's initial response. The transformation of institutional identity, language and symbols to help members of the French segment of the society recognise themselves generated identification and status concerns ... among those of non-British, non-French origin.'[34] Representatives of the third force sought recognition of their cultural contributions to Canada, and felt that they would be relegated to second-class citizenship status if the country was to be formally defined as bicultural and bilingual.

Prime Minister Trudeau's response was to alter the recommendations of the commission, which had called for a 'two nations' conception of the country whereby French Canada and English Canada were to be recognized equally as founding nations, with each enjoying majority status. Trudeau's solution was to adopt a policy of official multiculturalism within a bilingual framework. In doing so, he believed that language could be dissociated from culture and individuals would be free to decide whether or not to actively preserve their ethnic identities. Implicit in such an approach is the primacy of individual rights – the right of all individuals freely to dissociate themselves from their cultural communities. Moreover, the language of participation in Canadian society, between French and English, was left to individual choice. The idea that language was to correspond to sociological realities, as the B&B Commission implied, was abandoned. The community for the integration of an immigrant was Canada, defined as a single bilingual host society. In Trudeau's view:

> We cannot have a cultural policy for Canadians of French and British origin, another for Aboriginals, and still another for all the others. Although we will have two official languages, there will be no official culture, and no ethnic group will have priority ... *All men will see their liberty hindered if they are continuously enclosed in a cultural compartment determined uniquely by birth or language. It is thus essential that all Canadians, regardless of their ethnic origins, be required to learn at least one of the two languages in which the country conducts its public affairs.*[35]

Indeed, as Evelyn Kallen contends, the final policy outcome represented a middle ground to the multicultural and multilingual vision espoused by the third force and the two nations demand of Quebec nationalists of all stripes.[36] By separating language and culture, Canadian identity was said to be constructed on universal principles, relegating culture to the private sphere. In short, the federal government's policy objectives ran as follows:[37]

  i. The Government of Canada will support all of Canada's cultures and will seek to assist, resources permitting, the development of those cultural groups which have demonstrated a desire and effort to continue to develop a capacity to grow and contribute to Canada, as well as a clear need for assistance.
  ii. The Government will assist members of all cultural groups to overcome cultural barriers to full participation in Canadian society.
  iii. The Government will promote creative encounters and interchange among all Canadian cultural groups in the interest of national unity.
  iv. The Government will continue to assist immigrants to acquire at least one of Canada's official languages in order to become full participants in Canadian society.

New concerns over racial and ethnic equity led to a reiteration of the policy in the 1988 Canadian Multiculturalism Act by the Progressive Conservative government of Brian Mulroney. As Yasmeen Abu-Laban notes, the act furthered the impact of multicultural policy by focusing not only on cultural maintenance, but by more explicitly emphasizing concerns over discrimination. The act now contained a provision whereby the minister of multiculturalism could 'assist ethnocultural minority communities to conduct activities with a view to overcoming any discriminatory barrier and, in particular, discrimination based on race or national or ethnic origin.'[38] This response by the state was a result of greater concerns surrounding the changing composition of minority ethnic groups following recent waves of immigration. The new act, however, did little to change the general thrust of the original policy, and simply refined and strengthened the terms of recognition with respect to the contribution of cultural groups.[39]

While multiculturalism had been largely proceeding through federal funding of cultural projects, of more significance was the entrenchment of multiculturalism in the Canadian Charter of Rights and Freedoms in 1982. The existing policy of multiculturalism within a bilingual framework was reinforced. Under the interpretive clause in section 27, the constitution would henceforth 'be interpreted in a manner consistent with the preservation and enhancement of the multicultural heritage of Canadians.' Multiculturalism thus became 'a visible component of the patriated constitution,' leading to the perception among ethnocultural groups that they had achieved the status of 'legitimate constitutional actors.'[40] In Vince Wilson's words, 'Armed with long memories and the constitutional gains of 1982, these recently enfranchised "Charter Canadians" took our political decision-makers by surprise in serving notice that they were now serious players in the constitutional stakes.'[41] In short, the Charter:

> Struck a balance between Trudeau's concept of dualism and the concerns of third force Canadians ... On the one hand, dualism was constitutionally entrenched in the establishment of English and French as the official languages of Canada, and in the provision of English educational rights to the English minority in Quebec and the French minority elsewhere. On the other hand, Section 27 says that the Charter 'shall be interpreted in a manner consistent with the preservation and enhancement of the multicultural heritage of Canadians.' In short, the balance between bilingualism and multiculturalism established at the statutory level early in Trudeau's Prime Ministership was duplicated at the constitutional level in the Charter.[42]

Concurrent Nation-Building Strategies

Prior to proceeding with the comparative study, it must be noted that such policies cannot be assessed in the absence of a clear understanding of political processes related to the strategy of nation-building. This qualification is particularly salient in the Canadian case, where the precarious nature of pan-Canadian identity has been in itself somewhat of a 'national symbol' due to the persistent existential question in Quebec. Indeed, as will be shown below, policy-makers at the federal level charged with defining the bases of belonging in Canada have not only faced the challenges associated with the incorporation of diverse cultural identities, but have been confronted with a national minority with established political institutions within a well-circumscribed territory. This fact presents a qualitatively different challenge confronting Canada in comparison to the United States. As Christian Joppke makes clear, each society's actual response to immigration and polyethnicity does not merely stem from an abstract model that is subsequently applied to the real world: 'The concrete meaning of multiculturalism and its linkage to immigration differs significantly across these societies. These differences are conditioned by distinct traditions of nationhood, the specific historical contexts in which immigration has taken place, and the existing immigration regimes.'[43]

As such, Quebec, although formally a province of Canada, nevertheless merits independent consideration as it has negotiated extensive authority over immigration.[44] Moreover, Quebec constitutes a distinct political community with a well-defined collective societal project that includes the integration of immigrants. In short, Quebec should be viewed as a host society in its own right, with its own patterns of historical and cultural development, its own sense of nationhood, and a distinct discourse with regards to the general orientations and choices of society.

There are indeed political imperatives at work in such policy outcomes. Thus far, this chapter has attempted to shed light on the phenomenon of multiculturalism – distinguishing between its use as a general label for an emerging tradition in political thought and the actual name bearing its policy in Canada – in order to alleviate the ambiguities surrounding the concept, particularly in applied approaches in political theory that assess hard cases and specific policies. However, an assessment of Canadian multiculturalism cannot disregard the fact that in the final analysis it is a policy and not an ontological principle devoid of contingencies. The ideal of multiculturalism must not be confused with the Canadian policy, as this is prone to stifle debate concerning the value of the policy in framing citizenship status.

Returning to the normative backdrop for evaluating integration as developed above, it is clear that the Canadian strategy was related to both the goal of unity and the fostering of citizen dignity through the recognition of particular cultural affiliations. First, it seeks to achieve unity through a pan-Canadian nation-building project that emphasizes the primacy of individual rights in a constitutionally entrenched Charter of Rights and Freedoms, and a choice of language use applied across the country. Superimposed on individual rights is the official recognition to treat all constituent cultures equally. Such recognition, however, is largely a symbolic concession – the fabrication of an identity marker based on the voluntary adherence to particular cultural allegiances. In Morton Weinfeld's words, 'In the absence of any consensus on the substance of Canadian identity or culture, multiculturalism fills a void, defining Canadian culture in terms of the legitimate ancestral cultures which are the legacy of every Canadian: defining the whole through the sum of its parts.'[45]

Moreover, one of the main indicators of the withdrawal from a commitment to multiculturalism that Yasmeen Abu-Laban and Christina Gabriel[46] have observed is in cutbacks to ethnocultural groups.[47] A genuine commitment to cultural pluralism, at a minimum, requires more than a mere 'sponsorship' of diverse ethnocultural groups. Two points are worth mentioning here. First, the situation hardly qualifies as an example of the fostering of citizen dignity through recognition of a diversity of contributions to the country's self-understanding. Qualitative citizenship through participation and deliberation and interchange is hardly furthered with the federal government simply throwing money at the issue. When a policy can be made or broken by spending and cutbacks, then its commitment to deep philosophical principles needs to be questioned. Second, paying for allegiance in a top-down state-citizen framework is not what those promoting institutional recognition and accommodation had in mind. Canadian multiculturalism works only on a rhetorical level, when people believe they need not assimilate and shed their cultural sources of meaning. This symbolic function does have its virtues in terms of conditions for belonging; other than that, however, there is no real substance to the policy than the familiar pattern of groups being at the whim of federal spending. Moreover, as Abu-Laban and Gabriel illustrate, the new direction of the policy does not move to a more firm commitment for 'national inclusion and belonging' based on 'recognition and respect,' the original rationale for the policy, but on national and global competitiveness – in other words, multiculturalism as a commercially defined comparative advantage in a global economy. Indeed, the policy may be taking a more direct turn towards an instrumental application by strengthening national sovereignty, symbolically, in the face of global pressures: Canada's very own niche.

By forging a common identity throughout the country based on the sum of its parts, it was hoped that the identity marker for unity could be universal, the equal recognition of all cultures, within a regime governed by individual rights and bilingualism. In this way, adherence to particular cultural attachments could be voluntary for all *individuals*, while at the same time claiming to empower citizens of minority cultures through reductionist means; Canada's symbolic order was to be based on the negation of any particular cultural definition. Gilles Bourque and Jules Duchastel argue that the Canadian response, by conceptualizing citizenship in such terms, has in effect altered social relations to the point of damaging the exercise of democracy. The Canadian political community in this sense is predicated on the judicialization of social interactions, to the detriment of the deliberative aspects of representative democracy. The idea of public space for citizen participation, reflection, and deliberation within the political community is reduced to a narrow forum of rights-bearers. Deliberative assemblies give way to the 'legalization' of social relations,[48] preventing parliaments from being responsible for organizing social life and, ultimately, preventing citizens from identifying with others in the larger society.[49]

According to Kymlicka, the final outcome of Canadian multiculturalism as a symbol for identification is analogous to the situation in the United States in its failure to differentiate between national minorities and polyethnic communities. The fundamental difference between the two is that the former strive for self-determination while the latter seek inclusion. Canada's policy fails to address this distinction; multiculturalism becomes a mechanism to quell legitimate national aspirations and thus shares with the US model a certain homogenization of identity, albeit through cultural relativism. Kymlicka argues that the American reluctance to recognize minority nations is a direct result of its assimilationist model, as it fears that such recognition will trickle down to its polyethnic communities and thus undermine the bases for unity.[50] Canada's policy stems from similar fears; however, its response was to elevate the status of cultural groups to the same level as that of national minorities. Both policies are universal, both are bound by nation-building projects which stress unity, and both fail in any significant way to recognize territorially-defined group-differentiated rights as a federal principle.[51]

The Canadian model was not predicated on a genuine commitment to the ideology of multiculturalism as a pillar upon which to frame citizenship status; rather, the goal was unity in the face of a national minority challenge. Quebec's national identity was placed, constitutionally, alongside every other minority culture as a basis for identification.[52] Giroux effectively conveys this point:

The partial recognition of ancestral right reveals, *a contrario*, a refusal to recognise the Quebec nation ... As such, demands by national minorities, those of cultural communities, and those of the majority group are regarded, without being defined or explicitly taking into consideration the criteria of legitimacy attributed to a nation which allow for a viable and effective democratic order ... In effect, without valid criteria for inclusion and exclusion, all demands become acceptable; thus it becomes possible to pit group demands against one another and to transform pluralism into a zero-sum game.[53]

In Charles Taylor's terms, multiculturalism as such fails to appreciate 'deep diversity' in Canada, in which difference can be recognized on tiered levels in view of particular groupings' political aspirations and historical/territorial/linguistic realities. In adopting a strategy for unity similar in aims to the American approach – uniformity from coast to coast based on universal principles – the Canadian policy failed to recognize that national minorities, as opposed to polyethnic communities, seek to provide a 'centre' for identification, their own pole of allegiance necessary for unity and common purpose. In other words, national identity in Quebec assumes a self-determining project for society. The community of reference for all citizens under the banner of multiculturalism, however, is Canada. Bourque et al. summarize:

This ideology ... defines itself in relation to the territorial state: it circumscribes a community of belonging to the state within a country – Canada. It thus privileges, clearly, national dimensions of the production of community, even though the discourse struggles to find a coherent representation of the Canadian nation. This Canadian nationalism finds its full significance in its opposition to the 'counter-nationalisms' of Quebec and the Aboriginal peoples.[54]

The arguments expounded above rest on the notion that Canada's similarity to the United States flows from the implicit assumption that equality stems from an emphasis on the individual, and what such individuals share with others across the country. The Canadian constitution protects individuals from collective intrusions. It can be argued that the failure to achieve unity and common purpose is not inherent in the model of multiculturalism adopted. Rather, disunity is a product of federal dynamics: Canada is not a nation-state that can claim the status of a single and unified host society. As such, one can assess the policy independently of the Quebec question, which to a large extent may explain the motivation for the policy but not its actual effects as a model for integration. If we disregard the variable of multinationality in Canada, has multiculturalism been successful in integrating immigrants and ethnic groups? Indeed, if we begin with the assumption that Canada constitutes a single political community, or host society, we can then proceed to evaluate the success of multiculturalism without considering disunity in terms of the fragmentation of 'national allegiance.' Unity can thus be conceptualized as the extent to which minority groups feel as though they belong to a single community called Canada, and actually participate in the general affairs of the larger society.

As a response to critics who view multiculturalism as a divisive force in Canada, Will Kymlicka provides some empirical data that demonstrate the success of multiculturalism in terms of the integration of minority cultures.[55] Certainly, the line of criticism in this chapter does not challenge the integrative success of the policy. The claim is that, due to the imperatives of nation-building, for the purposes of unity in the face of the Quebec question, Canada chose to adopt a 'lowest common denominator' formula that rejected the recognition of culture as an aspect of belonging altogether. Trudeau's just society is predicated on the notion that any emotive attachment to a given political community or nation is destructive and retrograde, and that progress requires an emphasis on reason to serve as a guiding principle in any citizenship regime. If we look closely at Kymlicka's indicators for integration, however, although they demonstrate that integration has been rather successful, it came at the expense of the recognition and preservation of minority cultures – which in the final analysis is the defining feature of ideological multiculturalism.

The Canadian model operates according to the primacy of individual rights in a constitutional bill of rights, with an interpretive clause for the recognition of diverse cultural affiliations. This interpretive clause is the only significant feature that distinguishes it from the American model of assimilation. There is no democratic imperative for the recognition of diverse minority cultures besides a legal/procedural provision that may be invoked if the minority group in question chooses to do so. This is a key conceptual distinction between the Canadian and Quebec models and it stems from the nature of the expectations of democracy itself. The fact that Canadian identity – the way citizens relate to each other and to the state in determining societal preferences – is predicated on such terms implies that there is not a public culture on which minority cultures can make their mark. Again, multiculturalism in Canada does not reflect a recognition of minority cultures; rather, to be blunt, it rests on the denial of culture altogether in defining the limits and confines of public space. Public space is based on individual participation via a bill of rights. Returning to Kymlicka's assessment on the success of Canadian multiculturalism in terms of integration, we note a dearth of evidence regarding the extent to which minority cultures feel as though they have been able to persist in living according to the sources of meaning garnered by their cultural affiliations. In his defence, this undertaking would require a large-scale empirical study, and the fact that he was able to successfully operationalize 'integration' merits credit in its own right, as it deepens the conceptual discourse surrounding these models of integration. However, the success of minority groups within indicators such as 'naturalization rates', 'political participation,' 'official language competence,' 'intermarriage rates,' 'a lack of territorial enclaves of cultural groups'[56] are addressed to those critics who view multiculturalism as an obstacle to forging a strong Canadian identity. They do not speak to the explicit concern for the preservation and flourishing of minority cultures within the political community – the capacity of such groups to participate and affect the public affairs of the country without shedding their particular group identities. The debate itself thus takes place outside the imperatives of ideological multiculturalism. In other words, these criteria may very well be addressing a regime committed to assimilation.

The virtue of Quebec's model of interculturalism is that it strikes a balance between the requirements of unity and the recognition of minority cultures. Recognition is not limited to viewing a diversity of cultures as a 'problem', and treating them as static, essentialized, and separate groups that require a slice of the public purse and therefore must be budgeted for, and vulnerable to cutbacks. Quebec's model of integration is not assimilatory as the American approach, nor does it conceptually fall into cultural relativism and fragmentation in its commitment to cultural pluralism. The idea of empowerment as it pertains to marginalized ethno-cultural groups is such that integration is a necessary prerequisite to full participation in the construction of a common public culture as an identity centre. Identification with and participation through a variety of cultures is not ruled out as a basis for citizenship status, yet the possibility of enclosure and ghettoization is discouraged because the recognition of particular cultural identities is de facto the *recognition of the right and obligation to participate* in the polity, not the recognition of culture as existing in self-contained communities that are pre-political, in a vacuum of space and time. Recognition is an *outcome* of participation, the result of contributing to the development of a common public culture and to larger consensual bases of allegiance and identification, without rejecting the established symbolic order offered by Quebec society as it has evolved historically, in which members of minority cultures can make a difference regarding their status as citizens. In this sense, the unity and solidarity sought by any model of citizenship are viewed as a process, to be constructed by the various parties involved through exchange and dialogue, rather than a model that offers a pre-existing blueprint of recognition. Bhikhu Parekh is perhaps the leading theorist to stress this aspect of cultural diversity.[57] For Parekh, a liberal framework that states simply that culture matters to individuals is not sufficient for making the case that cultural diversity in itself is valuable. While the majority culture may internalize the fact that members of minority cultures warrant certain cultural rights, it fails to appreciate the value of cultural diversity whereby a sense of cultural contrasts also endows individuals with a deeper understanding of their own cultures and allows for reflection about larger questions of coexistence between people. Cultural diversity is thus valuable on top of the instrumental benefits that cultural contexts provide for individuals.

Interculturalism as a model for addressing polyethnicity represents a forum for citizen empowerment, not retrenchment. From the initial premise that a national culture consists of a 'daily plebiscite,' to draw from Renan's conceptualization, the Quebec model stresses the idea that the common public culture be inclusive of all groups in its changing and evolutionary fabric. Jeremy Webber has located this dynamic aspect of a national identity in the idea that communities are fostered through public debates in a common language through time. Shared values in themselves do not provide the sense of allegiance necessary for a national community to thrive. Indeed, disagreements about the major orientations of society are perhaps emblematic of a healthy political community because they demonstrate that citizens are concerned with the state of the community. The democratic quality of a constantly changing political community lies precisely in the idea that citizens are able to identify with and make an impact on the current streams of public debate in society – and this requires that citizens interact within the framework of a common vernacular.[58] In short, we turn to Joseph Carens, who states it succinctly: 'In integrating immigrants, Quebec is transforming not only their identity but its own as well.'[59] As such, the French language is not meant to define a static culture into which immigrants and cultural communities are expected to melt. Rather, French is the conduit through which the disagreements, contentions, and conflicts inherent in a culturally diverse society can be aired in a situation of normal politics. In the end, participation implies some degree of political conflict. The political community is based on a shared language, and challenges to the prevailing tenets of the national culture are not viewed as threatening, but are encouraged as a healthy and normal effect of democratic deliberation.

As discussed above, two general considerations are salient in assessing the models as they pertain to polyethnicity and democratic citizenship. First, the model must consider unity as a basis for democratic stability, which provides a shared sentiment, a common ground for dialogue and, generally, dispositions amenable to the exercise of liberal citizenship. In other words, a pole of allegiance that acts as an identity centre of convergence is required for active participation in a democratic polity. Second, the recognition of difference and a respect for the sources of meaning of minority cultures is an integral element of equal citizenship status – of citizen dignity or empowerment. For traditional liberal thought, such goals are incompatible. The involvement of group-differentiated recognition is said to mitigate the former ideal, where equality stems from shared adherence to universal principles and culture is treated with benign neglect in the public sphere. Recognizing cultural distinctions shatters unity and renders citizens unequal.

This position is not meant as a radical argument for postnational identity politics; indeed, the normative merits of unity in any given state have been explicitly acknowledged. Nor is it meant to prescribe a formula for unity in a specifically federal context. It seeks to demonstrate the merits of interculturalism as an alternative model for integration, and that Canadian multiculturalism has been and continues to be a product of nation-building efforts rather than a genuine commitment to the main tenets of ideological multiculturalism. It is an aspect of a political strategy by the central state to forge a strong commitment, by its citizens, to Canada as a single and unified political community. Canadian multiculturalism should not be viewed as an example of the emerging ideology of multiculturalism and its implications for the redefinition of the legitimacy of nation-states in the case of polyethnic societies. The main principles of Canadian citizenship are not that far off from those of the United States, or Australia and Germany, for that matter.[60] Indeed, the place of culture in Canadian conceptions of citizenship is liberal: it is about building a nation based on universal principles. A model of cultural pluralism along the lines of Quebec interculturalism makes a more serious effort to balance the requirements of unity with the preservation, recognition and flourishing of minority cultures. The enduring problem confronting the Quebec model, one that would have to be taken into account in any future attempts at empirical verification, is the idea of competing interpretations of citizenship by those targeted for integration in the first place. As Micheline Labelle and Joseph Levy have illustrated in interviews with leaders of ethno-cultural groups, there is continuing ambivalence with regards to the legitimacy of the Quebec model.[61]

The Quebec model is unique in that it is embedded in a larger project for national affirmation. The fact that it can legitimately be included as a model for integration at the very least demonstrates the strides that Quebec has made in the area of citizenship, and perhaps such conceptual overviews can spark some interest in more empirically-based research in the future. Whether or not such research can be undertaken in a context of competing models of citizenship, within a single territory, should not undermine efforts to include the model of interculturalism in debates about recognition and integration in liberal democracies. Indeed, Quebec intellectuals, in formulating the boundaries of the national project, have been engaged in a rich debate about the bases of belonging in the Quebec societal culture. It is to this debate that the discussion will now turn.

Citizenship Discourse in Quebec: Societal Culture at Work

The parameters of national identity in Quebec must be assessed in the context of its minority status within Canada. As noted above, Quebec's status as a nation is not recognized formally in the Canadian constitution: it is considered to be a province, equal in status to the others, and individuals in Quebec are to enjoy the same fundamental rights as do those in the rest of Canada. Debates in Quebec concerning the defining characteristics of national identity have thus taken place in a setting in which it has to compete with a larger political community that demarcates formal citizenship. Unlike most established nation-states, national identity in Quebec faces the added burden of accounting for institutional and symbolic barriers that are externally imposed. Moreover, its very legitimacy is questioned by a significant proportion of its population because of the ambiguous nature of belonging in a hybrid political community. Debates surrounding the socio-cultural versus civic or liberal character of national identity are easily dismissed by some since the national movement itself is concentrated mostly around one socio-cultural grouping – francophone Quebeckers. Indeed, Quebec's national project is at times dismissed as reactionary, retrograde and 'ethnic'[62] because historically, nations and states have been cotermi-nous; thus the larger 'state' must be a reflection of some 'nation' that finds its clearest expression at the level of the central government, which in the final analysis represents the institution that determines cit-izenship laws.[63]

Others view Quebec's efforts at defining the contours of citizenship as but another reflection of efforts to broaden the normative impact of citizenship discourse along the lines of the widespread growth of iden-tity claims on central institutions of citizenship, and not as a competing centre for determining the very boundaries of citizenship. From this perspective, Quebec's demands are interpreted as merely another set of claims on citizenship, similar to those of social movements more gener-ally. The key assumption here is that the 'challenge' posed by Quebec nationalism rests among other developments that 'unsettle' nation-state citizenship, leaving little room for the conclusion that Quebec itself is involved in its own debates about how to craft contours of membership based on the nation form.[64]

The very discourse of managing diversity in Canada through the institution of citizenship, from a Quebec perspective, is thus persis-tently coloured by the bias that the central institution of citizenship remains the preserve of the Canadian political community, and that Quebec national identity is but an object to be managed in the larger canvas of diversity. This is the backdrop against which debates about managing diversity within Quebec, and reconciling it with Quebec's conception of itself as a nation, take place. Those debating the contours of Quebec's national identity, by contrast, seek to define the political subject in the specific context of the Quebec political community.

Like all nations, absolute consensus as to the substance of shared identity in Quebec does not exist. The main problem with regards to the boundaries of Quebec's national identity relates to its justification for nation-state status, or more broadly stated, for some arrangement that recognizes its claim to sovereignty. The paradox is that the more civic or liberal the movement becomes, and the more it moves away from its thick socio-cultural roots towards the trend of postnational citizenship, the more its justifications for sovereign status are weakened. On the other hand, others have argued that it is precisely the move towards a socio-political conception of the nation, demarcated by the territory of Quebec, that demonstrates the political community's commitment to liberal democracy and its credentials as a societal culture without 'internal restrictions.'[65] According to Jocelyn Maclure, the narratives and counter-narratives that have nourished the collective self-awareness of the Quebec nation have been characterized by constantly shifting and alternating self-interpretations and political projects.[66]

Since the Quiet Revolution, interpretations and debates around Quebec's national identity have for the most part taken place in line with those of most societies in a period of late modernity. The main concern has been with the burgeoning plurality of constituted identities and its impact on the project for political sovereignty. Nationalism in Quebec has thus faced the task of being re-conceptualised to accommodate the multiplicity of collective projects that compete with particular belonging based on the socio-cultural nation. This is a familiar debate that in many respects has prompted scholars to point to the phenomenon of postnationalism.[67] In Quebec, however, the debate is rendered more complex because of the project for political sovereignty. Fernand Dumont, for example, doubts the validity of a shift towards territorial and civic conceptions of the nation and claims that it is sociologically inauthentic. For Dumont, the nation is, by definition, a product of memory, history and culture. Quebec, in this sense, does not constitute a nation. He preferred to call it a political community that 'houses' the French-Canadian nation:

> We currently speak of the Quebec nation. If our English co-citizens in Quebec do not feel as though they belong to our nation, if many allophones reject it, if Aboriginals refuse it, can I just include them by the magic of vocabulary? History has fashioned a French nation in America; by what sudden decision do we think we can change it to a Québécois nation? Defining the nation by territorial boundaries is to affirm that the state corresponds to it; a verbal and perfectly artificial construction of political tacticians.[68]

Addressing the implications of 'thinning out' national identity on the project for political sovereignty, Nicole Gagnon contends that the traditional socio-cultural markers of the French-Canadian nation in Quebec should inform the societal project, arguing against the trend of postnationalism for 'assimilation as the normal and necessary destiny of the majority of the children or grandchildren of immigrants.'[69]

This perspective, however, has very few adherents among Quebec intellectuals, who contend that it is precisely the legitimating necessities of the project for national sovereignty that discredits an emphasis on strict socio-cultural representations of the nation and require openness to liberal and pluralist conception of collective consciousness. Michel Seymour, seeking to move the debate past its civic versus ethnic paradigm, proposes a socio-political conception of the nation that at once demarcates it from absolute universal markers while maintaining a commitment to late modern developments in Quebec society by accepting that no national imaginary can be legitimate if it excludes any portion of the population. For Seymour, a nation that is purely civic can only be a nation that is already recognized as sovereign. The identity construction of the national movement, while not necessarily resting on objective sociocultural markers, nevertheless is conceptualized as a political project in the context of the quest to achieve sovereign status. This is the key marker and debates cannot simply rest on an ethnic/civic continuum. If the nation is identified as ethnic, then it excludes a good portion of society for membership, de-legitimizing the movement altogether. If it is conceived as a civic collectivity, then what is the fundamental justification for distinct sovereign status? For Seymour, the key is to recognize that a significant linguistic community constitutes a majority on a given territory. This constitutes a distinct political community that is shared with minority groups, which – and this is a key component of his socio-political argument – does not rule out the cultural, moral, and historical foundations of the majority linguistic grouping yet at the same time recognizes, through open political and social processes, the contributions of minority groups in shaping and reshaping the narratives of the political project in progress.[70] In short, the main consensus in Quebec is that the national movement is clearly not ethnic in orientation, yet it connects to a long tradition of cultural assertion. As we have seen, this is the thrust of the model of interculturalism.

Although reconciling the national with the postnational foundations of any society is a difficult theoretical task, the balance lies in recognizing that the socio-political aspects of the nationalist movement in Quebec must be interpreted in the context of its predicament as a societal culture whose defining characteristics cannot be separated from its condition as minority nation that has yet to achieve the status of a nation-state. Debates about the postnationalist character of Quebec nationalism cannot fundamentally be grasped without reference to this paradox of self-interpretation. The question of belonging in most liberal democratic nation-states is addressed through the central institution of citizenship. Debates surrounding the postnational markers of identity in such states, in an era of social pluralism and compounded identities, do not have to contend with the prospect of conveniently accommodating diversity by stripping citizenship of its particular 'national' bases and defining it along universal entitlements that transcend national identity. In the Quebec case, by contrast, the movement itself, as a process of definition and redefinition, rests upon interpretations of belonging that attempt to delineate it from a plurality of collective identities that are defined by a central institution of citizenship whose boundaries are set by the central Canadian state. In this sense, managing internal diversity in Quebec can only be reconciled with the project for sovereign status if it assumes that the Quebec political community constitutes a 'centre for convergence.' Any conceptualization of a national model in Quebec cannot conceive the universal premises of postnationalism (whether this takes the form of individual rights based on personhood or a cultural pluralist model that does not recognize the primacy of any majority socio-cultural markers of identity, such as Canadian multiculturalism), without conceding that its project is no different from any grouping that seeks differentiated recognition from the larger institution of citizenship.

The official position in Quebec with regards to markers of belonging to the political community has been given form in two key government documents on the topic of Quebec citizenship.[71] Without delving too deeply into the intricacies of such policies, it suffices to say that Quebec's position on the construction of citizenship and, broadly speaking, on the contours of membership, differentiates itself from Canada's approach to diversity by stressing a 'common public culture', civic participation, and a pole for cultural convergence that is absent in official Canadian multiculturalism.[72] Moreover, whether the classic formulation of a moral contract is employed or more recent manifestations of the model that stress civic rights, (a more broadly defined strategy of integration that stresses citizenship, as shown by attempts to drop the term 'cultural communities' in favour of the inclusive appellation Québécois), the main idea is that integration involves reciprocity, empowerment and interculturalism. As such, there is an emphasis on language, which is viewed as a bearer of culture but also as a common good that must be considered as a rallying point for all residents of Quebec, delimiting the public space for democratic expression and debate. However, according to Danielle Juteau, the very adoption of the language of citizenship signifies a shift from a pluralist conception of the community to a conception of belonging that merges with nationality:

In spite of a shift from a cultural to a territorially based definition of the community, I argue that the citizenship presently developed is anchored in a homogenized notion of cultural belonging, as the Quebec State is attempting to define a 'universal' national identity that would subordinate all others. The national model of citizenship is preferred over the postnational, the republican over the pluralist, the undifferentiated over the differentiated, at least when it comes to cultural identity.[73]

Juteau contends that while Quebec flirted with a more unmitigated commitment to cultural pluralism in the early 1990s, the latest discourse centred on citizenship represents a shift to a more homogeneous conception of the nation that is contrary to the international trends pushing liberal democratic nation-state towards multicultural rights and differentiated postnational identities. Dimitrios Karmis concurs with this understanding of identity in Quebec in the contemporary period, noting that there is a persistent strain, within the civic strand of national identity in Quebec, which alternates between Jacobin-style republicanism and integrationist nationalism. For Karmis, the notion that the construction of the nation in Quebec is based on ethnic definitions, along the lines of Trudeau's view, is a debate that has seen its last days. The real tension lies within the civic camp.

The past ten years have seen alternating conceptions that lie somewhere in the middle of integrationism and republicanism. We contend, however, that the basic thrust of interculturalism continues to hold in Quebec's model of integration. For integration nationalists, Jacobinism represents a defensive-minded approach to identity. In its place, francophone Quebec is interpreted as a strong linguistic and cultural space, open to pluralist liberal democratic citizenship as a shared good across the political community that is open to the contribution of all cultures. Moreover, this model recognizes certain collective rights of national minorities (such as the English-speaking community and Aboriginal peoples).[74] The French language is valued both as a bearer of a cultural heritage, as well as its public function of facilitating solidarity and deliberation and point of convergence for various ethnocultural communities. The formal model of interculturalism emerged in the 1990s along these lines, and it is coming to fruition.[75]

Karmis concurs with Juteau, however, that developments during the last Parti Québécois government (1998–2003) have moved the model somewhat closer to republicanism, particularly in the 2000 consultation document presented by the PQ government at the Forum national sur la citoyenneté et l'intégration. This approach places relatively more emphasis on unity, consensus and cohesion in its treatment of plural-ism. We contend, however, that this distinction is of minimal conse-quence, and does not represent a wholesale redefinition of belonging as is suggested by Juteau.

However, as Micheline Labelle and François Rocher observe, the election of the Liberal party of Quebec in April 2003 has resulted in the downplaying of the instrument of citizenship for the purposes of man-aging ethnocultural diversity. In place of civic discourses that referred to 'Quebeckers of all origins' and 'Quebec citizens as a result of im-migration,' the government has returned to the use of the category of 'cultural communities' in order to scale down the broad political impli-cations of a discourse centred on citizenship and the nation. This has been accompanied by a budget of $21 million centred around five main areas of intervention, while slashing spending in thirty-eight others. Moreover, the Liberal party has explicitly included Quebec's commit-ment to the larger federal order in recent documents,[76] no doubt con-tributing to the reduction of a more ambitious vision for Québécois citizenship in the area of immigrant integration. This represents the most explicit attempt to reduce the role of the Quebec state in managing ethnocultural diversity, as a distinct host society in Canada. While the moral contract is still present in the discourse, the government has del-egated much responsibility to actors in civil society and to third parties more generally as a result of its cost-cutting measures. Furthermore, the Semaine de la citoyenneté was replaced by the Semaines de rencontres interculturelles, and on February 5, 2005, the Quebec Ministry of Immi-gration and Relations with Citizens was renamed the Quebec Ministry of Immigration and of Cultural Communities. Labelle and Rocher lament such developments to the extent that they treat the issue of inte-gration as though immigrants were clients, to be named as the subjects of government services, as opposed to full citizens in a wider concep-tion of belonging in Quebec society.[77] From our perspective, however, the danger lies in the potential for such measures gradually to cede this area of responsibility to the aggressive Canadianization of the central government; in other words, to step outside of the parameters of the debate around republicanism versus cultural pluralism altogether. By slashing the budget, delegating such responsibilities to the private sec-tor and civil society, and implicitly defining citizenship around the Canadian political community (read federal government), the very notion of Quebec as a host society, with a distinct model of integration that is intercultural, is in danger of waning in significance. This is a prominent policy area for the state and for Quebec society in general. It is about questions related to substantive citizenship, whether or not the designation of citizenship is explicitly employed. The present orientation of the policy, while still committed to the main premises of the model of interculturalism, is nevertheless the most significant reduction of commitment by the Quebec government to the management of ethnocultural diversity. It remains to be seen whether this path will continue to be followed.

As shown in this chapter, Quebec's construction of boundaries must always account for a centre of convergence due to its status as a movement, a political project, in the process of definition within a larger citizenship regime. Both integrationist nationalism and a move towards more republican conceptions of the Quebec model cannot, by their very logic of representing a counter-movement, adopt unmitigated postnational markers of belonging. In the end, Quebec does not simply face the question of diversity, but must navigate through the question of diversity while justifying its very existence as a nation in a larger sociopolitical setting that does not formally recognize this fact, and tends instead to undermine it. Postnational belonging comes after national belonging is taken for granted: Quebec cannot simply skip this step. Quebec has demonstrated its commitment to the values of democracy, liberal justice, and cultural and national pluralism; it has abandoned exclusive ethnic markers of belonging both in official national models and intellectual discourses; it cannot, however, commit existential suicide by proposing the end of the nation form in the structuring of political sovereignty; this road is reserved for nation-states whose existence is not in question.

The debate is essentially about the quality of democratic citizenship in a multinational state. Thus there is no empirical imperative to treat the Canadian state as a 'cooperative scheme in perpetuity,' as traditional liberals tend to do. In Quebec, the idea of cosmopolitan democracy simply does not hold, because it lacks the crucial step of full sovereign status and it would constitute a tacit admission that there are no particularities in Quebec that merit specific legislative approaches and community imperatives. Indeed, cosmopolitan citizenship is in itself a state-building device among a system of states that are secure in the status quo – it is what majoritarian nations practise already, with a strong dose of 'patriotism' – and it tends to discredit national movements like Quebec. It is not merely postnational, but we would argue that it is post-democratic as well, in a substantive sense, as it succumbs to the promise of a universal liberalism that undermines democratically-initiated diversity among political communities.

As such, the process of citizen formation, in its horizontal conceptualization, is seriously weakened by the central state, which serves as the universal guarantor of non-participation for minority groups in Quebec. This turns the virtue of the multination on its head. What starts off as an experiment in universal liberalism simply degenerates into a regime that fosters apathy and state protection to those that do not wish to enter into the established public space – the dominant societal culture. During the last decade and a half, the majority group in Quebec follows activities in Ottawa almost in a monitoring capacity, constantly demanding change and frequently electing a majority of legislators from a sovereignist party to sit in the House of Commons. Minorities, on the other hand, consistently vote for a default party, the one least likely to foster a commitment to a more substantial engagement to the political community defined within the territory of Quebec. This troublesome electoral pattern is symptomatic of an unhealthy state of citizenship which divides more than it unites. Paradoxically, as long as Quebeckers are divided, national unity is assured – hardly a model of belonging and stability worthy of the term citizenship. Canadian citizenship provides a formal opting-out clause for citizens that wish not to participate in Quebec's public life. It is not merely the case that free citizens choose to reject any emotive attachment and sources of solidarity provided by national allegiance – this electoral trend is evident in most contemporary liberal democracies. The issue, rather, goes right to the heart of citizenship. There simply cannot be concern about strengthening public engagement and deliberation towards consensus-building in Quebec because a robust conception of citizenship runs contrary to the effects of the national integration strategy consolidated in the majority nation. The following chapter will more closely examine citizenship in a multinational context.

5 Citizenship and Democracy: Negotiating Membership

The Political Sociology of Citizenship: Contemporary Debates and Challenges

In recent years, political and social thought has witnessed a significant revival in citizenship analysis, particularly in relation to the political sociology of liberal democratic societies. Several world events, both domestic and global, have contributed to an expansion of the landscape of citizenship theory by altering the basic conditions of national citizenship (in both its 'thick' and 'thin' variants). These phenomena include: the challenge of accommodating national minorities within multinational democracies; the growing prevalence of identity politics, with non-territorial groups increasingly making particular and collective citizenship claims; the universalization of a 'rights' discourse that supersedes authoritative claims to sovereignty of the nation-state; the formation of supranational institutions such as the European Union; the changing ethno-cultural composition of states due to mass migration; and the increasing salience of security issues. Such developments have forced liberal theorists to account for identity formation and boundary fluidity that operate above and below the context of the nation-state.[1] In light of such challenges, the fundamental problem for theorists of citizenship lies in locating a principled basis for delineating the boundaries of political membership. What draws a body of citizens together into a coherent and organized political community – and preserves their allegiance?

For much of the twentieth century, liberal political philosophy has treated questions of justice and liberty from the perspective of undifferentiated individuals.[2] Citizenship in this view is based on a set of universally-applied procedural rules and identity is relegated to individuals, privately pursuing their own conception of the good life. Citizenship is a status, where individuals are endowed with a set of rights, and justice is a remedial value: an autonomous and responsible moral agent may pursue his/her life chances without infringing on another's. Indeed, the seminal study of citizenship that dominated thinking through much of the postwar period was put forward by Thomas Humphrey Marshall, who stated that free and equal citizenship was achieved through the codification of a set of rights, where the state ensures that citizens are treated as full and equal members of society.[3] For Marshall, citizenship in liberal democracies consists of an evolutionary process in which those possessing membership seek to widen the scope of entitlements from civil, to political, and finally, to social rights. Since citizenship represents the acquisition of entitlements from the state, the set of rights enjoyed by citizens is assumed to be a matter of common agreement within a territorial nation-state.[4] This conception is often referred to as 'passive' citizenship, because it stresses negative entitlements without an obligation to participate in public life.[5] Moreover, it assumes the existence of fixed territorial boundaries that demarcate the political and social relations of the citizenship regime.

Political theory has recently turned to a more serious consideration of the sorts of social identities that are relevant to politics, paving the way for the reformulation of liberal thought away from the abstract individual to an emphasis on socio-cultural contexts and particularities.[6] In this view, citizenship is given a more substantive meaning that presupposes a commonality between citizens – a thicker, more robust collective identity – that permits them to transcend their self-interested lives and strive for the common good through active engagement and participation. Collective life implies more than a 'rights-relationship' with other members and with the state; it entails social identities that are expressive of various collective allegiances, which in themselves carry particular duties and obligations. The notion that liberal citizenship simply requires procedural rights to be sustained has been criticized along two general lines. These will be explored in turn.

Identity and Liberalism: The Emergence of 'Thick' Bases of Belonging

Some liberal theorists question the extent to which citizenship can be reduced to entitlements in a vertical state-citizen relationship. An emphasis on rights, while constituting an important aspect of legal entitlement, fails to foster certain dispositions expected of engaged citizens, and, more importantly, denies citizens the ability to participate politically as agents that are culturally and socially constituted. In short, liberalism has trouble accounting for identity as the basis for membership or, more specifically, the public recognition of identity, as communitarians have convincingly argued. Individuals, in this conceptualization, cannot easily be disentangled from their particular cultural contexts, which provide a framework for choices and aspirations, and foster certain dispositions necessary for collective endeavours: trust, communication, solidarity, to name a few. As such, these questions speak to the internal social dynamics of political communities and attempt to determine whether certain socio-cultural identities are being under-represented and not recognized within a system of formal universal and individual rights-based recognition. In the end, such identities are assumed to be constitutive of the political and social agent, and the institution of citizenship needs to accommodate such attachments to achieve the ideal of full and equal membership that underpins liberal political communities.

This emerging approach to liberal citizenship generally contends that citizenship includes more than mere entitlements. Rather than a strictly vertical notion pitting the individual citizen in a relationship to the state, where rights are ends, citizenship discourse has moved to include horizontal conceptions that attempt to link members of society in a relation of rights and obligations to the state and to each other. As such, citizenship theory has come to incorporate a more robust conception of civic membership in a political community, with a greater emphasis on political agency and the recognition of identity as a constitutive aspect of citizenship.[7] Indeed, Alan Patten addresses such concerns and provides a minimal set of questions for any liberal theory of citizenship that includes a *membership* question (who is to be granted this status?), an *entitlement* question (what rights are implied by virtue of this status?), and a *social expectation* question (what responsibilities, dispositions, and identities are expected of one who holds this status?).[8]

This is a clear departure from Marshall's rights-based approach. Through this expanded perspective, citizenship provides the framework in which individuals and groups commit emotionally and existentially to a given political community. Citizenship is expected to act as a linking mechanism – a source of fellow-feeling and solidarity – that predisposes people to achieve common endeavours.[9] It plays an independent normative role to the extent that the promotion of citizen dispositions is a matter to be addressed by public policy in the active recognition and promotion of various identities. States can no longer simply rely on a set of individual rights in assuring liberty and equality. The resurgence of questions relating to citizenship thus tends to temper the ambitions of theorists in achieving a grand theory of citizenship because, unlike political parties or interest groups, the institution of citizenship makes a claim to being the only genuinely inclusive institution; it provides a source of unity that underpins the effective functioning of democratic institutions, constitutes a framework for evaluating the dictates of justice, and accounts for distributive questions. Citizenship, in the end, is meant to unite what political parties and interests groups divide. Citizenship as a cohesive force, fostering dispositions that are meant to bind members of society – what Kymlicka has called 'the mystery of the ties that bind' – is rendered much more complex in its horizontal conceptualizations.[10]

Horizontal conceptualizations of citizenship thus challenge the postwar liberal response to inclusive citizenship because they introduce new cleavages between members of a political community – cleavages that Marshall's entitlements are ill-equipped to address. Marshall's conception can assume that the bundle of rights 'won' by citizens is a matter of common agreement because he took class to be the underlying cleavage that citizenship was meant to address.[11] The rational individual in Marshall's view was concerned mainly with material entitlements, and this was claimed to hold true across cultures, identities, or any collective grouping. National identity and citizenship are correlated, and this dual political identity is simply assumed to supersede other particularistic collective allegiances. Citizenship as a horizontal linking mechanism, however, includes various divisions that cannot be resolved merely by addressing socio-economic concerns. Proponents of various models of cultural pluralism, in liberal, communitarian and postmodern traditions, thus contend that neutral difference-blind rights do not recognize or accommodate particular group identities that are essential for citizenship to fulfill its function as an overarching political identity that provides concrete measures of inclusion.[12] The main distinction is the extent to which *substantive* identity is considered to be an integral aspect of citizenship, versus citizenship as a mere organizational rule – a *shallow* conceptualization of the relationship of individuals to the state and to one another – with constantly shifting interests and associations.[13]

The salient aspect of new identity claims on liberal polities, particularly in contemporary understandings of citizenship, is that they are not reducible to the negotiation of interests in a strictly pluralist model. Conflicts surrounding the recognition of identity, social and cultural, can be far more damaging to the integrity and stability of a political community than are conflicting interests. Conflicts played out in the arena of citizenship, as opposed to treatment in normal channels of political resolution, reflect a growing sense that institutions designed for inclusiveness may be inadequate, and democracy is not fulfilling its function as a mediating device for diverse interests, since interests are not at cause. In other words, identity claims imply a redefinition of political community altogether – a challenge that traditional majoritarian liberal democracy and representative institutions are ill-equipped to resolve. Distinct cultural backgrounds may produce variation in the quality of citizenship within a liberal polity, liberal majorities may not be impartial or neutral in actual policy outcomes, and public deliberation may be limited to those sharing the dominant cultural worldview.

Questioning Citizenship 'Spaces'

A second set of questions that challenge an individual rights-based approach to liberal citizenship is the notion that political communities themselves are an open question with regards to the very agents that determine the boundaries of citizenship. In other words, if every individual is the same in the eyes of the law, then why should specific states that represent particular political communities exist? This set of issues has scholars debating the very notion of the nation-form as a purveyor of rights; as a place for fellow-feeling and solidarity; as an organizing principle for representation. Generally, it asks questions about why communities should be organized along certain parameters if liberal rights apply to humankind universally. In other words, this set of questions looks at the very organizing principles, sociological and legal, of political units that frame citizenship status. One fundamental issue has been the challenge associated with minority national identities, whose demands cannot be accommodated within the framework of multicultural citizenship, since such groupings constitute a societal or organizational culture in their own right, and are not objects for more authentic integration through a tinkering of liberal citizenship. For liberal nationalists, nations provide members with meaningful ways of life across a wide spectrum of human activity. Such identities are operating within a framework that is institutionally complete, in many cases implying a strong moral case for secession based on the principles of popular sovereignty, national self-determination, and democratic legitimacy. In the end, liberal nationalism rests on the notion that the basic premise of liberalism – that individual citizens are endowed with the ability to determine the good life for themselves – is contingent on particular contexts and experiences as members of national groupings. One particular problem has been the multinational state, where scholars have been vigorously debating questions about justice, unity, and stability through the framework of citizenship.

Why must liberty, equality, and welfare in the liberal tradition be undertaken by distinct nation-states, and are these particular 'spaces' for citizenship set in stone or do they reflect other considerations that liberal emphases on individual rights cannot address? Among liberal theorists, questions about the bases of belonging to a political community have coincided with a re-conceptualization of the links between citizenship and national identity. Phenomena captured by terms such as postnationalism, transnationalism, and cosmopolitanism suggest a waning of the nation form as the primary marker of membership and mode of belonging to a political community. New issues with regards to the very boundaries of citizenship have emerged alongside questions about justice and rights, which in abstract formulations simply presupposed the existence of bounded political units within which individuals exhibit a shared sense of purpose.[14] Indeed, this approach has occupied liberal thought for most of the latter half of the twentieth century, and liberals have been altogether weary about the legitimating bases for group rights. Citizenship, identity, and culture, once thought to converge as the legitimating basis for a stable political community, have disaggregated in new and multiple configurations of belonging that have put a strain on distinct 'national models' of integration, forcing states to explicitly define markers of allegiance and explore their self-understanding as political communities worthy of citizen engagement and commitment.

While these novel trajectories have been drawn and states have been proceeding with concrete initiatives that outline the entitlements, obligations, and boundaries of citizenship, the matter of democratic self-government, both in a large sense (of peoples) and at the individual level (political participation or societal engagement) has not yet caught up in practice or in theory. Current notions of representation, deliberation, mobilization, psycho-social sentiments of belonging, and territorial boundaries have continued to rely on the ideals established by national citizenship and on territorial notions of representation and sovereignty. The response by theorists has been to dilute belonging away from pre-political, cultural markers to more inclusive civic models of citizenship. Yet political communities have not been reformulated away from the nation-form to some sort of local or global organizing principles for legitimate political action.[15] The next section will offer some reflections on the tensions associated with conceptions of citizenship in multinational democracies.

Multinational Democracies

One catalyst for this expanded conception of citizenship has been the development of a field of study that isolates multinational democracy as a distinctive type of political association. James Tully, in introducing *Multinational Democracies*, outlines four attributes of multinational democracies. First, these political associations consist of two or more nations that seek not only group rights, but actual self-government and self-determination as it is understood in international law. This does not necessarily imply outright secession, but may involve internal measures that include constitutional recognition and accommodation of their status as a nation. Second, multinational democracies are not confederations of independent nation-states. They exhibit an overlap of jurisdictions, modes of participation, representation, and national identities of citizens that are open to negotiation.[16] Third, the nations and the larger multination are constitutional democracies. Fourth, multinational democracies are also multicultural in the broad sense of the term, consisting of minority groups that seek recognition of their particular identities. Struggles over minority and multinational diversity typically compete and are subjects of democratic negotiation as well.[17]

The emergence of such associations, and the widening and reformulating of citizenship theory away from strict individual rights, has opened new avenues for theorists of citizenship in that both a plurality of group identities and territorially demarcated national communities must be accommodated within a single democratic political system.[18] Several layers of group recognition thus exist, creating an inherent tension within multinational democracies. On one hand, the dispositions that are to be fostered by citizenship may be undermined with the existence of two or more political communities. If citizenship is meant to provide an overarching identity or loyalty to a given political community, then the existence of two or more nations fundamentally challenges uniform models of citizenship because both claim to provide this overarching identity. Indeed, in the case of Quebec and the rest of Canada (ROC), there exist parallel citizenship regimes: Canada as a 'political space' for citizenship constitutes a theoretical anomaly. As the previous chapter demonstrated, Quebec has formulated its own particular model of cultural pluralism – interculturalism – that, although not constitutionally binding, nevertheless informs its policies of integration and competes directly with Canadian multiculturalism as a symbolic centre for citizenship. Through protected social programs, Quebec has also been able to promote its distinctiveness in the realm of social citizenship by framing the content of social entitlements and fiercely resisting pan-Canadian national standards in the area of social policy.[19] Moreover, Quebec has negotiated extensive control over immigration, including the determination of selection criteria and a network of immigration offices abroad.

On the other hand, to complicate matters, there exists a level of ambiguity in the Canadian citizenship regime with regards to accommodating socio-cultural minorities that compete directly with Quebec's demands for recognition as a distinct societal culture and, by implication, a host society for integration. The confusion lies in the conceptual difficulties associated with the institutional implications of recognizing group rights in liberal democratic polities. By what criteria are distinct socio-cultural groupings appropriate subjects for institutional self-government, or constitutional recognition, as opposed to remaining objects of centrally-directed cultural policy through certain collective rights provisions? The Canadian case is rendered more complicated by a complex and more differentiated cross-cutting of collective identities. Canada's self-understanding, through official, constitutionally-protected multiculturalism, does not concede that national identity in Quebec constitutes a centre for allegiance that supersedes other particular loyalties and identities in Canada. In other words, it denies that belonging in Quebec can be qualified as citizenship, in the normative as opposed to legal sense of the term. One of the primary difficulties throughout the constitutional negotiations in Canada since 1982 has been the difficulty in reconciling the non-territorial demands of 'Charter groups'[20] with a traditional territorial conception of Canadian federalism. The persistent constitutional impasse finds Quebec competing with non-territorial identities for constitutional recognition. Cultural pluralism and multinationalism are thus in direct conflict and citizenship status in Canada is at stake. Indeed, at least one defining feature of Canadian citizenship is the persistence of a plurality of contests over recognition.

How does one establish a principled basis for delineating the boundaries of political membership in the specific case of multinational democracies, which are characterized by overlapping layers of identity that complicate the demands on citizenship? Much of the theory associated with answering this question invariably reverts to 'thin' conceptions of citizenship that call for the promotion of novel civic or political identities, or ways of relating to the larger democratic polity that incorporate various identities, as the unifying element of citizenship. These approaches seek to affirm and include particular identities by recognizing the imperative of diversity, while simultaneously providing a universal basis of allegiance. In essence, they superimpose a new, more inclusive notion of identity[21] for a specifically multinational context, with several caveats:

i. without falling back to a set of difference-blind rights as the constitutive element of citizenship – in other words, the community is a monolith, and the state exists to provide rights-enforcement services. Allegiance should be framed according to this principle rather than through a vague conception of collective agency;

ii. without asserting the primacy of national identity at one level (the multination), or the other (the minority nation), which would involve a denial of the existence of the multination altogether, or would simply resolve the problem by advocating secession;

iii. without getting bogged down in the seemingly infinite exercise of promoting the recognition of all particularistic or minority identities regardless of their territorial claims – a radical pluralist approach that makes no substantive distinctions between competing demands on citizenship; and,

iv. without advocating a 'third way': that is, a republican approach that draws upon Rousseau and Aristotle in asserting the primacy of a dominant identity that overrides the private loyalties of citizens. While offering a solution for pluralism, this view presupposes a bounded territory and does not offer specific solutions to the challenges of multinational democracies. The dominant identity is assumed to emanate from the idea that the privilege of citizenship inclines participants to address the common good of society as opposed to participating on the basis of self-interest.

In short, these responses tend to avoid the extreme poles of liberal universalism and ethnic, or pre-political, conceptions of nationalism, claiming that both subvert the idea of civic community in a multinational setting. The common strand among these approaches is that citizenship status is a policy area to be managed and promoted by the state in terms of how it chooses to recognize various collective agents in defining the political community. Policies can reinforce, promote, affirm, and recognize certain ways that citizens relate to the state and to each other.

These views, however, do little to advance the notion that citizenship can be reformulated away from simply widening the net of civic membership. There still remains a nation-state, in its traditional manifestation, that arranges the boundaries of citizenship according to thinner conceptions of belonging that may be more inclusive – and may even accept differentiated group rights as an integral aspect of citizenship – but does not genuinely address the persistence of specifically 'national' minorities. A re-conceptualization of citizenship that is differentiated at the level of national identity involves an acceptance that the very recognition and non-recognition of minority nations is not something to be *managed* by a centralizing demos, but to be negotiated between equal partners, each constituting distinct deliberative poles and each framing *particular* citizenship status. It must be emphasized, however, that this institutional scenario does not rule out the possibility of multiple linkages and integrated policy areas if these are the results of negotiation.

Indeed, Michael Keating, a foremost thinker of minority nationalism, argues that these challenges require novel institutional responses that go beyond much contemporary political and social theory, and further than mere attempts to consolidate citizenship along the principles of majority nationalisms, which often define themselves as civic or patriotic expressions of belonging. Thinner conceptions of belonging, without altering the basic ordering principles of the nation-state and its relationship to citizenship, are simply cosmetic responses to a much larger phenomenon. Within this traditional conception of the nation-state, minority nationalist movements are treated as reactionary, illiberal, and a threat to equal citizenship.[22] For Keating, the contemporary era is characterized by a pluralism of national identities that fundamentally challenges the established framework of political order – that of the homogenizing nation-state as a product of a Westphalian legacy. He characterizes this emerging era as post-sovereign, where the nation form prevails as an organizing political identity, yet is fluid and entails distinct levels of sovereign authority and representation.[23] Indeed, surveys illustrate that there is little in the way of distinction between the liberal values of those who identify with minority nations and those who connect with the majority in Canada, the United Kingdom, Spain, and Belgium. Such minority nations have demonstrated the de-ethnicized character of their movements, and it is precisely for this reason that they legitimately claim a niche as global societies in an integrating world, and to go beyond basic cultural accommodation in their demands.[24]

Embedded in a democratic tradition, Keating notes that the traditional nation-state obliges citizens in minority nations to be subject to decisions in which they can never form a majority. Treating minority nations as distinct deliberative communities or public spaces, as opposed to mere manifestations of some primordial ethnic/cultural reaction to the forces of universalization, is thus strengthening democracy, not contributing to its sudden unravelling.[25] To the charge that forging some sovereign space for minority nations would unleash a postmodern wave of claims for national self-determination, Keating responds that building and mobilizing a nation is a long process that occurs only under certain social conditions, with strong sources of political activism and social mobilization. Moreover, many such movements do not seek a retrenchment from integrated political and economic relationships or a return to the nineteenth-century nation-state; rather, plurinationality as a normative principle implies the coexistence of multiple political communities rather than a single demos, stressing union rather than unity and paving the way for constitutional asymmetry. Three implications offered by Keating assist in summarizing the persistence of minority nations and their fundamental claims,

> as authority is dispersed and there is no ultimate site of authority but several, then self-determination itself takes on a new meaning. It is the right to negotiate one's position within the emerging complex order, as the subject rather than the object of constitutional debate. A second implication is that there will be no 'end' to the process of constitutional negotiation and no solution to the 'problem' of nationalities ... A third implication is that political order will become increasingly asymmetrical as the varied claims to self-determination and the various normative orders cannot be arranged hierarchically or assimilated to a common model.[26]

In the next section, we offer some reflections on a novel approach based on authentic multinational citizenship in Canada, in which the nation form remains integral to the institution of citizenship, with implications relating to territorially-based representation and channels of accountability. In this approach, the central state no longer defines the boundaries of citizenship but instead acts as a mediator in the process of negotiation of citizenship status – the extent to which the multination will conform to the desires of its constituent units.

Citizenship and Multinationalism in Canada

The challenges associated with the management of diversity in Canada touch a variety of intellectual traditions and several disciplines. The notion that pluralism has come to challenge the privileged place of national identity as the legitimate order of contemporary liberal democratic political communities is a subject of debate within and among fields as diverse as political science, law, sociology, history, social anthropology, and international relations. Moreover, the idea of diversity itself engenders a multitude of avenues of thought, ranging from cognitive self-understanding vis-à-vis others (identity) to the place of collective projects in interstate relations and internationalized commercial and social transactions. Indeed, diversity has become somewhat of a rallying cry for those opposed to homogenizing forces that are taking place on two fronts. First, cultures are increasingly converging and interacting with one another due to phenomena generally associated with globalization. Many scholars thus propose a reassessment of the particularistic national markers of identity within political communities (or, at least, argue for a retention of the tools to govern and intervene on behalf of these collective goods), and some even envision an international convention that would recognize culture as a collective good for which states can legitimately intervene to respond to globalizing pressures.[27] Second, we are witnessing increasing legitimacy attached to 'thin' conceptions of liberal citizenship, or postnational citizenship within liberal democracies, that value civic membership above particular pre-political (ethnic) markers of belonging, and individual rights-based polities over collective social projects.

Christian Joppke and Ewa Morawska have observed that there seems to be a convergence among liberal democracies towards sociological multiculturalism as fact, and efforts at political integration based on the twin pillars of a public language and individual rights as a response by state actors.[28] Diversity in this sense has come to be associated with models of citizenship that acknowledge cultural pluralism within states, allowing for citizenship to be defined through particular cultural attachments as opposed to top-down definitions of citizenship that reflect homogeneous majority cultures as a precondition for belonging.

However, detaching culture from definitions of citizenship has not resulted in differentiated group rights for socio-cultural identities as a pillar of citizenship; identity largely remains a private matter.

Again, the Canadian case lies at the crossroads of these two developments. Canada faces diversity on both fronts. In many ways, Canada must navigate through questions surrounding a plurality of nation-based forms of representation and sovereignty while simultaneously addressing issues related to self-understanding, belonging and, more generally, citizenship, in a setting characterized by diverse social and cultural identities. As a multinational democracy, debates surrounding diversity in Canada often tend to stop short at sorting out the various layers of diversity (national, ethnocultural, social groups) without actually taking a step further to find solutions for the management of diversity.[29] Moreover, these distinct layers of diversity are frequently pitted against one another, and political projects or solutions made in their names are employed to undermine other legitimate expressions of diversity.

On the one hand, Canada must manage the question of national diversity, a challenge that most other liberal nation-states do not have to grapple with to the same extent. To formulate it differently, in the language of Kymlicka's theory of multiculturalism, Canada contains separate 'contexts of choice,' national identities that are instrumental to individuals' well-being, thus tailoring political institutions accordingly.[30] On the other hand, Canada is also involved in crafting the boundaries of citizenship: it must address questions related to immigrant integration, cultural pluralism, and ethnocultural diversity. Kymlicka's conceptual categorization relating to the distinct policy implications of national minorities and ethno-cultural groups makes an important contribution to the way we comprehend citizenship, yet, addressing one problem in a multinational state invariably limits the options available in dealing with the other. Kymlicka indeed concedes that self-government rights for national minorities pose a theoretical problem for liberal citizenship, as opposed to what he considers to be the more straightforward task of recognizing culture as a primary good for citizens, within a liberal framework, and thus integrating members of ethnocultural group on the basis that, first, they seek integration and second, they must be allowed to flourish as members of their particular cultures.

This is the fundamental challenge confronting Canada today, and any attempt to sort through the issue of diversity must account for this entanglement. Conceptually, the question of diversity itself must be disentangled to reflect distinct political and social projects, and methodologically, a multinational democracy such as Canada is precisely the case with which to evaluate such projects, since the term diversity means different things to different social and political actors. The distinct challenges associated with the various layers of diversity in Canada will be assessed in turn in the following sections.

Citizenship Activity in a Multinational Setting: Negotiating and Enriching Boundaries in Competing Arenas

Distinct forms of citizenship activity in Canada can be characterized as *convergent* versus *oppositional* in their relations with the state. This is evident when comparing Canadian and Quebec models of integration – multiculturalism and interculturalism respectively – which place varying levels of emphasis on the principle of individual rights relative to deliberation, consensus, and deliberative outcomes. Indeed, the Quebec case may be considered unique in that the very basis of its citizenship regime may be associated with attributes of social mobilization more generally, since many of its social attitudes are intimately tied to collective action.[31] In other words, the defining features of the political community of Quebec, with regards to citizenship and the dispositions that support it, may in themselves be considered units of study in social and political mobilization, as opposed to the strict lens of citizenship, which cannot account for mobilization that seeks to question the legitimacy of the central state. The democratic project for sovereign status, for its own version of citizenship (within or outside of the federation) encompasses non-territorial group identities.

Conceptually, the polity itself resembles a case of collective sentiment and action, with goals linked not to specific minority identities, but to the fostering of a democratic community *sui generis*. Quebec and ROC, as competing minority and majority centres of citizenship activity, condition identities and their relative levels of participation and allegiance because the layered nature of belonging 'forces' citizens perennially to answer questions about existential affirmation within the larger polity. Distinct pockets of citizenship activity emerge from the fact that national identity in the larger multination is not defined instrumentally – it is mired in a relatively closed process of negotiation and self (re)-definition – and these condition the defining characteristics of citizenship in ways that are not replicated in traditional nation-states. In a manner which challenges modern precepts of the nation-state, multinational democracy makes negotiations for defining citizenship status an open-ended process. Yet the formal citizenship regime in Canada does not recognize this phenomenon, and directly undermines Quebec's efforts to bolster and enrich horizontal links between members of their particular political community.

Ramon Maiz and Ferran Requejo,[32] two prominent philosophers, note that a glaring flaw in much of political theory as it relates to questions of cultural pluralism lies precisely in the tendency to treat identities as preordained objective facts. Indeed, a relational as opposed to a substantial view of group identities is a more fruitful conceptualization, in that it allows for a clearer understanding of processes of active participation and deliberation that shape such identities over time. A view that considers cultures and nations as processes of political construction must thus add a complementary democratic dimension to any discussions of the liberal dimension that rests on the recognition of rights. In developing a normative approach, we must thus address the conditions present within the public spaces of such societies in order to evaluate the process of citizenization itself. We argue that the multinational democracy is an ideal setting with which to assess the political dimensions of such developments.

While Maiz and Requejo, however, argue that this theoretical account that emphasizes democracy ought not to distinguish between cultural groups and nations as subjects of study, claiming this distinction to be artificial, we argue that this conception is necessary precisely because of democratic institutions that legitimately reflect a plurality of politically-constituted groups. In a multination state, conceiving the polity as one large public space in which group identities work themselves out in a relational process neglects the fundamental distinction that some groups are already constituted politically, with a range of institutions and patterns of democratic participation and legitimacy. The constructionist view that seeks to view group identities in the abstract is thus difficult to apply in the hard cases of multinational democracies. Group identities negotiate their place in the polity, through democratic processes, yet a failure to distinguish between territorially based nations and cultures suffers from the conceptual and empirical shortcomings of denying the existence of the multinational democracy altogether. Disregarding 'deep diversity,' in other words, has the effect of denying a good part of the citizens in internal nations the ability to bring their particular life experiences with them into the coexistence of the multination. Again, the multination is conducive to an active citizenry because contexts of choice are positioned relationally, and institutionalized, within a single state. These contexts of choice are qualitatively distinct precisely because, in themselves, as societal cultures, they constitute a sort of first-order citizenship that plays itself out in majoritarian systems of representation.

As Jane Jenson has aptly described it, this approach to the study of politics can be conceptualized as 'agency-centred and action-focused.'[33] In defining interests and articulating strategies, the social and political activities of minority ethnic groups involve a process of (re)formulating identities in a given polity. As such, citizenship activity is reflected in the manner and form through which individuals and groups struggle to mobilize, decide which interests are to be prioritized, search for allies, articulate policies that will accommodate their interests, and determine whether to pursue an advocacy role through political parties, members of Parliament, interest groups, legal channels, and so on. Yet in multinational democracies, the ambiguous nature of the boundaries of allegiance adds a new layer of identity into these processes of identity formation. The actual strategies employed by these groups, as well as their substantive interests, may interact with and be conditioned by the fact that territorial national identities themselves are open to redefinition in the larger multination. The reciprocal aspects of citizenship are thus undermined by policies relating to self-definition of the central state. In the Canadian multination, the formal status of citizenship and citizenship as 'activity' do not complement one another; they occur in distinct public spaces that undermine each other. This point will be developed further below.

Empiricists might do well to borrow from political philosophy and attempt to trace the effects of collective identity – or social cohesion based on shared national sentiment – on such pockets of citizenship activity, particularly in the case of multinational democracies. The Canadian case suggests the possible implications of such an approach. The societies of Quebec and the ROC enjoy similar levels of economic development, share the same democratic traditions, and, more generally, exhibit many of the values found in advanced industrialized states. Indeed, the fact that these distinct sociological entities share a government at the federal level might, on the surface, preclude any differences in the substantive social and political integration of minority ethnic groups in Quebec and ROC. Several scholars, however, have argued that shared values are not sufficient in themselves as precursors to citizenship boundaries and subsequent democratic institutions.[34]

This is not a question of divergence in terms of the basic tenets of liberal citizenship. Furthermore, this should not preclude the idea that Quebec and ROC have distinct citizenship regimes.

The phenomenon of collective national consciousness is a permanent feature of Quebec's self-definition. Charles Taylor is surely the foremost proponent of an approach that stresses the normative aspects of collective identity in the construction of citizenship. Taylor's view is that national allegiance is an inherent feature of modern democratic political communities. Individuals are given a sense to their lives, a 'horizon of meaning'[35] within a collective identity. In other words, citizen dignity cannot be divorced from a sense of belonging to a particular national group. In his words, 'The language/culture that defines our identity must be one that can command our allegiance. We have to see it as valuable. If it comes to be depreciated in our eyes and if it remains the indispensable pole of our identity, we are in a catastrophic position, one in which we cannot avoid depreciating ourselves, tied as we are to an impoverished culture.'[36]

The salient point here is his conceptualization of democracies on a procedural/substantive continuum. Of course, the continuum is an ideal model. The former implies that social principles are designed without reference to any collective good as a goal for society. Individuals enjoy neutral rights where such rights are trumps, and are usually codified in a Bill of Rights that takes precedence over legislative sovereignty. Individuals are assumed to be active citizens in that they may act within the limits of such procedural safeguards without any infringement on their aspirations and demands. In a sense, they are free from the demands of society, to the extent that the rights of other individuals are not encroached upon. This view is in line with T.H. Marshall's conceptualization of citizenship. In contrast, the substantive model assumes that certain collective initiatives may supersede the rights of individuals because some collective goods as end goals are seen as indispensable for society. For Taylor, it is this 'sharing of fate' which gives meaning to democratic citizenship: 'This citizen is free in the sense of having a say in the decisions of the political domain, which would shape his and others' lives. Since participatory self-government is itself usually carried out in common actions, it is perhaps normal to see it as properly animated by common identifications. Since one exercises freedom in common actions, it may seem natural that one values it as a common good.'[37]

The fundamental difference between these ideal democratic models is that the former favours the ethic of right rather than that of the good.

Again, Taylor's moral philosophy is not at issue here. The point is that citizen dispositions may be more conducive to one or the other of these two models, and this affects individual and group mobilization, in terms of both substance and strategy, at the level of civil society. The variation in emphasis on collective initiatives is thus an important indicator of the quality of active citizenship in a multinational democracy. Elsewhere, Taylor has identified this procedural/substantive divide as constituting the foremost distinguishing factor between the societal cultures of Quebec and ROC. The Canadian constitutional impasse is not merely a product of distinct visions regarding the bases of national unity. Rather, it stems in part from competing arenas of citizenship activity that are sociologically distinct and not reducible to an overarching and imposed procedural conception of citizenship.

Common citizenship status is not merely a function of instrumental attempts by states, at either level, to foster a sense of allegiance, through nation-building projects, explicit models of integration, or measures that promote civic participation such as military service, mandatory voting, standardized secular education, and so on. The contention is that the struggles and negotiations involved in identity formation and deliberation in a multinational context are in themselves processes of citizenization, forming distinct pockets of citizenship activity, precisely because they take place within, and compete directly with, separate contexts of choice. Multinational democracies may well contribute to citizen-formation by virtue of the fact that they force minority nations to continuously assert their particular identities, and in turn force majority nations to respond. 'Normal' politics between social actors and the state are infused with identity questions, creating a situation in which political demands become intertwined with the defining constitutional aspects of citizenship status. Once the relationship is deemed 'settled', by fiat as in the case of Canada, then citizenship is stunted. The minority nation's citizens are deprived of a better part of their agency; they are citizens in status only – hardly an accommodation of robust citizenship promised by multiculturalism and the 'liberal culturalist consensus.' Their capacity for outcomes based on deliberation, and the belief that political and social engagement may result in some form of consensus as to the main orientations of their political community, is cut out from under them in advance. Policies are developed for, rather than with, such groups. This observation is all the more urgent in the case of a national minority like Quebec, since their very democratic process and the flourishing of a societal culture, as necessary ingredients of qualitative citizenship, are simply not allowed to be worked on their own initiative.

Citizenship models do not merely define the contours of membership in a linear sense; the relationship may be reversed. Since Canada as a multination formally employs a unitary model of citizenship, then varying substantive forms of political mobilization between social actors, across political communities, may reveal a causal relationship in which citizenship status itself becomes the dependent variable, since the defining contours of citizenship are conditioned by the process of layered identities competing for public recognition while simultaneously practising 'normal' politics. In other words, a horizontal conception of citizenship may not be something that is somehow created instrumentally to serve the purposes of democracy and allowing for common endeavours to flourish. This is one significant failing of much political theory on diversity and citizenship. Rather, it implies a pre-existing level of commitment and allegiance to a given sociological entity. The theoretical problem lies in identifying this predisposition. The multination allows us to assess the explanatory role of certain social indicators (levels of solidarity, cohesion, allegiance to the common good) in fostering distinct centres, or pockets, of citizenship activity because it provides a comparative basis for measuring social and political activity across more than one political community. The sociological category we call nation may indeed be in the details – the forms of processes of engagement and deliberation. Empirically, Canada as a multination serves as an excellent experimental laboratory for observing the way citizenship activity is filtered through distinct political communities that participate within a monistic citizenship regime. Strict nation-states, by contrast, confine the potential for assessing citizenship activity in the sense that we have to start off with assumptions about pre-existing levels of horizontal and vertical commitments. There is no basis for comparing dispositions of members of distinct political communities because membership itself is pre-defined.

We will clarify what this approach might look like. I belong to political community X, which corresponds perfectly to territorial nation-state X, where my citizenship status is defined formally. This instrumental set of democratic rules or institutions that can formally be called citizenship, through which I participate, mobilize socially, make individual or group claims on the community, act responsibly with the common good in mind, act in a self-interested manner, practise civil disobedience, display extreme apathy, and so on; but it provides no comparative empirical reference for assessing the horizontal and vertical strength of citizenship status. Whatever its form ('ethnic' nationalism, republican, difference-blind liberalism), the nature of my particular dispositions – my allegiance to political community X – can only be measured in reference to fixed contours of citizenship determined within the confines of nation-state X. There is no other testing ground. I am not existentially involved in the struggles and processes of negotiation, on a spatial plane, through which my identity as a member of this community was formulated. As such, if I display a sense of extreme apathy, and the theorist asks the question 'Why is this individual experiencing such extreme indifference towards the common good of his/her community?', the answer will invariably involve some form of counterfactual reasoning. The response might look something like this:

> 'because an individual-rights based citizenship regime does not promote civic allegiance, rather, it fosters adversarial vertical and horizontal relationships';

> 'the community is defined on an ethno-cultural basis, and this is reinforced through an active nation-building project that has not successfully integrated you. You feel a sense of exclusion from the larger society because you cannot identify with particular indicators of belonging (language, history, culture) that are shared by the majority thus you experience a sense of apathy',

> 'as a woman/ blue-collar worker/ member of a minority race or cultural group/member of the gay community/member of a minority religious faith ... etc., your particular social-cultural identity is not explicitly recognized through the institution of citizenship, therefore your status as an oppressed minority group, the identity through which you participate in the political community, is denied altogether as a private concern. This non-recognition produces your sense of apathy';

> 'the instruments of the state (public education, social policy, legal framework) have not adequately promoted republican values that would inculcate you to subordinate all particular loyalties to the common good of the larger community. You are not a politically active agent because you don't know how to be one and the community is not structured along civic lines. You prefer to experience the good life as a client of the state, in strictly private endeavours, and this is the source of your apathy.'

What these responses indicate is that there is no way of assessing how citizen disposition might otherwise have been produced because the institution of citizenship does not vary spatially within the nation-state as a unit of study. There is no territorial 'other' with which to compare qualitative differences in citizenship activity. The empirical aspects of identity formation that supposedly explain citizen dispositions are limited to either: an interpretive chronological retrieval of key moments in the historical development of the nation, which have presumably shaped variation in political cultures and citizen dispositions within the nation-state over time; or, normative theoretical insights based on counterfactual assumptions about what citizen dispositions might look like if they were defined by other models of citizenship (i.e., republican, liberal, pluralist ...) – an approach that draws from experiences that we have observed in other democratic nation-states.

The case of multinational democracies, however, might look something like this. I belong to political community Xi, which shares an overarching model of citizenship with political community Xii, and together constitute the larger multination X. My citizenship status is defined formally at the level of X. This instrumental set of democratic rules or institutions that can formally be called citizenship, through which I participate, mobilize socially, make individual or group claims on the community, act responsibly with the common good in mind, act in a self-interested manner, practise civil disobedience, display extreme apathy, and so on, are the same whether I am a member of community Xi or Xii. Whatever its form ('ethnic' nationalism, republican, difference-blind liberalism), the nature of my particular citizen dispositions can be compared empirically with the nature of citizen dispositions of members in community Xii, because although we share citizenship space, I am existentially involved in the struggles and processes of negotiation of identity definition and redefinition in relation to political community Xii. As such, in contrast to the unitary nation-state, and its universal markers of membership, this very process of identity negotiation forces citizens to condition their dispositions in ways that might vary from political community Xi to political community Xii. For example, I might be more likely, as a member in a majority political community, to feel as though my identity is not threatened; therefore I concentrate on rights-claims, either as an individual or as a part of a group. Horizontal cohesion is less of an explicit concern because it is assumed that other citizens also seek entitlements from the state since the very legitimacy of the national state is taken for granted. My dispositions might reflect more of an emphasis on entitlements and less on protecting certain defining characteristics – certain collective goods – of a corporate national identity.

Whether or not this direct hypothetical conclusion from the Quebec/Canada relationship is accurate is just one theoretical scenario. The issue is that the multination provides us with a valuable testing ground on which to make assessments about 'principled bases of membership' that go beyond normative resolutions about how to re-create identity for the sake of cohesion. In short, the tendency of multinational democracies inherently to threaten the bases of unity may be precisely what keeps constituents of the multination on their toes as active citizens. Again, instability is not the only variable that ought to inform our evaluation of citizenship in multinational democracies. Forging a citizenship model that denies this inherent diversity is thus counterproductive: unity comes at the expense of a more robust citizenship, and at times it is even imposed.

Diversity in Canada: The Quebec Question

Canada's formal attempts to manage diversity have culminated in defining characteristics of the country that emphasize homogeneity at the expense of national diversity. With regards to Quebec's status as a national minority, the issue was said to have been settled once and for all with the entrenchment of a Charter of Rights and Freedoms which defines the country in terms of individual rights, as well as recognizing certain group rights for socio-cultural groups with the aim of addressing discrimination and regional unevenness. With regards to cultural pluralism, Canada has entrenched official multiculturalism as an interpretive clause in the Charter. This approach has endured over many years, and in order to trace back the debates around which this vision was adopted, it is necessary to assess the impact of Pierre Elliott Trudeau, acknowledged by many to be the architect of this approach to diversity in Canada.[38]

Trudeau's experiences with earlier, pre-Quiet Revolution variants of French-Canadian nationalism leaves us with a large body of his thought on national identity. As a proponent of enlightenment thought, he promoted the ideals of individual liberty, autonomy, justice, and equality – values that did not limit themselves to particular communities but applied universally, to all individuals regardless of spatio-temporal contingencies. Trudeau rejected the nation-state model, preferring the foundations of the modern state to be based on universalizing and individualist liberalism. He thus contrasted the 'sociological nation' – which he associated with reactionary and emotive politics – with the 'juridical nation', based on universalism and reason. National identity was depicted as an outdated loyalty, which narrowed interests and undermined the progression of civilization. Quebec neo-nationalism was thus deemed to constitute a threat to progressive politics and certain to lead to a cycle of never-ending conflicts that would hinder reconciliation and unity. For Trudeau, a federal state was most conducive to the development of the juridical nation and the exercise of reason in politics.[39] However, Trudeau himself, several years earlier, had defended the principle of Canada as a multinational state in *Canadian Forum*.[40]

The pillars of Trudeau's thought culminated in the formal construction of pan-Canadian nationalism based on multiculturalism, official bilingualism, and, above all, the primacy of individual rights as entrenched in a Charter of Rights and Freedoms. Although culture is recognized as constituting individuals through formal multiculturalism, fundamental to their autonomy and equality, the vision sought by Trudeau did not allow for any particular collective status based on historical, cultural, linguistic, or territorial claims as defining political markers of attachment to Canada. We have already shown, in chapter 4, how the pan-Canadian treatment of diversity through multiculturalism, official bilingualism, and individual rights serves as a counterforce to Quebec's aspirations for national status. This vision of Canada has endured and, since 1982, has left a mark on Canada's self-understanding that makes it extremely difficult to allow for innovative approaches to the management of diversity, particularly with regards to some form of constitutional formula that disaggregates the countervailing tendencies of acknowledging socio-cultural diversity simultaneously with national diversity.

The Canadian approach to the management of diversity, although pluralist and postnational in rhetoric, paradoxically undermines the substantive aspirations of distinct societal cultures by misinterpreting the meaning of 'equal status,' linking it with homogeneous and universal legal provisions – in effect, contributing to the perseverance of the Westphalian model. Through the central institution of formal citizenship, Canada has successfully carved out the national boundaries of the country from coast to coast, based on a rights-regime which has not undergone the process of acceptance and consensus that even a proceduralist liberal thinker like Jürgen Habermas deems necessary for any political community to thrive. As Michael Ignatieff reminds us, 'All peoples will refuse to surrender what is precious to them – land, religion and language – even when the compensation offered them is equality of citizenship as individuals.'[41] Diversity, however, can mean many things to many interpreters. The fundamental question when it comes to the management of diversity in Canada is not 'what is Canada's position on pluralism?' Rather, a commitment to diversity that accounts for its multi-layered character would look something like this, 'How does Canada accommodate demands by distinct national groupings that constitute the country to determine the boundaries of diversity within their respective polities?' In other words, at the pan-Canadian level, the central state and its use of the institution of citizenship would exhibit a stronger commitment and effort to manage the challenges associated with diverse modes of belonging by acknowledging its limits as an arbiter of citizenship status through constitutional adjustments. Short of such measures, diversity in the Canadian context, defined by multiculturalism in a bilingual framework, formal equality of provinces, and a Charter of Rights and Freedoms, is not postnational or cosmopolitan or universal in orientation, but filling in for a national void.

A genuine commitment to postnational identity in Canada, which as a multinational state would seem a likely candidate, would be to resist the top-down nation-building temptations of traditional nation-states and allow for diverse political communities to work out the delicate balance between collective goods and individual rights themselves. In several liberal democratic nation-states, where citizenship was traditionally congruent with the boundaries of national belonging, states have accepted pluralism as a sociological reality and have adapted by thinning out the requirements of membership. This is an empirical development whose roots cannot be explored here. In Canada, however, the institution of citizenship itself has recently been employed with the aim of 'making a nation.' It is a process whose peak in industrializing Europe was undertaken by states even before the development of Marshallian political, civil and social rights, when a vertical relationship between citizen and state was the norm, and states simply set out to assimilate diverse identities into an elite-driven conception of nationality.[42] This legacy does not bode well for a politics committed to diversity, regardless of what the rhetoric of multiculturalism and the present manifestation of federalism in Canada suggest.

Identity and Belonging in the Multination

The Canadian model thus creates a distortion between formal citizenship and active citizenship that is unsuitable for a globalizing world.

Quebec citizenship is not an opportunity grab to convince citizens of the merits of outright secession in the perceived propitious institutional setting of federalism. Quebeckers are divided and compounded citizens in ways that citizens in ROC are not. In a globalized world with a splintering of identities away from settled national citizenship, belonging needs to be 'named,' whereas in the past it was merely a residual category, the outcome of democratic rights and liberal justice through territorial representative institutions. Yet the latter approach is precisely what the central Canadian state is undertaking in a nation-building initiative. Unity, paradoxically, comes at the expense of meaningful citizenship.

Postnationalists argue that the nation no longer defines the political subject as constitutive of a collective project. But then, what defines the boundaries of the political community, territorial conceptions of sovereignty and representation, if not, at the very least, remnants of the nation form? Regardless of the extent to which national identity is decoupled from citizenship, the nation form still structures our cognitive understanding of political categories, particularly in relation to territorial modes of representation, deliberation and policy outcomes. This is the crux of the dilemma for most liberal democratic nation-states. The overwhelming response has been to recreate the nation away from exclusive pre-political markers towards inclusive rights-based conceptions that recognize few collective attributes of membership, except for instrumental ones such as a common language and the respect for the basic laws of the state.[43] In short, substantive culture as the essence of the nation has largely been replaced by the procedural culture of liberalism itself. In the end, liberal states are reverting to liberal solutions, throwing rights at the issue of diversity and widening the private sphere.

Even Jürgen Habermas, the recognized champion of postnational citizenship, conceded that his preferred notion of 'constitutional patriotism' was not devoid of certain collective attributes that precede process and form. In Habermas's view, public spaces demarcated by rational social communication and devoid of thick socio-cultural markers of citizenship nevertheless require a common language and some consensus with regards to the parameters of the common political culture. In essence, the term postnational itself causes some confusion to the extent that it implies a state of affairs that has moved beyond monistic conceptions of belonging. Even Habermas himself, in refashioning belonging based on a procedural patriotism, assumes that there is a political community upon which such consensus and deliberation takes place. For him, the exercise of sovereignty defines the parameters of citizenship, as opposed to flowing from pre-political ethnic identities. This does not imply, however, that political communities can be constructed anywhere and at any time regardless of time and space as long as a procedural constitution is in place. The main contribution of Habermas to redefinitions of the nation is indeed the very notion that citizens converge around a constitution which is deemed as somewhat of a victory – that there is widespread consensus as to the legitimacy of the basic laws governing a political community. For Habermas, it is the process of citizenization itself that leads to such ends.[44] In the Canadian case, this consensus is absent and the process of deliberation is stunted – the present constitution is simply instrumental and even a nuisance among a large portion of Quebeckers and Aboriginals – and in many areas of public policy, including questions surrounding the status of citizens, debates often take place independently of the other in distinct political communities, through distinct languages, historical memories, and representative institutions.

Moreover, in a multinational context, universal approaches that dilute socio-cultural attachments in the management of diversity actually work against minority nations and contribute to undermining diversity, to the extent that national diversity is not acknowledged as constitutive of the country and more specifically, as constitutive of citizenship status. As Michael Ignatieff has noted with respect to Aboriginal claims in Canada, 'At the moment, might lies with the majority and right with the minority. Mutual recognition must rebalance the relationship, with both power and legitimacy finding a new equilibrium. Then, and only then, will we be able to live together in peace in two countries at once, a community of rights-bearing equals and a community of self-governing nations.'[45] They cannot be considered separate issues, as the actions aimed at one set of problems invariably touch the other. If postnationalism can be equated with the logic of liberalism itself, in which citizenship is defined by fundamental rights based on a universal conception of personhood, then this serves the political purposes of a central government that wishes to impede the existence of a plurality of distinct centres of citizenship, host societies, or societal cultures that seek self-determination.

For those proponents who view cultural diversity as a Canada-wide area of management, Quebec's appeal for national recognition is antithetical. A model of cultural pluralism such as Canada's policy of multiculturalism within a bilingual framework does not specifically recognize national belonging as a basis for citizenship, at least in its socio-cultural expressions.[46] For Quebec, on the other hand, certain aspects of pre-political nationalism cannot be divorced from its socio-political project because of its particular status as a minority nation, or societal culture within Canada. Debates on the merits of diversity in Quebec have proceeded in conjunction with those in the rest of Canada, but the model of social and political integration itself must, by defini-tion, recognize the primacy of a national centre for convergence. Quebec is a postnational state to the extent that its version of national belonging allows room for a plurality of identities and individual rights. Indeed, any differentiated conception of citizenship, in order to remain true to its liberal foundations, can never accept the loss of a basic level of indi-vidual liberties, the prospect of 'internal restrictions,'[47] or a 'lexical pri-ority' of individual rights, to use Rawls's formulation. Differentiation of citizenship based on national group rights, however, implies that it is not up to a centralized institution of citizenship to determine such restrictions; citizenship is not a guardian to keep internal nations in line. Citizenship is a device for inclusion; it is not meant to serve as a patron-izing tool as though one conception of political community can legiti-mately serve as the liberal guarantor of another. Canada is not the guarantor of individual rights for its minority national groupings, and this is not the purpose of multinational democracies – to keep nations at bay. Quebec cannot, however, adhere to a radically postnational model that disregards all collective initiatives because its raison d'être as a dis-tinct political community within the Canadian federal arrangement stems, like all nation-states that are reformulating the demarcations of national identity, from socio-cultural markers such as language, mem-ory, history and, most importantly shared democratic institutions which serve as the basis for self-determination. Quebec national identity is rec-ognized as a collective good, and, as such, has to constitute the object of state policy as long as Quebec is deprived of its own constitution, or a Canadian constitution which receives Quebec's endorsement and rec-ognizes its status as a societal culture.

Citizenship in Canada, from a normative perspective, must thus be conceptualized as an institution which serves as a standard-bearer for public engagement. Within separate national political communities, this would permit the development of discursive will-formation through deliberation and participation in civil society, where citizens would have the capacity to reveal publicly who they are and what they stand for – an expressive form of activity as opposed to strict instrumen-tal activity.[48] As regards the institution of citizenship, these communities would determine the boundaries of membership, responsibilities, and entitlements without interference, and it would be the result of legitimate democratic processes. Choosing a formal rights regime, if so desired, would thus be based on negotiation and consensus as to its form, and the balance between collective and individual rights that it prescribes. With respect to the multination, citizenship would be based on the unitary principle, to reiterate Keating's distinction, and the level of political integration between the communities would stem directly from the bottom up – as the result of qualitative horizontal citizenship that recognizes the merits of citizens that reveal a minimum level of commitment towards one another. The liberal dispositions, as discussed earlier, would be allowed to flourish *within particular communities*. Institutionally, citizenship at the level of the multination would be based on mutual justification, in a setting of reciprocal recognition.

Under the present structure of Canadian citizenship (official bilingualism, ten equal provinces, individual rights, multiculturalism), claims are framed as interests and the polity becomes an adversarial ground for diverse interests which are predetermined; those who wish to make group claims simply slot themselves into a recognized social, economic or cultural category and look to the central state. Witness the repeated discourse of a secessionist party representing the majority of Quebeckers in the federal Parliament, the Bloc Québécois; their duty is to 'stand for Quebec's interests,' as though the political community of Quebec can be reduced to a set of interests that the central government weighs with other interests, and the elected representatives of Quebeckers constitute a mere lobby group. This is the extent of instrumental membership to Canada that must be addressed with a novel conception of citizenship specific to multinational democracies. Substantive citizenship is brought into being through its exercise, not through its subjugation. A sense of belonging to any political community is garnered by engagement in struggles over a myriad of material, social and cultural questions, not by the act of begging for recognition from a central government. Negotiations regarding the extent of nation-to-nation integration presuppose an affirmation of the very existence of distinct centres of citizenship activity.[49]

The Road Ahead

The socio-cultural foundations of this or that nation competing within a single territory is an old debate. The Quebec project is about allowing all cultures to participate in its construction for future generations. The basis of societal culture is not essential, it is in construction. The distinction in Quebec is that there is a strong will that this common public culture, its development, not be hindered by the arbiters of central citizenship who give citizens of Quebec a way out of the project to strengthen pluralism and democracy to advance their own political agenda. The multinational state incarnates the very ambiguity of the relationship between liberal democracy and nationalism. Multiculturalism, cosmopolitanism and postnationalism, and constitutional patriotism are inadequate as bases for citizenship in multinational democracies. The problem has thus far persisted precisely because citizenship has not really been disaggregated away from individual rights based on personhood on one end, and the distinction between recognition of minority cultures versus the self-affirmation of societal cultures on the other. The process of citizenization is perpetuated in the multination – this is precisely its virtue – it is the missing civic link that state-centric theories lack. All that is required is an acknowledgment that representatives negotiate the boundaries of membership at the multinational level, having taken their cue from a democratic process that included a potential for full social and political engagement that is not reducible to the articulation of mere interests, and without the divisiveness of offering an alternative nation-building vision, in an open-ended process. Contrary to those who view minority nationalism in its nineteenth-century manifestations, this is indeed the recipe for a genuine political relationship between political communities that share a long history, demonstrate similar values, and have expressed the will to live together. It is not a retrograde vision intent on closing a society off from a more enlightened other. It is, rather, a democratic project, in the first instance carving out the boundaries of community so that claims made upon citizens are self-assumed, as opposed to the imposition of the rules of membership, with citizens seen as clients/targets of the central state, constantly clamouring for their interests to be heard.

Diverse identities are indeed characteristic of modern liberal societies, and this has forced observers to re-conceptualize the institution of citizenship. However, simply merging the Quebec national question along with other identities that make claims on the institution represents a political strategy by the Canadian state that does little to offer promise for the future. Canada must be postnational, not by a universe of homogeneous rights, but by acknowledging the existence of several citizenship centres that are national in form to the extent that they are given the capacity to determine the boundaries of citizenship usually associated with unitary nation-states. A move away from the formal nation-state model need not imply a retreat from the national bases of belonging to democratic political communities as the foundation for citizenship. Quebec remains mired in debates about the character of its national sentiments; it does not have the option of offering a radically postnational basis of belonging. Given the institutions of a nation-state, Quebec as a societal culture can then choose to manage diversity in whatever fashion it sees fit in a liberal democratic setting. Evident in its present initiatives, even in the face of such glaring obstacles, it has demonstrated that its commitment to cultural pluralism is beyond reproach. Short of such developments, the ambiguous nature of belonging and self-understanding in Quebec and the constant confusion with regards to its place in Canada will persist, to the detriment of Quebec citizens vis-à-vis those of other political communities. In the end, even in a postnational age, it is the national form that lends legitimacy to liberal citizenship; it provides the foundational elements of popular sovereignty, accountability, empowerment, and representation, and the institutional capacity for decision moments that, at the very least, lend depth and a finite element to public deliberation. Short of this equation, citizenship comes to be impoverished.

The trend of postnationalism does not signal the end of sentiments of attachment to political communities on a more substantive level. There remains an element of national identification in legitimate liberal democratic conceptions of citizenship. The top-down forging of homogeneity through disassociated rights, however, can no longer take hold in a vacuum, as national minorities in the contemporary period simply will not allow this to take place. Such processes in most European cases of national integration proceeded prior to the consolidation of liberal democracy. The process of generating a satisfactory model that accommodates diversity in a multinational state can only achieve the stature of a procedural basis of belonging (or patriotism) if the process itself has been adhered to by all parties. In that way, the final product that defines the basic laws, the configuration of political relations, the acknowledgment and recognition of national groupings, the system of representation, and so on, is a point of pride and consensus for all parties involved.

Some might argue that this vision for the multinational state is simply secession under another name. This contention is mistaken, since it rests on a classical notion of the nation-state – the sense that it is the result of a natural progression and is therefore immutable. Multinational democracies must live with the prospect of potential secession because of the imperative of self-government rights, the dictates of popular sovereignty and democracy, and the fact that citizens are entitled to debate the boundaries of their political communities. A multinational democracy must endow active citizens with the freedom to choose their existential futures as political agents. If the will to stay together is strong, as majority nationalists in Canada seem to imply in their quest for national unity, then this should not be an issue. Multinational citizenship is precisely the arrangement in which this will is allowed to be revealed, while avoiding a domineering and constraining constitution or the constant prospect of zero-sum referendums. Citizenship implies willing participants as members, not as subjects. The next chapter will highlight recent developments in Canadian federalism and citizenship. It will conclude with a specific framework through which we believe Canada may yet be endowed with a self-understanding premised on multinationalism.

6 Contemporary Challenges and the Future of Canada

'Since [the 1995 referendum], the only consensus to emerge is that we should postpone everything – whether it be separation or a renewed union – until we have all thought further. The fervent desire to find either common ground or the terms of divorce has been replaced by a tacit contract of mutual indifference.'[1]

– Michael Ignatieff

This attitude of mutual indifference that Ignatieff identifies, from our perspective, is symptomatic of the deficient state of Canadian federalism and citizenship. Recent developments have done nothing to address the flaws that have led to the current impasse. Indeed, the constitutional debate in Canada is confined to scholars and pundits, while politicians avoid using the term 'constitution' altogether, except in regards to the prospect of Quebec secession, where the term 'constitutional democracy' is often employed. For Quebeckers, Canada is increasingly becoming an instrumental association. For the rest of Canada, Quebec is but a spoiled child, the land where concessions must be made and threats of secession are ever present. No doubt contributing to this malaise in Canada in the past few years and in the era following the constitutional rounds was the emphasis on Plan B by the governing Liberal party – the idea that the federal government charges itself with 'keeping Quebec in its place,' ignoring its demands and aspirations as an internal nation, and maintaining a consistent pattern of heavy-handed centralization and nationalization of the polity. We are of the view that this strategy will only hasten a rupture in Canada; it is going against its multinational grain, and is based on a level of political cynicism by Ottawa that can only be qualified as irresponsible. It is, in effect, a classic case of the perils of majority nationalism which any multinational federation is in danger of experiencing when the perceived imperative of national unity confronts federalism and differentiated citizenship. Some even prefer to call it imperial, but we will leave that word out of the discussion at the present time.

This chapter will highlight some recent developments in Canadian federalism and citizenship, from the consolidation of the present constitutional order through non-constitutional renewal, to a closer look at the Supreme Court's ruling on the legitimacy of Quebec's unilateral secession and the invocation of the Clarity Act as the central government's response. Finally, we propose to tread into the tumultuous waters by proposing a possible way out of the impasse that at once allows Quebec to express its right to self-determination without reverting to a the process of a referendum while making an attempt to restore mutual confidence and trust between Canada's founding members.

Consolidation of the Present Constitutional Order

Non-Constitutional Renewal

With the consolidation of the Canadian political community through the instruments outlined above and the failure of two federal initiatives for constitutional renewal in the late 1980s and early 1990s (the Meech Lake and Charlottetown accords), a centralizing vision under the leader- ship of Jean Chrétien emerged under the guise of non-constitutional renewal. While Canadian federalism is replete with bilateral relations between Ottawa and Quebec, leading many observers to contend that this signals the flexibility of the federal system to accommodate asymmetrical provincial needs,[2] the Plan B approach favoured by the Liberal government represented an attempt to wield the federal spending power in order to coordinate public policies within provincial jurisdictions in an era of fiscal retrenchment at the centre. While spending increased during the tenure of Paul Martin as leader of a minority Liberal government, there was a renewed emphasis on the use of the federal spending power to craft policies to Ottawa's liking, through the setting of conditions for national standards or by outright intrusions into provincial jurisdictions.

This approach to intergovernmental relations was based on the premise that constant attempts to address constitutional issues, particularly in relation to Quebec's demands, are a threat to national unity.

The federal Liberal government of Jean Chrétien thus adopted an ever-centralizing approach to reforming the federation, under the guise that Canadians wanted good government above all. Indeed, in the Liberal party's 1993 election platform – there was no mention of the continuing constitutional impasse. There would be no more mega-constitutional reform, since this was perceived to be the failed policy course of the federal Progressive Conservative party. Prime Minister Chrétien went as far as to state that even a sovereignty vote in Quebec would not lead him to consider opening up constitutional talks.[3] Towards the end of the 1995 referendum campaign, when it seemed as though the yes vote may be more significant than expected, Chrétien conceded that a recognition of Quebec's distinctiveness would accompany a no result. This was reminiscent of Trudeau's strategy of promising a reformed constitution on the eve of the 1980 referendum campaign. Yet Chrétien's intervention was a lot less ambitious; there was no talk of a grand constitutional makeover.

After the referendum was won by the no side by a slim margin, Chrétien continued to refuse to open the constitutional file. Instead, Quebec was recognized as a distinct society within Canada via a parliamentary motion in December 1995, and in February 1996 Parliament passed a bill in which the federal government guaranteed that it would not make any constitutional changes that would affect any of the major regions, including Quebec, without their consent. Finally, the federal government undertook a renewal strategy for the federation. This approach, however, continued to stress a prominent role for centrally directed governance. According to Harvey Lazar, while renewal meant increased federal-provincial cooperation and a new public management model[4] for the delivery of services that stressed efficiency, markets, partnership, and communities, it did not make efforts to include any notion of asymmetry into the federal structure.[5] While Lazar contends that this was the only politically viable option for reform, since it could simultaneously assure the rest of Canada that there would be no special status for Quebec while demonstrating to Quebec that the country was not stuck in a static federal system that was inflexible, we argue that this approach simply perpetuated the idea that the constitutional order in Canada was not going to be changed. The process was directed by Ottawa, and the target citizens were undifferentiated Canadians from coast to coast, in order that they may receive equal levels of services regardless of messy constitutional issues that were left unresolved. Thomas Courchene effectively summarizes the main motivation from Ottawa during this period of fiscal retrenchment: 'The underlying reality, fully recognized by the provinces, was that Ottawa was both fiscally able and politically more-than-willing to invade provincial jurisdictions if the provinces did not adopt a pan-Canadian approach to their collective actions. This might not prevent federal intrusions, but it would at least make them politically more difficult.'[6]

We submit that such an approach may very well have been undertaken if Canada was a unitary state and not a multinational federation. The strategy was driven by fiscal constraints, not by an imperative to accommodate the country's multinational make-up, as the previous constitutional rounds had attempted. Federalism is primarily about sharing sovereignty, not about delivering efficient services to citizens, as though this is a cure-all for unresolved questions about political community in a larger sense. Legislative and administrative solutions to problems of government services simply included the provinces because they had to: the provinces were responsible for those files. According to Jennifer Smith, non-constitutional renewal is anti-federal in its intention and outcomes, and severely disregards the federal principle in both legal and normative terms. She argues that the Quebec position on constitutional issues has been remarkably consistent over time. Simply foregoing well-established constitutional rules and conventions only galvanizes opposition, which serves as a constant reminder of certain benchmarks with which to evaluate the strength and relevance of federalism in Canada. Smith also raises important issues regarding the role of non-constitutional renewal in subverting the legal protections afforded to weaker provinces, creating a hierarchy among provinces in their relations with Ottawa. Finally, non-constitutional renewal creates ambiguity with respect to accountability of the governors to the governed – a situation in which citizens are left increasingly in the dark as to which order of government is responsible for a given policy initiative.[7]

In short, non-constitutional renewal signals the absence of a federal vision for Canada; it is an ad hoc strategy that reveals more about the failure of accommodating diversity as a federal principle than its stated intention to address distinct needs without rocking the boat of Canadian constitutionalism. The idea that it signals flexibility and an evolving nature of federalism is a fallacy. Federalism in Canada is as flexible as the central government wants it to be, and it evolves within very narrow boundaries that do not include any input from Quebec.

Recent developments in the era of Paul Martin's minority Liberal government did not usher in a fundamental change from Ottawa. The election of a Liberal government in Quebec, and the entrance of Paul Martin in Ottawa in 2003, was perceived as more conciliatory to Quebec and led observers to hope for a new era in Ottawa-Quebec collaboration, but did not address the main dividing lines of Canadian federalism. The question of fiscal imbalance remains unresolved, the federal government continues to play an aggressive role in the area of health, and the focus on a new deal for cities has the federal government once again treading into provincial jurisdictions. The general orientation remains: the provinces are considered junior partners, to be consulted in a system of agenda-setting directed by Ottawa. Moreover, in the Liberal party's election platform of 2004, social programs are equated to Canadian values, defining the very essence of the Canadian nation.[8]

Perhaps the most significant development has been the establishment of a formal institution embodying pan-Canadian provincialism: The Council of the Federation. It was spearheaded by the Liberal government of Jean Charest, and established formally in December 2003, in part to tackle the issue of vertical fiscal imbalance,[9] which has been persistently disregarded as non-existent by the central government. In the short term, the agenda of the Council of the Federation is the improvement of the healthcare system and the strengthening of the economic union. For François Rocher, however, this does not signal a new approach based on partnership. Rather, it simply institutionalizes existing practices among the provinces. Rocher does contend, however, that this avenue goes against the grain of traditional Quebec responses over the last four decades, which rested on two objectives: recognition and autonomy.[10] In this sense, while short-term goals may be achieved, nothing is undertaken to resolve the root of the problem as Quebec has always perceived it: a centralizing agenda from Ottawa.

In September 2004 optimism for the merits of collaboration once again emerged with the signing of a bilateral Health Agreement between Ottawa and Quebec. In short, the ten-year, $41 billion deal signed with the provinces contained a clause that exempted Quebec from accountability provisions imposed on other provinces. While the agreement does signal a moderate move away from the inflexible approach pursued under Jean Chrétien, it still remains a mere administrative response to a much larger phenomenon. Indeed, Quebec intellectuals were quick to point out that this case is one of asymmetry in result only, since Quebec only managed to secure full control over a field of policy that lies within its jurisdiction in the first place. In a situation of *a priori* constitutional asymmetry, Quebec would not have to strike a deal in order that it may govern in its area of competence for its citizens

Indeed, we are of the view that federal asymmetries can be concretely summarized in two forms. First, there are asymmetries of a constitutional and juridical nature (*de jure*), emphasizing the division of powers, and second, there are asymmetries of an administrative nature (*de facto*), which are more easily reversible. The latter correspond to agreements stemming from practical considerations or as the result of negotiated mutual agreements between representatives of the two orders of government. To this day, Quebec has demanded changes that are guaranteed into the future by proposing *de jure* modifications, yet has been forced to be content with agreements that could be modified according to current power relations – relations that are invariably unfavourable to Quebec. This has led to the signing of *de facto* agreements without any formal guarantees for the long term.[11]

In the Canadian context, if we exclude the articles of an asymmetrical nature already included in the Constitution Act of 1867, (for example, article 133 concerning the use of the English and French languages, articles 93A, 94, and 98 of the Constitution Act of 1867, paragraph 23(1) of the Canadian Charter of Rights and Freedoms and article 59 of the Constitutional Act of 1982),[12] the scope of asymmetrical federalism has been essentially limited to agreements of a non-constitutional nature, such as, the Quebec Pension Plan (1964), the agreements on immigration (Cloutier/Lang, 1971; Bienvenue/Andras, 1975; Cullen/Couture, 1978; Gagnon-Tremblay/McDougall, 1991), manpower training (1997), and the more recent health agreement (2004).

From a Quebec perspective, asymmetrical federalism has for the most part been seen by sovereignists as a strategy to demobilize nationalist forces and as paltry compensation for the all-too-frequent central intrusions in the fields of jurisdiction exclusive to Quebec. The main contention can be summed up like this: What good does it do to be satisfied by piecemeal powers when Quebec could have a single state capable of administering all of its responsibilities? As for the federalist forces in the Quebec political scene, asymmetrical federalism is presented as a last hope, allowing for a revival of Quebeckers' confidence by pointing to the flexibility that can characterize federalism. In the absence of making permanent gains by way of constitutional modifications, these federal forces still believe in the possibility of finding a formula that is tailor-made for Quebec within the Canadian federation.

However, it will remain far from an accomplished reality as long as opposition to asymmetrical federalism continues to be ensconced.

The Supreme Court Ruling re Quebec's Secession and the Clarity Act

With a strong electoral showing in 1997, the Chrétien Liberals sought to obtain a favourable ruling on a reference to the Supreme Court of Canada on whether or not Quebec had a right to secede unilaterally, either in Canadian or international law.[13] The ruling took the federal government by surprise. Attempting to re-establish the principle of continuity in constitutional discourse, the Supreme Court took a global view and recognized four main defining aspects of the Canadian federation: federalism, democracy, constitutionalism and the rule of law, and the respect for minorities. In paragraph 51, the Court made clear that although such principles are not explicitly noted in the constitution, 'the principles dictate major elements of the architecture of the Constitution itself and are as such its lifeblood.' In paragraphs 84 and 85 of its ruling, the Supreme Court affirmed that a constitutional modification could permit a province to secede. While the court conceded in paragraph 87 that 'the results of a referendum have no direct role or legal effect in our constitutional scheme,' it maintains that 'It would confer legitimacy on the efforts of the government of Quebec to initiate the constitution's amendment process in order to secede by constitutional means.'[14] If repatriation of the constitution in 1982 restricted Quebec's liberty to exercise its right to self-determination, the Court ruling can be viewed as a corrective measure. Paragraph 88 provides the most significant example of this:

> The clear repudiation by the people of Quebec of the existing constitutional order would confer legitimacy on demands for secession, and place an obligation on the other provinces and the federal government to acknowledge and respect that expression of democratic will by entering into negotiations and conducting them in accordance with the underlying constitutional principles.

Quebec officials and intellectuals interpreted the ruling with some optimism, since it allows for the possibility of relations between Quebec and the rest of Canada to be more open, and it makes possible a revitalization of the democratic foundations of the Canadian federation. The ruling had the potential to pave the way for a return to the norm of continuity as a permanent feature of future constitutional developments. The Court emphasized that the rest of Canada has a clear obligation to negotiate with Quebec should Quebeckers decide to demand constitutional change, with or without the legal backing of the Canadian constitution. As such, the ruling served to revitalize the traditional Quebec position that the federal principle in Canada must respect continuity of past constitutional practices, among which Quebec is to be treated as a distinct negotiating partner and not a mere sub-division of the federation. In paragraph 92, the ruling asserts that

> The rights of other provinces and the federal government cannot deny the right of the government of Quebec to pursue secession, should a clear majority of the people of Quebec choose that goal, as long as in doing so, Quebec respects the rights of others.

Contrary to the Supreme Court's ruling in 1982, which discredited it in the eyes of many Quebeckers by allowing for repatriation without Quebec's consent, the reference regarding the secession of Quebec has helped restore the Court's credibility. In essence, the Supreme Court validated a widely-shared consensus in Quebec that it constitutes a nation within Canada, with the implied capacity to determine its future democratically, in line with the spirit of dualism and a tacit admission that Canada is fundamentally a multinational democracy, regardless of the strict confines of the constitution. James Tully summarizes the thrust of this sentiment:

> The condition of liberty of a multinational society rests on the fact that its members remain free to initiate discussions and negotiations with regards to possible amending formulas to the structure of recognition in place and, as a corollary, the other members have an *obligation* to respond to those legitimate demands. A member that seeks recognition as a nation (in a form that is itself open to objection) is free to the extent that the possibilities for discussion, negotiation and amendment are not impeded, in practice, by arbitrary constraints. The constitution of a society that endures such obstructions can be likened to a strait-jacket or a structure of domination. This situation of an absence of liberty is revealed, in Canada, as much by the case of Quebec as that of First Nations.[15]

For Samuel LaSelva, a significant contribution of the ruling is the fact that the Court denied the notion that secession is a purely political matter, and recast it as a broader constitutional issue. Rather than adopting a narrow legalistic approach, the Court addressed the 'internal architecture' of the constitution when it proceeded to define the four underlying legitimating principles. Moreover, as LaSelva contends, by exploring a broader approach to constitutionalism and pluralism in Canada, away from the narrow purview of the Charter, the Court also validated the legitimacy of continuity by tracing the principles relating to the protection of minorities and the federal idea back to the intentions of the Confederation agreement.[16] Again, Canada is not inherently stuck in this present constitutional order. For optimistic observers, this presented a grand opportunity to recapture the founding principles of the country.

However, rather than seizing the opportunity to build on the ruling by engaging in dialogue about Quebec's future in Canada, in good faith and in order to avert a potential referendum, the response of the federal government took a familiar route: it enacted the heavy-handed Bill to Give Effect to the Requirement for Clarity as Set Out in the opinion of the Supreme Court of Canada in the Secession Reference, otherwise known as the Clarity Bill or Bill C-20. This response in effect disregarded the notion that Quebec's right to self-determination is legitimate and that Canada has the obligation to negotiate should a referendum process result in a yes vote. Instead, Ottawa keyed in on the requirement for clarity in both the wording of the referendum question as well as on a legitimate majority, which the Court had left to political actors to decide. The law's stated goal is to prescribe the conditions and methods under which the federal Parliament could determine the clarity of a referendum question on secession and also establish the criteria for what qualifies as a clear majority. In doing so, the federal government killed off any opening with regards to a truly established ethos of negotiation as a foundational new beginning for legitimate federalism and again decided that the ends of federal practice would be determined by imposing a dominant vision at the expense of others in a unilateral and arbitrary manner. Indeed, while many observers note that the federal Parliament cannot legally endow itself with the privilege of simply determining the criteria through which it will deal with Quebec's constitutional future – as though such criteria need not concern Quebec's National Assembly or even involve Quebec at all – the actual power of the Clarity Act lies in its appeal to the Canadian electorate, as a display of forcefulness and intimidation.[17]

The Clarity Act demonstrates the folly of conceptualizing federalism and constitutional change in purely formal/legalistic terms. The

Supreme Court itself did not wade into the perilous exercise of determining clarity, precisely because the very act of determining clear principles is inherently political and must involve a dialogue between interested and affected parties in a federal system. The Clarity Act simply represents a pre-emptive strike against negotiating in good faith. An equivalent act would be for Quebec to simply draft a bill stating that the National Assembly does not recognize any constitutional authority over Quebec because, retroactively, the Quebec legislature has never been allowed to determine, *a priori*, the clarity of the terms employed in legal provisions establishing the federal state in the first place. All future disagreements (post-1867) with regards to constitutional interpretation would be considered void, since the issue of clarity itself was never considered by the National Assembly – as though constitutional law can ever be left without some ambiguity. Indeed, this constitutes the very notion of the political realm. Again, the Canadian federal system is turned on its head; rather than accommodating and encouraging the contributions of diverse visions for the country – the initial promise of a country founded on compromise – unity is consistently maintained through a single-minded, homogenizing vision that seeks constantly to remind Canadians that the 'inconveniences' of federalism will be dealt with harshly.

The Clarity Act is tantamount to a veto for the rest of Canada, akin to the power of disallowance whereby the Canadian parliament can simply override the National Assembly by a statutory act. Nor is the Clarity Act limited to the Liberal government's particular hard line approach to Quebec, as it is unequivocally supported by all major federalist parties in Ottawa, including the recently elected minority Conservative government led by Stephen Harper. This does not abide by the principles of federalism. Moreover, by endowing itself with the prerogative to determine whether a referendum question is clear or not, the federal government is limiting the constitutional and political options available to Quebeckers by reducing the possibilities to either all out secession or the status quo, and this is not acceptable. In addition, the federal government has determined that it alone would serve as the interpreter of what constitutes a clear majority, subverting the universally accepted 50 percent plus 1 formula and in effect paving the way for the very real prospect that some citizens' votes are more important than others. Again, this is not acceptable to Quebec, as it denies principles of justice and fairness that ought to characterize relations of power. With regard to spending practices for Canadian unity, Quebeckers have demonstrated in the 2004 and 2006 federal elections, with great conviction, that their allegiance is not for sale and they will not be bribed by the federal government.[18]

The intentions of the federal government are clearly political, yet the Clarity Act is presented as a straightforward response to a court ruling. In effect, it reasserts the Canadian Parliament's dominance in any referendum process before the Quebec National Assembly even decides to hold a referendum, and before it even determines the wording of the question.[19] For Rocher and Verrelli, this contravenes the principle of democracy. Democracy assumes a continuous process of deliberation, dialogue, discussion, and debate. By attempting to define terms with certainty, the context in which they operate is neglected, and in this case the complex context of a multinational democracy is simply deemed to be irrelevant. All constitutional ideas and debates are essentially open to some level of interpretation. For example, Rocher and Verrelli contend that the notion of distinct society, a cornerstone of the last round of constitutional negotiations, seemed clear to some and vague to others. Yet the federal government still held a referendum on such a complex provision in the Charlottetown Accord. If all political actors have to agree on the precise interpretation of the concept before the process of popular sovereignty is set in motion, then the democratic process is stunted altogether, because any particular negotiating partner can simply make the claim that something is not clear; therefore it should not be a subject of democratic deliberation in the first place. Moreover, this approach by the federal government directly undermines the other major aspect of the ruling – that all parties concerned must negotiate in good faith. Endowing a central body with the statutory power to simply close off the process altogether hardly qualifies as a gesture of good faith. Indeed, in paragraph 93, the Court made it clear that:

> ... other parties cannot exercise their rights in such a way as to amount to an absolute denial of Quebec's rights, and similarly, that so long as Quebec exercises its rights while respecting the rights of others, it may propose secession and seek to achieve it through negotiation. The negotiation process precipitated by a decision of a clear majority of the population of Quebec on a clear question to pursue secession would require the reconciliation of various rights and obligations by the representatives of two legitimate majorities, namely, the clear majority of the population of Quebec, and the clear majority of Canada as a whole, whatever that may be. *There can be no suggestion that either of these majorities 'trumps' the other.* A political

majority that does not act in accordance with the underlying constitutional principles we have identified puts at risk the legitimacy of the exercise of its rights.

The only clear aspect of this process for constitutional change is that the
federal government once again failed to grasp the underlying principles associated with 'two majorities,' preferring instead to return to
unilateralism and majority nationalism to bolster its approach. The
requirements of clarity must be weighed against the four principles
outlined by the Court, subject to negotiation. There is no precedent in
Canadian constitutionalism for recourse to a simple statutory act of
Parliament to severely alter the framework with which the negotiations
themselves take place.

The express aim of Bill C-20 is to inject the process with clarity, yet its
function as a heavy-handed instrument to thwart legitimate democratic
practice cannot be overemphasized. For example, the bill endows the
Parliament of Canada with the right to determine what constitutes a
legitimate threshold of support for secession. While only specifying
that an absolute majority is not sufficient, the bill goes on to add that
Parliament will also consider the percentage of eligible voters that took
part as well as 'any other matters or circumstances it considers to be relevant.'[20] The last qualification is particularly revealing, since this can
refer to virtually any factor that may have affected the referendum
result, even if an overwhelming majority voted for secession.

With regards to the actual question, the Clarity Act is self-effacing.
The bill makes clear that any mention of political or economic association with Canada, or wording that refers to a mandate to negotiate a
new relationship with Canada, will be considered void, since it is
deemed to be a scheme to obscure the real agenda of secession. Yet the
whole referendum process, as it has been designed and practised in
Quebec and in the Supreme Court's validation, is fundamentally an
exercise of democratic self-determination in order to provide a legitimate mandate to negotiate between equal partners – in effect recognizing the empirical reality of dualism as well as interdependence that
characterizes the multination. As such, a genuinely clear question is
one that includes an offer of partnership, or association, since the parties will, in fact, be negotiating a new relationship. If the National
Assembly, through all debates and deliberations surrounding the
wording of the question, decides to include an offer of association with
Canada, then that is the mandate they are asking for from the people.

That is the clear question that reflects the intentions of the representatives of the people of Quebec in setting in motion its right to self-determination. It is not up to the federal Parliament to determine clarity here, since forcing Quebec to word the question as the central government sees fit – with a straightforward reference to a break-up with Canada and nothing else – actually subverts the intentions of the whole process, thus making it less reflective of reality, undercutting democratically-achieved initiatives in Quebec, and actually obscuring an essentially clear and transparent process. A question that asked, for example, 'Do you wish to secede from Canada?' is much more ambiguous with regards to the process of negotiation that would follow: it simply is not a clear question, since it reduces a very complex process into either/or scenarios when such scenarios are unlikely to unfold. This aspect of the Clarity Act is thus but another mechanism to halt the democratic process for self-determination in Quebec before it is allowed to express itself and its intentions vis-à-vis the larger multination. Obviously, it makes no legitimate claims to settle the problem of clarity, as though there were solutions that an act of Parliament could devise. In short, the Clarity Act is merely a draconian measure introduced to appease the prevailing ethos of uniformity and centralisation in the rest of Canada. There is no legitimate justification, in either law or convention, for its application in a multinational federation.

The High Road

The cultural-ideological disagreements with regards to Quebec's specificity, the strong sense of territorial identity expressed by Aboriginal peoples, the consolidated individual rights-based national identity in Canada outside Quebec, and the persistence of regional tensions with regards to the representative institutions of the central government – all these issues continue to dominate the landscape of diverging visions of Canadian federalism. Moreover, inherent stresses and strains associated with division of powers are still around, particularly the encroachment into provincial areas of responsibility. There remains much work ahead to federalize the federation; the endurance of competing visions demonstrates that the defining aspects of the Canadian political community have yet to be accommodated. Indeed, the urgency of persisting with the affirmation of various conceptions of political space in Canada becomes evident when we recognize that territory remains one of the rare areas within liberal democracies where it is still possible to maintain representation and to demand accountability from political actors.

The endurance of diverging federal visions in Canada, far from threatening the country, is a positive tribute to the idea of federalism itself. Federalism represents more than an institutional arrangement. It is not reducible to political solutions that can be imposed by any one particular government or prevailing idea of political community, or to ad hoc deals that keep members in line. The Canadian experiment with federalism, rather than threatened by the political conflicts spawned by diverging visions, has been shaped and defined by the negotiation of distinct visions over time. This is the essence of the federal spirit. In the interests of federalism, Canada should embrace its diversity of views about political community and take solace in the idea that this is a system that, like politics more generally, cannot be resolved. The goal is to recognize this fundamental and unchanging condition of Canada's existence. However, democracy ought to be organized around territorial representation. We cannot lump sub-national movements together with other group-based movements. Otherwise the polity will truly resemble a postmodern assortment that lacks accountability and is responsible to no one but the prime minister, who may pick and choose which groups he deems to be relevant.

This period of so-called constitutional peace is an aberration, a low point for democracy in Canada. Indeed, as Roger Gibbins contends, 'mega-constitutional change is more likely to occur in the wake of Quebec's departure than it is to occur as a way to prevent that departure.'[21] The presence of the Bloc Québécois is consolidated in Quebec without anyone in Canada raising an eyebrow, preferring to conceptualize its powerful appeal as a 'protest party.' In the foreseeable future, no federal political party is willing to open constitutional talks for fear of electoral reprisal, and as long as this situation continues, Quebec will be left out and Canada will, *de facto*, have no central government that appeals to all Canadians, short of an instrumental body that serves its citizens as clients of the central state. This is the price to pay for dismissing federalism in Canada's national project and the principles upon which citizens identify with each other.

For the Canadian multination to flourish, we propose two developments that need to occur, beyond the incessant talk of recognizing cultural rights for Quebec, making special administrative deals that serve only to postpone the problem and merely affirm the powers that Quebec ought to control in the first place, and treating Quebec as a lobby group in a wider conception of Canada as a pluralistic national polity. First, it must be understood that Quebec is a constituted society – a societal culture, to use the familiar designation. Second, and related to the first, Quebec citizenship must be allowed to develop independently of Canadian measures that serve only to undercut its developments.

What we have in mind is a new course of action. We visualize an incipient process that might move the federation towards its multinational roots without relying on a stagnant federal government that continues its nationalizing course, or on a rupture caused by another referendum (which we deem legitimate as a course of action because of federal intransigence with regards to Quebec's right to self-determination and its failure to meet Quebec's needs within the federation).

Much political theory has been concerned with the ideas of mutual recognition, mutual reciprocity, democratizing nation-to-nation relations, and so on. This 'Canadian school of rights philosophy'[22] notes that Canada is at the forefront of recognizing the collective rights of peoples as opposed to strict recognition of individual rights. Even Michael Ignatieff has joined the fray:

> ... recognition of distinctiveness does not have to fragment the country. What ought to balance these distinctive provisions is a politics of reciprocity. If Quebec is granted certain rights in respect of its language and culture, the rest of the country has a right to expect the province to protect the cultures, languages and religions of its minorities. Reciprocity rather than strict symmetry for all is the way to move beyond a politics of concession and threat into a process of mutual recognition, in which each side acknowledges the distinctiveness of the other.[23]

As this discussion has demonstrated, however, many such characterizations of Canada's self-understanding remains confined to rhetoric and indeed can be qualified as academic in the broad sense of the term, since Canada has turned away from such principles in the contemporary period. Ignatieff goes on to contend that reciprocity implies that minorities must also recognize the status of the majority. We agree, but we reject that this point needs to be made at all, since in the case of Quebec, there is no question that it recognizes a negotiating partner. If what Ignatieff means by a 'politics of concessions and threat' is Quebec's desire to act on its right to self-determination, we contend that this is unavoidable since it is the majority that has closed off negotiations altogether. We propose a new approach to constitutionalism in Canada, and it may require more affirmative measures by Quebec. If, no matter how Quebec proceeds, its expressions of self-determination will be considered a threat, and the issue will be framed as a constant search for concessions, then mutual reciprocity is never possible. The majority perspective in Canada simply will not allow this to occur. Moreover, Quebec has demonstrated its strict commitment to liberal-democratic rights for its minorities, including the recognition of a special status for its English-language minority community,[24] yet Ignatieff still requires that the burden of proof lies with Quebec. Again, Canada is not Quebec's guardian in these matters. This attitude does not bode well for a politics of mutual reciprocity, or however the normative framework of two majorities is phrased. Indeed, in the following sketch of a possible way out – not, we might stress, a solution, but a starting point to the Canadian constitutional debate – there is an implicit test to measure Canada's resolve as to its actual commitment to the idea of reciprocity.

We propose a practical approach that would test this resolve. Although this is a hypothetical scenario, we believe that this sort of course of action is at once inevitable and desirable. It will avoid an acrimonious rupture and it will return the country to its rightful legitimate foundations. It seems that the primary obstacle as it stands now is twofold: English Canada's reluctance to step outside the boundaries of a centralized polity towards the acknowledgment of special status or the recognition of Quebec as a nation, and a lack of trust, between partners in constituting the country. As such, what is required is a galvanizing moment that can add a spark to some fundamental reforms. One obvious solution is a referendum on sovereignty, which might cause reform but will not do much to address the issue of severed trust. We propose a second tract. It may be idealistic, but it is based on constitutive realities of the country, and it will reflect many of the principles highlighted in this discussion. Most importantly, however, it is meant to restore mutual trust between the Canadian political communities without relying on federal political parties whose electoral fortunes cynically increase when stressing scenarios meant to 'keeping Quebec down.' Moreover, it pre-empts the high risk game of going through the uncertainties of a referendum.

Quebec is already constituted as a societal culture, having carved out a distinct citizenship regime; it is endowed with legitimate democratic representative institutions within a distinct arena of public debate[25]; it recognizes fundamental human rights and the historic collective rights of the anglophone and Aboriginal communities; and enjoys sovereignty in its areas of exclusive provincial jurisdiction, including in international relations. It has carved out a citizenship regime for itself, including the development of its status as a host society for integration of ethnocultural minorities and immigrants. Most importantly, its credentials for democratic self-determination based on popular will have already been legitimated by the Supreme Court of Canada. Quebec already has several organic elements of a formal constitution, which includes a Charter of Rights and Freedoms, enacted in 1975, an Election Act, a Referendum Act, and Bill 99, An Act respecting the exercise of the fundamental rights and prerogatives of the Quebec people and the Quebec state, which was put forward as a response to the Clarity Act and affirms the inviolability of the sovereignty of the National Assembly. The missing link, however, is full political sovereignty. In a multinational context, as we have been arguing, this option is neither necessary nor inevitable, yet it cannot be pre-empted by unilateral actions of the majority nation.

Building on the ruling of the Supreme Court, particularly on its spirit and its reference to the four foundational principles of the Canadian constitution (federalism, democracy, constitutionalism and the rule of law, and the protection of minorities), the approach we have in mind reflects a commitment to a true multinational democracy and an outcome that neither stunts citizenship in Quebec nor holds Canada hostage. For lack of a better term, we will call it a 'roadmap' to fulfilling Canada's promise. Many normative accounts of the accommodation of identities in multinational democracies, most notably by James Tully, Charles Taylor, and Will Kymlicka, propose that citizenship and the federation be structured along the lines of its constituent nations – in the sense that they may be self-determining within the larger political structure. In Canada, as this discussion has attempted to clarify, such measures stop short in academia; there is no foreseeable attempt that both the public and more specifically, the federal government, will consider reopening this perceived pandora's box. We propose an approach that may restore confidence in the country's institutions among Quebeckers, while addressing the question of mutual trust and the re-flourishing of the will to live together. Several assumptions need to be recapitulated. First, we assume that Canada will have to be structured along the normative principles of multinational democracy, or it will eventually cease to exist. Second, since the central government is quite content with proceeding with a constitution that simply disregards Quebec's terms for membership, we assume there will be no initiative from Ottawa – as long as the constant appeal of a national-unity threat continues to make inroads among English-Canadian voters. Third, we

assume that Quebec's legitimate right to self-determination is established, a principle that the Supreme Court of Canada legitimated but
did not invent – and that a referendum on its political and constitutional future will allow for nation-to-nation negotiations, as equal partners. Quebec is already constituted sociologically, with an organic
constitution and a citizenship regime, in a broad sense, that is distinct
from ROC. Finally, we assume that the Canadian conversation about
the limits of diversity and unity, in itself, is not a sufficient normative
foundation upon which to define the country. This would be sufficient
if Quebec consented to the constitution and it was a willing partner in
negotiating through the identity landscape of Canada. Moreover, on a
more political level, there is very little debate, again outside of a very
small circle of thinkers who have been pushing for a more faithful representation of multinationalism in this country. Quebec simply does not
have a conversation partner.

Bearing in mind such assumptions, the plan would proceed as follows. In the first phase, Quebec would adopt a formal constitution – one
that builds on its nascent and organic one, including present conventions adopted from the British system. This constitution would specify
the boundaries of Quebec citizenship, its orientations in terms of integration, its entitlements and obligations as a member state in the federation, its institutional relationships to its negotiating partners. This
formal constitution would serve as a symbol of self-determination that
Quebec has always sought, regardless of questions of recognition that
have not been on the table from ROC. It would be a vision for a multinational democracy spearheaded by the internal nation itself, as
opposed to the constant antagonistic positions that see the centre denying such diversity and the internal nation constantly begging for recognition; and, for the purposes of unity, it would qualify as a multinational
democracy in the sense established by Tully, respecting the three principles of mutual recognition, continuity and consent.

In the spirit of active citizenship and deliberative democracy, this
exercise in Quebec would signal a strong commitment to pluralism and
diversity. It would, in effect, reflect qualitative citizenship through a
widespread consultation and deliberative exercise that cuts across partisan lines and includes the major players in civil society. Unlike previous instances in which Quebec has sought constitutional reform in
Canada, this exercise would start from scratch, if you will, in order to
avoid limiting the question of Quebec's status to a partisan position. It
would be clear that Quebec citizens were asked to participate and con-

tribute, without ambiguity, in a self-determining community that has its own constitution. There would be no uncertainty, for example, about which model of integration is employed, or which language is designated for public space, or which minority rights are recognized, or Quebec's asymmetrical status in the federation. The process itself ought to be an exercise in democratic citizenship, in an attempt to reach as large a consensus as possible. Also, and again flowing from the judgment of the Supreme Court, it would involve a democratic process that assures Quebec's negotiating partner that it is not a tactic for secession: it is a genuine overture to reconstruct the federation according to just principles that respect self-government for nations that have a right to self-determination. Furthermore, it would go well beyond the divisive and acrimonious process of a referendum. Such a recourse leaves citizens with little input as to the negotiating position of Quebec, other than to provide a mandate.

In this scenario, the legitimacy of Quebec's negotiating position would not be in doubt. Call it 'mega-constitutional' politics at the level of the internal nation, where the difficulty of reconciling national and social pluralism is not at play. Indeed, while the latter rounds of constitutional debate in Canada in the late 1980s and early 1990s deepened democracy in rejecting processes of elite bargaining and consolidating democratic deliberation, this has paradoxically led to a deepening of the political impasse. This is the case because, in a multinational federation, constitutionalism ought not to substitute for normal politics. The setting of mega-constitutional change ought not to reflect a pluralistic polity in a majoritarian liberal setting, where organized interests and identities compete for recognition in a polity that has never been constituted as a legitimate political community.

If Quebeckers do not want constitutional reform, as the central government continues to suggest, then this exercise in deliberation may result in a position that reflects an overwhelming desire to maintain the status quo. The process will require effective leadership that does not revert to cynical politicking at a partisan level. It must build upon the general Quebec consensus identified throughout this discussion, perhaps formalized through a constituent assembly. Finally, the outcome of the process – a formal constitution – may itself be put to a referendum if Quebec representatives choose to include this step in the overall process.

This process of formally endowing Quebec will also provide an opportunity for consultation, deliberation, and input from a plurality of diverse voices within Quebec society. It will allow citizens, groups, and representatives with the opportunity to contribute to the process of delineating the extent of Quebec's self-government vis-à-vis the larger federation, as well as providing a forum through which Quebec society can undergo a procedure of introspection. This avoids the pitfalls of ascertaining whether a referendum question is clear or not – since the outcome of the process will be the result of direct citizenship activity – or whether the referendum outcome will initiate formal constitutional change that will satisfy Quebec, or, whether the ROC will even negotiate a new relationship at all in the event of a positive referendum result. Again, the process of formally constituting Quebec may in itself involve a referendum on the final outcome of the codified text.

When Quebec terminates this process, with a constitution that has satisfied some measure of broad consensus, perhaps from major socio-political interests and collective identities as well as across the partisan spectrum, rather than initiate a popular referendum that aims to provide a mandate to renegotiate the federal pact, Quebec would extend an overture to Canada that asks representatives, *acting as a negotiating partner*, to ratify it. This would serve notice that Quebec is at once serious about self-determination as well as demonstrating its continuing desire to live together and be an active and flourishing member of the federation. Such an approach would force the ROC to acknowledge that Quebec seeks a partner with which to negotiate a relationship, building on Quebec's long-standing position of dualism. Finally, and this is perhaps the most important aspect of the proposed scenario, this overture would serve as somewhat of an olive branch. It would act as a galvanizing procedure that Quebec is not required to pursue, yet does so in order to demonstrate its commitment to association with Canada in an attempt to restore a sense of mutual confidence and trust that is presently lacking. In doing so, Quebec understands that it is not a linear, take-it-or-leave-it proposition. The ROC may have some amendments to suggest, particularly in the sections that address the extent of association and the boundaries of citizenship in Quebec. The key here is that mega-constitutional practices are not necessary at the level of the multination; internal nations may initiate a constitutional proposal that allows for the constitution of a 'people' to be further expressed without the danger of attempts to nationalize a multinational society out of universal principles and away from the federal idea.

If the critical response to this framework is that such a process is politically impossible, then it will confirm the continuing force of majority nationalism in contemporary Canada. There are, of course, obvious obstacles in this approach. First, Canada will most likely not accept this overture; it means that they would have to find some representatives to contribute to a ratification of the Quebec constitution, requiring an acknowledgment that Canada is a multinational community to begin with. This is no easy task considering the view of the political community in the ROC. Also, as long as Quebec does not threaten to secede, Canada does not listen. We submit that the country is living on borrowed time if its national unity strategy continues as it has, rolling the dice that Quebec does not win another referendum. This is not a legitimate basis for relations. There is no reason to believe that this needs to be an acrimonious project that requires a cynical response from Ottawa. From Canada's perspective, this would avoid a gamble on a referendum which would throw the relationship wide open. Moreover, it would point out that the ongoing nation-state strategy is deficient for this age, as it has been unsuitable for Quebec throughout the country's history. Quebec will not go away, and this process towards restructuring the federation possesses the foundation for a perfect compromise that avoids the pitfalls of a hard line approach by either partner.

Quebec has been at the forefront of cases of flourishing internal nations, carving out its own citizenship regime, demonstrating a strong commitment to democratic processes, and engaging in a societal project that other internal nations seek to emulate.[26] It has managed to achieve all this through a level of intransigence in Canada that has defined and structured the country according to its own vision, changing only in degree and not in kind throughout the country's existence. It is time to break the constant cycle characterized by deadlock. It is time for both parties to take the high road. For Quebec, it must continue to act as a leader for internal nations on how to forge a democratic polity in the face of larger obstacles; it must demonstrate that self-determination includes substantive commitments to liberalism and an evolving constitutive process that values democracy above all. For the ROC, it is time to recognize that denying Quebec its majority status will only lead to an acrimonious rupture whose ends are unclear. Canada must understand that Quebec's affirmation is not inimical to the preservation of the country. It is not a zero-sum game. The extent of association, however, must be negotiated before the level of mutual confidence and trust that bind the political communities together are severed beyond repair. This is a key step, since the will to live together may not be sufficient once that symbolic threshold is crossed. The high road is a two-way street. Quebec must make additional efforts to assure that its minorities are represented in the process of formally constituting itself. Its relationship to the rest of the country ought to be deliberated in a more legitimate procedure than a mere referendum question would imply. And its solid record in respecting liberal democracy ought to remain unblemished. The formal constitution process puts all of this on the table. With regards to Canada, whatever negotiating partner emerges, whatever procedure is adopted, one clear principle must take precedence; it must internalize the notion that it is not ratifying and subsequently negotiating a new deal as a majority. It must begin to see itself as a partner, in the spirit of dualism to which Quebec has always adhered. They may not ratify the document, or reject the process altogether, but in the scenario outlined here, this would only hasten the rupture.

It is obvious that this plan relies more heavily on principles and ideas than it does on power politics in proposing a way forward out of the present impasse. We are aware that political scientists must be cognizant of both these structuring variables, yet we contend that part of the problem in Canada is that central authorities refuse to heed any principled advice of those engaged in studying the boundaries of the Canadian conversation. A cynic of multinational democracy might reject this plan altogether as nonsensical. The storyline of the critic might go something like this: First, Canada is under no obligation to participate in what is a process that may be merely a guise for secession. The will for such radical change is simply non-existent. Second, Quebec is a divided society with regards to its status as a self-determining nation. There exist no processes of deliberative democracy, consultation or active citizenship, that will achieve some magical formula that can be called the result of a broad consensus. The process may actually be counter-productive, revealing the divided character of Quebec society and giving Ottawa more ammunition to maintain the status quo of undifferentiated citizenship and territorial federalism across the country. Third, there is no such entity as English Canada which can serve as a negotiating partner for Quebec. The present structure of the federation simply does not allow for this, since it does not recognize that Canada is a multinational federation. The plan will inevitably fall upon deaf ears. Such ideas are, at best, merely sociologically interesting and idealistic, lacking any actual real-world political salience. Canada cannot become an experiment in a global system of sovereign nation-states that mandates a strong central sovereign. And finally, even if Canada accepts this overture and finds some body that can legitimately represent the ROC, the ratification process itself might be problematic. The ROC in this scenario will feel as though it is presented with a fait accompli – a constitution developed without its participation. The political jockeying associated with the ratification process will simply return the country to a mega-constitutional quagmire that will inevitably result in Quebec's declaring an impasse and either holding a subsequent referendum on sovereignty or unilaterally opting for secession. Canada will never accept this scenario when it can take its chances with the status quo.

From Quebec's perspective, cynics might object to the plan mainly with regards to the imperative to extend a right of ratification to Canada. If Quebec enjoys the right of self-determination, why should the ROC have a say in its choices for the future? Others might even object to the idea that the substance of constitutional reform ought to require a measure of broad consensus altogether. These critics might point out that a government that has achieved a majority in the National Assembly can legitimately proceed with whatever project for self-determination it deems appropriate. In this view, deliberative democracy will simply muddle the process as it has in the latter stages of the last constitutional rounds in Canada. Quebec may want to employ the instruments of deliberative democracy if it so chooses, in developing its own constitution, but this step is necessary only after Quebec has stated its intentions to exercise its right to sovereign status. Finally, there may be a significant segment of Quebec society that is satisfied with the status quo and refuses to participate in the process to formally endow Quebec with a constitution in the first place. Any outcome would thus be rejected as illegitimate because there could never be a significant consensus right at the start.

All of these concerns are warranted. However, we maintain that this exercise in Quebec citizenship activity and a process of formal constitutionalism is necessary. First, Quebec self-determination is real and it must eventually express itself institutionally. We take this to be self-evident. The institutions of the Canadian federation at present do not allow this to occur, beyond very limited administrative deals based on an agenda set by Ottawa that stresses national standards, continues to implement a doctrine of provincial equality in a restrictive sense, and defines citizenship along the lines of undifferentiated individuals. Second, the ROC is not likely to take the initiative in structuring the federation along multinational principles. Quebec must take the high road by asserting its right to self-government legitimately while at the same time showing a commitment to association with the ROC as equal partners – in other words, a genuine allegiance to a multinational polity. As we perceive it, amidst the difficulties associated with the imperatives of power, any future arrangement between Quebec and the ROC will have to be built upon a restored sense of trust and mutual confidence. This plan, with all its shortcomings, is premised around the idea of reciprocity; this is the key ingredient that requires restoration if the promise of Canada is to be fulfilled.

In terms of process, this plan represents a compromise between the extreme poles of mass participation and elite accommodation[27] in Canadian constitutionalism. As previously discussed, one of the obstacles to constitutional reform in Canada is the norm that it must involve mass input from a variety of participants at the level of the Canadian political community. This book has argued that a hierarchy ought to exist between elected and accountable representatives, and organized interests and identities in the realm of civil society, *at the level of the multination*. The plan put forward makes it clear that mass input ought to proceed in the act of formally constituting the internal nation through democratic deliberation. However, the extent of association at the centre – negotiations between sovereign partners – should be carried out by representatives of the respective national groups.

Finally, we also concede that it is likely that the ROC will refuse to participate from the start. To add our own bit of cynicism to the equation, it is clear that such a response will only add to Quebec's arsenal of justifications for hastening the process of achieving sovereignty. The fact that a legitimate exercise of existential introspection and deliberative democracy in Quebec is wholly rejected, without considering the actual substance of that process, only multiplies Quebec's long list of grievances with regards to Canadian federalism. Moreover, while democratic deliberation is presently in vogue as a way out of the quagmire among many pundits and intellectuals involved in the Canadian conversation,[28] this will not occur unless some threshold that upsets status quo federalism is crossed. Quebec's initiative to endow itself with a legitimately conceived constitution would qualify as such an endeavour. In other words, while the force of arguments for multinational democracy remains unheeded by Canadian political actors, this process in Quebec might open some eyes to the fact that Quebec is serious about exercising self-determination, by injecting a moderate degree of power politics into the mix – perhaps just what is required to jump-start the process of democratic deliberation. Ideas and principles eventually make a breakthrough in the field of power politics. This may be a way for Quebec's contribution to help push the process forward.

Notes

1. Introduction: Exploring Multinationalism

1 Joseph H. Carens, 'A Contextual Approach to Political Theory,' *Ethical and Moral Practice* 7 (January 2004), pp. 117–32; Carens describes the purpose of this approach: 'A contextual approach to political theory has five interrelated elements. First, it involves the use of examples to illustrate theoretical formulations. Second, it entails the normative exploration of actual cases where the fundamental concerns addressed by the theory are in play. Third, it leads theorists to pay attention to the question of whether their theoretical formulations are actually compatible with the normative positions that they themselves take on particular issues. Fourth, it includes a search for cases that are especially challenging to the theorists own theoretical position. Fifth, it promotes consideration of a wide range of cases, and especially a search for cases that are unfamiliar and illuminating because of their unfamiliarity.'

2 For more on the resilience of the nation form as an avenue for political and social mobilization, sovereignty, and citizenship, see Walter Connor, 'National Self-Determination and Tomorrow's Political Map,' in Alan C. Cairns, John C. Courtney, Peter MacKinnon, Hans J. Michelmann, and David E. Smith, eds., *Citizenship, Diversity and Pluralism: Canadian and Comparative Perspectives* (Montreal and Kingston: McGill-Queen's University Press, 1999); and Michael Keating, *Plurinational Democracy: Stateless Nations in a Post-Sovereignty Era* (Oxford: Oxford University Press, 2001).

3 Will Kymlicka, *Politics in the Vernacular* (Oxford: Oxford University Press, 2001).

4 For a good overview of this debate, see Stephen Mulhall and Adam Swift, *Liberals and Communitarians* (Oxford: Blackwell, 1992).

5 Amy Gutmann, *Identity in Democracy* (Princeton: Princeton University Press, 2003), p. 2.

6 See Charles Tilly, ed., *The Formation of National States in Western Europe* (Princeton: Princeton University Press, 1975); and Heather Rae, *State Identities and the Homogenisation of Peoples* (Cambridge: Cambridge University Press, 2002).

7 See Yael Tamir, *Liberal Nationalism* (Princeton: Princeton University Press, 1993); Will Kymlicka, *Multicultural Citizenship: A Liberal Theory of Minority Rights* (Oxford: Oxford University Press, 1995); Jeffrey Spinner-Halev, *The Boundaries of Citizenship: Race, Ethnicity, and Nationality in the Liberal State* (Baltimore: Johns Hopkins University Press, 1994); and David Miller, *Citizenship and National Identity* (Oxford: Polity Press, 2000).

8 The term *societal culture* is attributed to Will Kymlicka, who defines it as 'culture which provides its members with meaningful ways of life across the full range of human activities' (*Multicultural Citizenship*, p. 76).

9 Will Kymlicka, 'Introduction: An Emerging Consensus?', *Ethical Theory and Moral Practice* 1, no. 2 (special issue on 'Nationalism, Multiculturalism and Liberal Democracy'), pp. 143–57.

10 Iris Marion Young, *Justice and the Politics of Difference* (Princeton: Princeton University Press, 1990); see also Melissa Williams, *Voice, Trust and Memory* (Princeton: Princeton University Press, 1998).

11 Avigail Eisenberg and Jeff Spinner-Halev attribute the rise in prominence of ascriptive groups in liberal theory in the 1980s to the attractiveness of communitarian thinking, the increased political activism of religious conservatives in the United States, and the rise of nationalism in Eastern Europe after the fall of the Berlin wall in 1989; see *Minorities Within Minorities: Equality, Rights and Diversity* (Cambridge: Cambridge University Press, 2005), pp. 1–15.

12 See, for example, Seyla Benhabib, *Situating the Self: Gender, Community and Postmodernism in Contemporary Ethics* (New York: Routledge, 1992); and Chantal Mouffe, *The Return of the Political* (London: Verso, 1993).

13 Immanuel Kant (1795), 'Towards Perpetual Peace,' in *Practical Philosophy* (Cambridge: Cambridge University Press, 1996).

14 David Held, *Democracy and the Global Order: From the Modern State to Cosmopolitan Governance* (Stanford: Stanford University Press, 1995).

15 See Gutmann, *Identity in Democracy*; Ramon Maiz, 'Democracy, Federalism and Nationalism in Multinational States,' in Ramon Maiz and William Safran, eds., *Identity and Territorial Autonomy in Plural Societies* (London: Frank Cass, 2000); Ferran Requejo, 'Political Liberalism in Multinational States:

The Legitimacy of Pluralism and Asymmetrical Federalism,' in Alain-G.
Gagnon and James Tully, eds., *Multinational Democracies* (Cambridge: Cam-
bridge University Press, 2001), pp. 110–32; and Bhikhu Parekh, *Rethinking
Multiculturalism* (London: Macmillan, 2000).

16 Kenneth McRoberts notes a significant disjunction between the rich theory
   on multinational federation by scholars in Canada and its actual application at the political level. See Kenneth McRoberts, 'Canada and the Multinational State,' *Canadian Journal of Political Science* 34, no. 4 (December
   2001), pp. 683–713.

17 See Michel Seymour, *Le pari de la démesure: l'intransigeance canadienne face au
   Québec* (Montreal: L'Hexagone, 2001).

2. Historical Foundations and Evolving Constitutional Orders

1 Seymour Martin Lipset, *Political Man: The Social Bases of Politics* (Baltimore:
  John Hopkins University Press, 1981), p. 64.

2 Alain-G. Gagnon and Can Erk, 'Legitimacy, Effectiveness and Federalism:
  On the Benefits of Ambiguity,' in Herman Bakvis and Grace Skogstad, eds.,
  Canadian Federalism: Performance, Effectiveness and Legitimacy (Don Mills,
  Ontario: Oxford University Press, 2002). Gagnon and Erk cite the Supreme
  Court of Canada's ruling on the legality of Quebec secession under the
  Canadian constitution and in international law as an example of the tensions between legality and legitimacy: 'To be accorded legitimacy, democratic institutions must rest, ultimately, on a legal foundation. Equally,
  however, a system of government cannot survive through the adherence to
  the law alone. A political system must also possess legitimacy, and in our
  political culture, that requires an interaction between the rule of law and
  the democratic principle' (Supreme Court of Canada, 1998, *Reference re the
  Secession of Quebec*, August 20, p. 66)

3 See Dominique Clift, *Quebec Nationalism in Crisis* (Montreal and Kingston:
  McGill-Queen's University Press, 1982).

4 See Michel Seymour, 'Rethinking Political Recognition,' in Alain-G. Gagnon,
  Montserrat Guibernau, and François Rocher, eds., *The Conditions of Diversity
  in Multinational Democracies* (Montreal: Institute for Research on Public
  Policy, 2003). Seymour develops an approach to recognition politics that is
  based on Rawlsian liberal thought yet goes beyond ethical individualism
  as a normative position.

5 See John Rawls, *A Theory of Justice* (Oxford: Oxford University Press, 1972).

6 Wayne Norman, 'Justice and Stability in Multinational Societies,' in Alain-

G. Gagnon and James Tully, eds., *Multinational Democracies* (Cambridge: Cambridge University Press, 2001), pp. 108–9.

7 As the Supreme Court stated, the status of 'province' as understood in the Canadian constitution does not limit Quebec's right to self-determination. See Stephen Tierney, *Constitutional Law and National Pluralism* (New York: Oxford University Press, 2004).

8 Cairns notes that the constitution of 1982 signalled a shift from a 'government's constitution' to a 'citizens' constitution.' Yet this is largely a phenomenon that has engrossed English Canada, since it was not the dominant concern of a large majority of Quebeckers. See Alan Cairns, *Charter versus Federalism: The Dilemmas of Constitutional Reform* (Montreal and Kingston: McGill-Queen's University Press, 1992).

9 Peter Russell asked, 'Can Canadians be a Sovereign People?' in R.S. Blair and J.T. McLeod, eds., *The Canadian Political Tradition* (Toronto: Nelson Canada, 1993), pp. 4–19. Russell argues that in the Confederation Debates, sovereignty of the people was not the overarching moral theory in the founding of the country. While this normative position is almost universally accepted today as the legitimating principle of liberal democracies, Russell claims that Canada still lacks this myth. 'The idea that a constitution, to be legitimate, must be derived from the people, a dreadful heresy to our founding fathers, has by our time become constitutional orthodoxy for Canadians ... We might celebrate this accord were it not for one crucial blemish when it is applied to the Canadian context. Not all Canadians have consented to form a single people in which a majority or some special majority have, to use John Locke's phrase, "a right to act and conclude the rest." In this sense, Canadians have not yet constituted themselves a sovereign people. So deep are their current differences on fundamental questions of political justice and collective identity that Canadians may now be incapable of acting together as a sovereign people' (p. 5).

10 Ibid., p.13.

11 Janet Ajzenstat provides a forceful assessment of the decline of governments as uniquely legitimate constitutional actors in Canada. Describing the 'decline of procedural liberalism' following the failed Meech Lake and Charlottetown rounds, she notes that 'Because the constitution-making arena is now a forum for political demands in Canada, participation is increasingly portrayed as a democratic right, comparable to the citizen's right to have a say in the ordinary business of politics. It is assumed that the competition of interests in the constitutional forum is like that in electoral and legislative politics. The distinction between constitutional law and ordinary legislation is eroded, and as a result the idea grows that con-

stitutional reform can never be anything but a battle of ideological and particular interests.' See 'Decline of Procedural Liberalism: The Slippery Slope to Secession,' in Joseph H. Carens, ed., *Is Quebec Nationalism Just?* (Montreal and Kingston: McGill-Queen's University Press, 1995), p. 131. Although we share this general view of Canadian constitutionalism, we argue in contrast that privileging a procedural liberal constitution that is purportedly built upon a conception of immutable justice while targeting citizens on a pan-Canadian level fails to meet the requirements of justice in the context of multinational federations. Indeed, procedural liberalism that knows no boundaries may simply reflect an expression of majority nationalism. While social interests need not enter the constitutional game and can be accommodated with a neutral procedural framework, the business of constitutional reform does indeed rest with the duly elected representatives of the country's constituent nations.

12 For more on the notion that the constitution cannot be conceptualized as an institution that captures the very essence of belonging in Canada, see Richard Simeon, 'Meech Lake and Visions of Canada,' in Katherine E. Swinton and Carol J. Rogerson, eds., *Competing Constitutional Visions: The Meech Lake Accord* (Toronto: Carswell, 1988).

13 James Tully, *Strange Multiplicity: Constitutionalism in an Age of Diversity* (Cambridge: Cambridge University Press, 1995).

14 Barry Cooper has argued that in order to grasp fully the constitutional problems confronting Canada, the substance, or 'the purpose or meaning of the country,' as opposed to strictly assessing the form of the regime, is paramount. While Cooper views this substantive constitutional vacuum as the product of a void left by Canada's colonial links to Great Britain, his approach essentially captures the idea that constitutions are not simply about governance and law. For him, constitutions are the outcome of distinct 'centres of articulated action' which provide for the existence of legitimate representation. In this sense, constitutions cannot create political communities from above. See Barry Cooper, 'Theoretical Perspectives on Constitutional Reform,' in Anthony A. Peacock, ed., *Rethinking the Constitution: Perspectives on Canadian Constitutional Reform, Interpretation and Theory* (Don Mills, Ontario: Oxford University Press), 1996.

15 See James Tully, 'Understanding Imperialism Today: From Colonial Imperialism through Decolonization to Post-Colonial Imperialism' (working manuscript, forthcoming, 2007).

16 Douglas V. Verney, *Three Civilizations, Two Cultures, One State; Canada's Political Traditions* (Durham: Duke University Press, 1986), p. 174. Verney notes that such historiographies are evident in history textbooks on Canadian government, which are distinct in French and English Canada.

17 Jennifer Smith, 'Political Visions and the 1987 Constitutional Accord,' in
    Swinton and Rogerson, eds., *Competing Constitutional Visions*, p. 271–2.
18 See Hilda Neatby, *The Quebec Act: Protest and Policy* (Scarborough: Prentice-
    Hall, 1972); Philip Lawson, *The Imperial Challenge: Quebec and Britain in the
    Age of the American Revolution* (Montreal and Kingston: McGill-Queen's
    University Press, 1989); and Alain-G. Gagnon and Luc Turgeon, 'Managing
    Diversity in 18th and 19th Century Canada: Quebec's Constitutional Devel-
    opment in Light of the Scottish Experience,' *Commonwealth and Comparative
    Politics* 41, no. 1 (March 2003), pp. 1–23.
19 Cairns, *Charter versus Federalism*, pp. 34–5.
20 Quoted in Verney, *Three Civilizations, Two Cultures, One State*, p. 204.
21 See Garth Stevenson, *Community Besieged: The Anglophone Minority and
    the Politics of Quebec* (Montreal and Kingston: McGill-Queen's University
    Press, 1999), ch. 2.
22 Brian Young, *The Politics of Codification: The Lower Canadian Civil Code of
    1866* (Montreal and Kingston: McGill-Queen's University Press, 1994), p.16;
    quoted in Guy Laforest, 'The Historical and Legal Origins of Asymmetrical
    Federalism in Canada's Founding Debates: A Brief Interpretive Note,'
    Asymmetry Series (Institute of Intergovernmental Relations, School of Policy
    Studies, Queen's University, 2005), p. 3.
23 Janet Ajzenstat, Paul Romney, Ian Gentles, and William D. Gairdner, *Can-
    ada's Founding Debates* (Toronto: Stoddart, 1999), p. 468; quoted in Laforest,
    'The Historical and Legal Origins,' p. 3.
24 The primary reference here is Kenneth C. Wheare, *Federal Government*, 4th
    ed. (London: Oxford University Press, 1963).
25 See José Woehrling and Jacques-Yvan Morin, *Les constitutions du Canada et
    du Québec* (Montreal: Les Éditions Themis, 1994).
26 Donald V. Smiley, 'The Two Themes of Canadian Federalism,' in R.S. Blair
    and J.T. McLeod, eds., *The Canadian Political Tradition*, 2nd ed. (Scarbor-
    ough: Nelson Canada, 1993), pp. 45–61.
27 Verney, *Three Civilizations, Two Cultures, One State*, p. 221. For a more thor-
    ough exposition of the compact theory, see Ramsay Cook, *Provincial Auton-
    omy, Minority Rights and the Compact Theory, 1867–1921*, Study no. 4 of the
    Royal Commission on Bilingualism and Biculturalism (Ottawa: Queen's
    Printer, 1969).
28 Smiley, 'The Two Themes of Canadian Federalism,' p. 48.
29 See Louis Balthazar, 'Quebec's International Relations,' in Alain-G.
    Gagnon, ed., *Quebec: State and Society*, 3rd ed. (Peterborough: Broadview
    Press, 2004); and Claude Morin, *L'art de l'impossible : la diplomatie québé-
    coise depuis 1960* (Montreal: Boréal Express, 1987).

30 Richard Simeon and Ian Robinson, *State, Society and the Development of Canadian Federalism* (Toronto: University of Toronto Press, 1990), p. 278.
31 The general amending formula (section 38), applicable to most constitutional provisions, allows for constitutional changes to be undertaken with the support of the House of Commons, the Senate, and seven provincial legislatures representing at least 50 per cent of the Canadian population. Sections 41, 43, 44, and 45, however, contain more specific amendment procedures ranging from unanimity (the House of Commons, the Senate, and all provincial legislatures), bilateral (the House of Commons, the Senate, and those provincial legislatures affected by the amendment), federal unilateral (the House of Commons and the Senate alone), and provincial unilateral (only by the provincial legislature affected). Reform of the amending formula itself is subject to the unanimity procedure. This formula was imposed on Quebec, which from that moment on had to abide by rules that could be potentially devised and adopted by other member states, resulting in a significant loss in terms of liberty of action in this area. See James Tully, 'Liberté et dévoilement dans les sociétés plurinationales,' *Globe* 2, no. 2 (1999), pp. 31–2.
32 See Keith Banting and Richard Simeon, eds., *And No One Cheered: Federalism, Democracy and the Constitution Act* (Toronto: Methuen, 1983).
33 R. Simeon, in Swinton and Rogerson, eds., *Competing Constitutional Visions*, p. 299.
34 James Tully, 'Liberté et dévoilement dans les sociétés plurinationales,' pp. 31–2.
35 See Cairns, *Charter versus Federalism*, for a detailed exposition of such developments and their implications for Canadian federalism.
36 R. Simeon, 'Meech Lake and Visions of Canada.'
37 See James Tully, 'The Unattained Yet Attainable Democracy: Canada and Quebec Face the New Century,' *The Desjardins Lectures*, McGill University, 23 March 2000.
38 See Michel Bélanger and Jean Campeau (commissioners), *Report of the Commission on the Political and Constitutional Future of Quebec* for more on this interpretation (Quebec City: Commission sur l'avenir politique et constitutionnel du Québec, 1991), p. 34.
39 For more on Trudeau's political philosophy, see Pierre Elliott Trudeau, 'The Practice and Theory of Federalism,' in Michael K. Oliver, ed., *Social Purpose for Canada* (Toronto: University of Toronto Press, 1961), pp. 371–93; and Stephen Brooks, James Bickerton, and Alain-G. Gagnon, *Six penseurs en quête de liberté, d'égalité et de communauté : Grant, Innis, Laurendeau, Rioux, Taylor et Trudeau* (Quebec City: Presses de l'Université Laval, 2003).

40 James Tully, 'Let's Talk: The Quebec Referendum and the Future of Canada,' The Austin and Hempel Lectures, Dalhousie University and the University of Prince Edward Island, 23 and 27 March 1995.
41 Guy Laforest, *Trudeau and the End of a Canadian Dream* (Montreal and Kingston: McGill-Queen's University Press, 1995).
42 For more on the role of the federal government in shaping the Canadian nation, see Philip Resnick, *Letters to a Québécois Friend* (Montreal and Kingston: McGill-Queen's University Press, 1989).
43 Alan C. Cairns, 'My Academic Career,' in Gerald Kernerman and Philip Resnick, eds., *Insiders and Outsiders: Alan Cairns and the Reshaping of Canadian Citizenship* (Vancouver: University of British Columbia Press, 2005), p. 342.
44 Peter Russell, 'The Political Purposes of the Charter of Rights and Freedoms,' *Canadian Bar Review* 61 (1983), pp. 1–33.
45 Laforest, *Trudeau and the End of a Canadian Dream*, pp. 134–5.
46 Janet L. Hiebert, *Limiting Rights: The Dilemma of Judicial Review* (Montreal and Kingston: McGill-Queen's University Press, 1996).
47 Ibid., p. 137.
48 Rainer Knopff and Fred L. Morton, 'Nation-Building and the Canadian Charter of Rights and Freedoms,' in Alan C. Cairns and Cynthia Williams, eds., *Constitutionalism, Citizenship and Society in Canada* (Toronto: University of Toronto Press, 1985), pp. 133–82.
49 Richard Simeon and Daniel-Patrick Conway, 'Federalism and the Management of Conflict in Multinational Societies,' in Alain-G. Gagnon and James Tully, eds., *Multinational Democracies* (Cambridge: Cambridge University Press, 2001), p. 343.
50 Russell, 'Can the Canadians Be a Sovereign People?' p. 16.
51 See Alain-G. Gagnon and Hugh Segal, eds., *The Canadian Social Union Without Quebec: 8 Critical Analyses* (Montreal: Institute for Research on Public Policy, 2000).
52 The referendum question read as follows: 'Do you agree that Quebec should become sovereign, after having made a formal offer to Canada for a new economic and political partnership, within the scope of the Bill regarding the future of Quebec and of the agreement signed on June 12, 1995?' The sovereignty question was to be asked in conjunction with an offer for a political and economic partnership with Canada that would follow a Yes vote. Ottawa would have a year to decide to agree to a political settlement. If no agreement could be reached, Quebec would proceed to full independence.
53 Premiers' Framework for Discussion on Canadian Unity (Calgary Declaration), 14 September 1997.

54 See Alain-G. Gagnon, 'Working in Partnership for Canadians,' in Gagnon and Segal, *The Canadian Social Union Without Quebec*, pp. 129–54.

55 See *A Framework to Improve the Social Union for Canadians: An Agreement between the Government of Canada and the Governments of the Provinces and Territories (except for Quebec)*, Ottawa, 4 February 1999.

56 Donald V. Smiley, *The Federal Condition in Canada* (Toronto: McGraw-Hill Ryerson, 1987), pp. 180–1.

57 Cairns, *Charter versus Federalism*, p. 83.

58 Alain Noël, 'Is Decentralization Conservative? Federalism and the Contemporary Debate on the Canadian Welfare State,' in Robert Young, ed., *Stretching the Federation: The Art of the State in Canada* (Kingston: Institute of Intergovernmental Relations, 1999), p. 197.

59 See also Jacqueline Ismael and Yves Vaillancourt, eds., *Privatization and Provincial Social Services in Canada: Policy, Administration and Service Delivery* (Edmonton: University of Alberta Press, 1988).

60 Michael Keating, 'Challenges to Federalism: Territory, Function and Power in a Globalizing World,' in Robert Young, ed., *Stretching the Federation: The Art of the State in Canada* (Kingston: Institute of Intergovernmental Relations, 1999), p. 15.

61 Ibid., p. 21.

62 Gilles Bourque, Jules Duchastel, and Éric Pineault, 'L'incorporation de la citoyenneté,' in *Sociologie et Sociétés* 31, no 2 (Fall 1999), pp. 50–1.

63 Keating, 'Challenges to Federalism,' p. 27.

64 See Alain Noël, 'Without Quebec: Collaborative Federalism with a Footnote?' Policy Matters, IRPP 1, no. 2 (March 2000).

65 For a converging interpretation, see Claude Ryan, 'The Agreement on the Canadian Social Union Seen by a Quebec Federalist,' in Gagnon and Segal, eds., *The Canadian Social Union Without Quebec*, pp. 209–25.

66 Alan B. Simmons and Kieran Keohane, 'Canadian Immigration Policy: State Strategies and the Quest for Legitimacy,' *Canadian Review of Sociology and Anthropology* 29, no 4 (1992).

67 Noël, 'Without Quebec,' p. 10.

3. The Federal Principle in Canada

1 Daniel Elazar, 'How the Prismatic Form of Canadian Federalism Both Unites and Divides Canada,' *Jerusalem Center for Public Affairs* (Daniel Elazar online library), 1999. 'The systematic approach seeks to define everything comprehensively, to set boundaries. The prismatic approach, recognizing how all of the universe is interconnected, seeks, rather, to

establish separate cores and to understand how each core has to be perceived and responded to differently from different perspectives. Boundaries need not be so clear. Interaction is more important than definition; hence, the emphasis on multiple polities related to one another, united yet separate, a logical contradiction from the perspective of systematic philosophy, but a clear reality from the perspective of prismatic thought. The end result was that Canada has no common systematic construct at its foundations' (Web document, unpaginated: www.jcpa.org/djeindex.htm).

2 Jane Jenson, 'Citizenship Claims: Routes to Representation in a Federal System,' in Karen Knop, Sylvia Ostry, Richard Simeon, and Katherine Swinton, eds., *Rethinking Federalism: Citizens, Markets and Governments in a Changing World* (Vancouver: University of British Columbia Press, 1995), p. 103.

3 Alan C. Cairns, 'The Politics of Constitutional Conservatism,' in Keith Banting and Richard Simeon, eds., *And No One Cheered* (Toronto: Methuen, 1983), p. 46.

4 See, for example, James R. Mallory, 'Five Faces of Federalism,' in J. Peter Meekison, ed., *Canadian Federalism: Myth or Reality?*, 3rd ed. (Toronto: Methuen, 1977).

5 François Rocher and Miriam Smith, 'The Four Dimensions of Canadian Federalism,' in Rocher and Smith, eds., *New Trends in Canadian Federalism*, 2nd ed. (Toronto: Broadview Press, 2003), pp. 21–44.

6 See Michael Burgess and Alain-G. Gagnon, eds., *Comparative Federalism and Federation: Competing Traditions and Future Directions* (London: Harvester Wheatsheaf, 1993) for a comparative examination of federalism and federations.

7 See Ronald Watts, *Comparing Federal Systems*, 2nd ed. (Montreal and Kingston: McGill-Queen's University Press, 1999).

8 Edwin R. Black, *Divided Loyalties: Canadian Concepts of Federalism* (Montreal and Kingston: McGill-Queen's University Press, 1975), p. 7.

9 Douglas V. Verney, *Three Civilizations, Two Cultures, One State: Canada's Political Traditions* (Durham, NC: Duke University Press, 1986), p. 164.

10 See Roger Gibbins, 'The Interplay of Political Institutions and Political Communities,' in David P. Shugarman and Reg Whitaker, eds., *Federalism and Political Community* (Peterborough: Broadview Press, 1989), pp. 423–38.

11 Preston King, *Federalism and Federation* (Baltimore: Johns Hopkins University Press, 1982); and Michael Burgess, 'Federalism and Federation: A Reappraisal,' in Burgess and Gagnon, *Comparative Federalism and Federation*, pp. 3–14.

12 William Livingston was among the first to note that federalism involves

more than formal institutions, contending that institutional outcomes, or policy fields, can in some part be explained by federalism as a characteristic of society; see William S. Livingston, 'A Note on the Nature of Federalism,' *Political Science Quarterly* 67 (1952), pp. 81–95; and *Federalism and Constitutional Change* (New York: Oxford University Press, 1956).

13 For a more developed treatment of this approach, see Burgess and Gagnon, eds., *Comparative Federalism and Federation: Competing Traditions and Future Directions*.

14 Black, *Divided Loyalties*, p. 9.

15 See Richard Simeon, *Federal-Provincial Diplomacy: The Making of Recent Policy in Canada* (Toronto: University of Toronto Press, 1972).

16 For more on the emerging field of study on multinational democracies, see Alain-G. Gagnon and James Tully, eds., *Multinational Democracies* (Cambridge: Cambridge University Press, 2001); and Alain-G. Gagnon, Montserrat Guibernau, and François Rocher, eds., *The Conditions of Diversity in Multinational Democracies* (Montreal: The Institute for Research on Public Policy, 2003).

17 See Will Kymlicka, *Finding Our Way: Rethinking Ethnocultural Relations in Canada* (Oxford: Oxford University Press, 1998); and Phillip Resnick, 'Toward a Multinational Federalism: Asymmetrical and Confederal Alternatives,' in F. Leslie Seidle, ed., *Seeking a New Canadian Partnership: Asymmetrical and Confederal Options* (Montreal: Institute for Research on Public Policy, 1994), pp. 71–89.

18 Watts, *Comparing Federal Systems*, p. 35.

19 Peter Russell refers to such a process as 'macro-constitutional,' which is distinguished from constitutional politics to the extent that, first, negotiations aim at resolving not only specific constitutional proposals but the very nature of political community; and second, since it touches upon citizens' very identities and sentiments of belonging, this variant of political dispute tends to be exceptionally emotional and intense. See Peter H. Russell, 'Can the Canadians Be a Sovereign People?' *Canadian Journal of Political Science* 24, no. 4 (December 1991), pp. 691–709.

20 See Jennifer Smith, 'Informal Constitutional Development: Change by Other Means,' in Herman Bakvis and Grace Skogstad, eds., *Canadian Federalism: Performance, Effectiveness and Legitimacy* (Don Mills: Oxford University Press, 2002), pp. 40–58.

21 For a useful analysis of the role of General Murray in consolidating the distinct collective consciousness of the *Canadiens*, see Christian Dufour, *A Canadian Challenge* (Lantzville and Halifax: Oolichan Books and the Institute for Research on Public Policy, 1990).

22 Alfred LeRoy Burt, *The Old Province of Quebec* (Toronto: Ryerson Press, 1933), p. 186.
23 See John Bierley, 'The Co-existence of Legal Systems in Quebec: "Free and Common Socage" in Canada's pays de droit civil,' *Cahiers de droit* 20 (1979), p. 280.
24 See Alain-G. Gagnon and Luc Turgeon, 'Managing Diversity in Eighteenth and Nineteenth Century Canada: Quebec's Constitutional Development in Light of the Scottish Experience,' *Journal of Commonwealth and Comparative Politics* 41, no. 1 (March 2003), pp. 1–23.
25 For an exposition of this debate, see Philip Lawson, *The Imperial Challenge: Quebec and Britain in the Age of the American Revolution* (Montreal and Kingston: McGill-Queen's University Press, 1999).
26 Maurice Séguin, *Une Histoire du Québec* (Montreal: Guérin, 1995), p. 36.
27 James Tully, *Strange Multiplicity: Constitutionalism in an Age of Diversity* (Cambridge: Cambridge University Press, 1994), pp. 145–51. For more on the Whig philosophy of the ancient constitution, see John Pocock, *The Ancient Constitution and the Feudal Law: A Study of English Historical Thought in the Seventeenth Century* (Cambridge: Cambridge University Press, 1987).
28 Brian Young, 'Everyman's Trope: The Quebec Act of 1774,' in *Cahiers du PEQ*, no. 21, December 2001 (Quebec Studies Program, McGill University).
29 Jean-Pierre Wallot, 'L'Acte de Québec, ses causes, sa nature et l'Ancien Régime,' in ibid.
30 Hilda Neatby, *Quebec: The Revolutionary Age, 1760–1791* (Toronto: McClelland and Stewart, 1966), quoted in Wallot, 'L'Acte de Québec,' p. 7.
31 George F.C. Stanley, 'Act or Pact: Another Look at Confederation,' Proceedings of the Canadian Historical Association, 1956, p. 5; quoted in Kenneth McRoberts, *Misconceiving Canada: The Struggle for National Unity* (Don Mills: Oxford University Press, 1997), p. 5.
32 McRoberts, ibid.
33 See William Ormsby, *The Emergence of the Federal Concept in Canada, 1839–1845* (Toronto: University of Toronto Press, 1969). For more on Lord Durham's justification for a legislative union, see Ged Martin, *Britain and the Origins of Canadian Confederation, 1837–67* (Vancouver: University of British Columbia Press, 1995).
34 Led by Robert Baldwin, the Reformers defected from a cohesive English bloc over the issue of responsible government, which would be eventually inaugurated in 1849.
35 John A. Macdonald, quoted in Kenneth McRoberts, *Misconceiving Canada*, p. 8.
36 Arthur Silver, *The French-Canadian Idea of Confederation*, quoted in ibid., p. 12.

37 For insightful historical accounts of the Confederation Debates, see Donald
    Creighton, *The Road to Confederation* (Toronto: Macmillan of Canada, 1964);
    and William L. Morton, *The Critical Years: The Union of British North America,
    1857–1873* (Toronto: McClelland and Stewart, 1964).
38 Black, *Divided Loyalties*, p. 4.
39 See Alan C. Cairns, 'The Judicial Committee and its Critics,' *Canadian Jour-
    nal of Political Science* 4, no. 3 (1971), pp. 301–45.
40 For a particularly good overview of competing visions at the time of the
    Meech Lake Accord, refer to Katherine E. Swinton and Carol J. Rogerson,
    eds., *Competing Constitutional Visions: The Meech Lake Accord* (Toronto: Cars-
    well, 1988).
41 Franz Neumann, 'On the Theory of the Federal State,' in *The Democratic and
    the Authoritarian State* (Glencoe: Free Press, 1957).
42 For earlier assessments of distinct visions of the federal principle in Can-
    ada, particularly in the period preceding patriation in 1982, see Mallory,
    'The Five Faces of Canadian Federalism'; Black, *Divided Loyalties*; and Garth
    Stevenson; *Unfulfilled Union: Canadian Federalism and National Unity*, rev. ed.
    (Toronto: Gage, 1982).
43 Judge Loranger was an influential jurist who published a series of constitu-
    tional texts in 1883, in which he gave form to the compact theory as a last-
    ing constitutional interpretation.
44 Royal Commission on Aboriginal Peoples (RCAP), *Partners in Confedera-
    tion: Aboriginal Peoples, Self-Government and the Constitution* (Ottawa: Minis-
    ter of Supply and Services, 1993), pp. 22–3.
45 Tully, *Strange Multiplicity*, p. 142.
46 Ramsay Cook, *Provincial Autonomy, Minority Rights and the Compact Theory*,
    Study No. 4 of the Royal Commission on Bilingualism and Biculturalism
    (Ottawa: Queen's Printer, 1969).
47 Stanley, 'Act or Pact: Another Look at Confederation,' p. 2.
48 Stevenson, *Unfulfilled Union*, p. 56.
49 Henri Bourassa, *Le patriotisme canadien-français* (Montreal: La Cie de publi-
    cation de la Revue canadienne, 1902), p. 8.
50 Rocher and Smith, 'The Four Dimensions of Canadian Federalism,' pp. 24–
    5.
51 Cairns, *Charter versus Federalism : The Dilemmas of Constitutional Reform*, p. 45.
52 The Canadian Senate is largely ineffective as a central body for regional
    representation because members are federally appointed, it lacks the legiti-
    macy that would come from elections by the people, and does not strictly
    adhere to a principle that would guarantee it a suitable distribution of seats
    among the provinces.

53 Joan Boase, 'The Spirit of Meech Lake,' in D. P. Shugarman and R. Whitaker, eds., *Federalism and Political Community* (Peterborough: Broadview Press, 1989), p. 212.
54 Kenneth McRoberts, 'Canada and the Multinational State,' in *Canadian Journal of Political Science* 34, no. 4 (December 2001), pp. 683–713.
55 Quoted in Cairns, *Charter versus Federalism*, p. 38.
56 For a deeper treatment, see Louis Balthazar, 'The Faces of Quebec Nationalism,' in Alain-G. Gagnon, ed., *Quebec: State and Society, Second Edition* (Scarborough: Nelson Canada, 1993); and Michel Venne, ed., *Vive Québec? New Thinking and New Approaches to the Quebec Nation* (Toronto: James Lorimer and Company Publications, 2001).
57 Speech of 6 February 1865, *Parliamentary Debates on the Subject of the Confederation of the British North America Provinces*, 8th Provincial Parliament of Canada, 3rd Session (Quebec City: Hunter, Rose and Co., 1865), p. 29.
58 *La Minerve*, Montreal, 1 July 1867.
59 Quoted in Rocher and Smith, 'The Four Dimensions of Canadian Federalism,' p. 30.
60 For a more developed reflection on the appeal of asymmetrical federalism as a basis for Quebec-Canada relations, see Alain-G. Gagnon, 'The Moral Foundation of Asymmetrical Federalism: A Normative Exploration of the Case of Quebec and Canada,' in A.-G. Gagnon and J. Tully, eds., *Multinational Democracy* (Cambridge: Cambridge University Press, 2001), pp. 319–37.
61 Government of Quebec, *Quebec-Canada: A New Deal* (Quebec City, 1979), p. 42.
62 For an analysis of the Bélanger-Campeau Commission's impact, see Alain-G. Gagnon and Daniel Latouche, *Allaire, Bélanger, Campeau et les autres* (Montreal: Québec Amérique, 1992).
63 Rocher and Smith, 'The Four Dimensions of Canadian Federalism,' p. 32.
64 For an excellent overview of Aboriginal peoples' relationship to the federal system, see Frances Abele and Michael J. Prince, 'Aboriginal Governance and Canadian Federalism: A To-Do List for Canada,' in Rocher and Smith, eds., *New Trends in Canadian Federalism*, pp. 135–61.
65 Kiera Ladner, 'Treaty Federalism: An Indigenous Vision of Canadian Federalisms,' ibid., pp. 167–94.
66 Royal Commission on Aboriginal Peoples (RCAP), *Report of the Royal Commission on Aboriginal Peoples*, vol. 2 (Ottawa: Canada Communications Group, 1996), pp. 193–4.
67 James Tully, 'Aboriginal Peoples: Negotiating Reconciliation,' in James Bickerton and Alain-G. Gagnon, eds., *Canadian Politics*, 3rd ed. (Peterborough: Broadview Press, 1999), pp. 413–41.

68 Donald V. Smiley, *The Canadian Political Nationality* (Toronto: Methuen, 1967), p. 2.
69 Gibbins, 'The Interplay of Political Institutions and Political Communities,' pp. 423–38.
70 Joseph Pope, *Correspondence of Sir John Macdonald* (Toronto: Oxford University Press, 1921), pp. 74–5.
71 For more on the national policy and its nation-building capacities, see Stevenson, *Unfulfilled Union* pp. 180–1.
72 Smiley, *The Canadian Political Nationality,* p 5.
73 See Peter B. Waite, *The Life and Times of Confederation 1864–1867* (Toronto: University of Toronto Press, 1962), p. 116, cited in ibid.
74 See Doug Owram, *The Government Generation: Canadian Intellectuals and the State, 1900–1945* (Toronto: University of Toronto Press, 1986).
75 The program of the Cooperative Commonwealth Federation, adopted at the first national convention held at Regina, Saskatchewan, 19–21 July 1933.
76 Pierre Elliott Trudeau, *Federalism and the French-Canadians* (Toronto: Macmillan of Canada, 1968), p. 193.
77 The Task Force on Canadian Unity, *A Future Together: Observations and Recommendations* (Ottawa: 1979), p. 48.
78 R. Kenneth Carty and W. Peter Ward, 'The Making of a Canadian Political Citizenship,' in Carty and Ward, eds., *National Politics and Community in Canada* (Vancouver: University of British Columbia Press, 1986), p. 75. For a more in-depth analysis of Trudeau's political philosophy, see James P. Bickerton, Stephen Brooks, and Alain-G. Gagnon, *Six penseurs en quête de liberté, d'égalité et de communauté* (Quebec City: Les presses de l'Université Laval, 2003), pp. 129–57.
79 For a more detailed treatment of Trudeau's vision, see Hugh Donald Forbes, 'Trudeau's Moral Vision,' in Anthony A. Peacock, ed., *Rethinking the Constitution* (Toronto: Oxford University Press, 1996), pp. 17–39.
80 See Alain-G. Gagnon, 'Everything Old Is New Again: Quebec, Canada and Constitutional Impasse,' in Frances Abele, ed., *How Ottawa Spends: The Politics of Fragmentation, 1991–92* (Ottawa: Carleton University Press, 1991), pp. 63–105.
81 Daniel J. Elazar, *Exploring Federalism* (Tuscaloosa: University of Alabama Press, 1987), p. 66.
82 Charles Taylor, 'The Deep Challenge of Dualism,' in Alain-G. Gagnon, ed., *Quebec: State and Society* (Scarborough: Nelson Canada, 1993), pp. 82–95.
83 Michael Burgess, 'Managing Diversity in Federal Societies: Conceptual Lenses and Comparative Perspectives,' paper presented at the Conference on Federalism, Université du Québec à Montréal, Montreal, 1 April 2005.

4. Distinct 'National' Models of Integration

1 Will Kymlicka and Wayne Norman note that citizens' perceptions about their political communities, their sense of belonging and level of commitment, have become an increasingly salient concern for contemporary political theorists, and that this is partly due to the challenge of integrating minority groups in established liberal democracies. In their words, 'the health and stability of a modern democracy depends, not only on the justice of its institutions, but also on the quality and attitude of its citizens: e.g. their sense of identity, and how they view potentially competing forms of national, regional, ethnic or religious identities; their ability to tolerate and work together with others who are different from themselves; their desire to participate in the political process in order to promote the public good and hold political authorities accountable; ... Without citizens who possess these qualities, the ability of liberal societies to function successfully progressively diminishes.' Will Kymlicka and Wayne Norman, eds., *Citizenship in Diverse Societies* (Oxford: Oxford University Press, 2000), p. 6.

2 Will Kymlicka, *Multicultural Citizenship: A Liberal Theory of Minority Rights* (New York: Oxford University Press, 1995), p. 193.

3 Christian Joppke, 'Multiculturalism and Immigration: A Comparison of the United States, Germany and Great Britain,' *Theory and Society* 25 (1996), p. 449.

4 See Michael Sandel, *Liberalism and the Limits of Justice* (Cambridge: Cambridge University Press, 1982); J. Raz, *The Morality of Freedom* (Oxford: Clarendon, 1986); and Charles Taylor, 'The Politics of Recognition,' in Amy Gutmann, ed., *Multiculturalism and the Politics of Recognition* (Princeton: Princeton University Press, 1994).

5 Joppke, 'Multiculturalism and Immigration,' p. 452.

6 Iris Marion Young, *Inclusion and Democracy* (Oxford: Oxford University Press, 2000), p. 7.

7 For more on multiculturalism's challenge to liberal models of citizenship, see Andrea Semprini, *Le Multiculturalisme* (Paris: Les presses universitaires de France, 1997).

8 This point was made by André Laurendeau as far back as 1965, in the preliminary report of the Bilingualism and Biculturalism Commission. See 'André Laurendeau: à la recherche de l'égalité politique et de la justice sociale,' in James P. Bickerton, Stephen Brooks, and Alain-G. Gagnon, *Six penseurs en quête de liberté, d'égalité et de communauté : Grant, Innis, Laurendeau, Rioux, Taylor et Trudeau* (Quebec City: Les Presses de l'Université Laval, 2003), pp. 59–76.

9 See Young, *Inclusion and Democracy,* in particular ch. 3, where she provides a review of arguments which construct group specific justice claims as an assertion of group identity and argue that the claims endanger democratic communication because they only divide the polity into selfish interest groups.

10 Kymlicka, *Multicultural Citizenship,* pp. 174–5.

11 Wsevolod Isajiw, 'Social Evolution and the Values of Multiculturalism,' paper presented at the ninth biennial conference of the Canadian Ethnic Studies Association, Edmonton, Alberta, 14–17 October 1981, cited in Evelyn Kallen, 'Multiculturalism: Ideology, Policy and Reality,' *Journal of Canadian Studies* 17, no. 1 (Spring 1982), p. 52.

12 Taylor, 'The Politics of Recognition,' p. 25.

13 Will Kymlicka, *Théories récentes sur la citoyenneté* (Ottawa: Multiculturalisme et Citoyenneté Canada, 1992), p. 45 (our translation).

14 The Couture-Cullen Agreement, signed in 1978, would grant extensive powers in recruitment and reception to the Quebec government.

15 Joseph H. Carens, *Culture, Citizenship and Community: A Contextual Exploration of Justice and Evenhandedness* (Oxford: Oxford University Press, 2000), p. 128. Alan Patten highlights three main arguments that support collective language rights, particularly in vulnerable societal cultures. First, the 'public access' argument claims that citizens ought to be permitted to receive public services in their language. Second, the 'social mobility' argument recognizes that people ought to be able to communicate with the wider network of people in order to be able adequately to access a full range of social and economic opportunities. Finally, the 'democratic participation' version stresses the requirement that people ought to be able to deliberate and debate with their fellow citizens as a matter of contributing to the democratic process. For Patten, the second is most convincing, since it allows individuals to access the societal culture that provides the context of choice necessary for personal autonomy and well-being, since they may draw upon a wider range of opportunities and options. In any case, Patten provides a strong normative framework with which to evaluate the role of communication in the debate over individual and collective rights. See Alan Patten, 'The Rights of Internal Linguistic Minorities,' in Avigail Eisenberg and Jeffrey Spinner-Halev, eds., *Minorities within Minorities: Equality, Rights and Diversity* (Cambridge: Cambridge University Press, 2005), pp. 141–3.

16 Allophones are defined as members of Quebec society whose mother tongues are neither English (anglophone) nor French (francophone). It is a significant group with regards to any discussion of citizenship in that they are, in large part, subjects of integration for the host society.

17 Michael D. Behiels, *Quebec and the Question of Immigration: From Ethnocentrism to Ethnic Pluralism 1900–1958* (Ottawa: Canadian Historical Association, 1991).
18 Marcel Gilbert, *Autant de façons d'être Québécois. Plan d'action à l'intention des communautés culturelles* (Quebec City: Ministry of Communications, Direction générale des publications gouvernementales, 1981).
19 On 1 November 1999 the minister of citizen relations and immigration, Robert Perreault, attempted to recast the model by announcing a new course of action that would emphasize a 'civic contract,' more broadly defined. This new approach was designed to focus less on integration as a specific policy field and more on the 'needs of Quebec society in its entirety.' The reciprocity implied by the moral contract was not significantly altered, yet in fact the policy resulted in a decentralization of services of integration to more local geographical centers. Conceptually, the policy did not significantly alter the notion that integration is a reciprocal endeavour that involves obligations and entitlements for both the host society and minorities and immigrants. See Robert Perreault, 'Notes pour une allocution de Monsieur Robert Perreault sur la réforme des services d'intégration et de francisation' (Quebec City: Ministère de Relations avec les citoyens et de l'Immigration, 1999). (www.mrci.gouv.qc.ca/775_2.asp)
20 For more on the principles of the common public culture as it is understood in Quebec, see Julien Harvey, 'Culture publique, intégration et pluralisme,' *Relations* (October 1991); and Gary Caldwell, 'Immigration et la nécessité d'une culture publique commune,' *L'Action Nationale* 78, no. 8 (October 1988); see also Gary Caldwell, *La culture publique commune* (Quebec City: Éditions Nota Bene, 2001).
21 Gouvernement du Québec, *Au Québec pour bâtir ensemble. Énoncé de politique en matière d'immigration et d'intégration* (Quebec City: Ministère des communautés culturelles et de l'immigration du Québec, Direction des communications, 1990), p. 15 (our translation).
22 Gouvernement du Québec, Conseil des relations interculturelles, 'Culture publique commune et cohésion sociale: le contrat moral d'intégration des immigrants dans un Québec francophone, démocratique et pluraliste,' in *Gérer la diversité dans un Québec francophone, démocratique et pluraliste : principes de fond et de procédure pour guider la recherche d'accommodements raisonnables*, (1994), p. 11 (our translation).
23 Carens, *Culture, Citizenship and Community*, p. 131.
24 François Rocher, Guy Rocher, and Micheline Labelle, 'Pluriethnicité, citoyenneté et intégration: de la souveraineté pour lever les obstacles et les ambiguités,' *Cahiers de recherche sociologique* 25 (1995), p. 221 (our translation).

25 Ibid., p. 225 (our translation).
26 France Giroux, 'Le nouveau contrat national est-il possible dans une démo-cracie pluraliste? Examen comparatif des situations française, canadienne et québécoise,' *Politique et sociétés* 16, no. 3 (1997), p. 137 (our translation).
27 Gouvernement du Québec, *Gérer la diversité*, p. 13 (our translation).
28 Harvey, 'Culture publique, intégration et pluralisme,' p. 239.
29 Michel Pagé, 'Intégration, identité ethnique et cohésion sociale', in Fernand Ouellet and Michel Pagé, eds., *Pluriethnicité et société: Construire un espace commun* (Quebec City: Institut québécois de recherche sur la culture [IQRC], 1991), pp. 146–7 (our translation and emphasis).
30 Gouvernement du Québec, *La gestion de la diversité et l'accommodement rai-sonnable*, Ministère des communautés culturelles et de l'immigration, Mon-treal, quoted in Rocher et al., 'Pluriethnicité, citoyenneté et intégration,' p. 225.
31 Mouvement pour une école moderne et ouverte (MEMO), the Commission of the Estates General on the Situation and Future of the French Language in Quebec, Montreal, 23 October 2000.
32 See chapter 2 for a brief introduction to the recommendations of the Lau-rendeau-Dunton Commission, in which the primary concern of constitu-tional reform was to accommodate Quebec in a dualist conception of Canada.
33 Yasmeen Abu-Laban, 'The Politics of Race, Ethnicity and Immigration: The Contested Arena of Multiculturalism into the Twenty-First Century,' in James P. Bickerton and Alain-G. Gagnon, eds., *Canadian Politics*, 3rd ed., (Peterborough: Broadview Press, 1999), p. 466.
34 Raymond Breton, 'Multiculturalism and Canadian Nation-Building,' in Alan C. Cairns and Cynthia Williams, eds., *The Politics of Gender, Ethnicity and Language in Canada* (Toronto: University of Toronto Press, 1986), p. 48.
35 Pierre Elliott Trudeau, cited by Linda Cardinal and Claude Couture, 'L'immigration et le multiculturalisme au Canada: la genèse d'une problé-matique', in Manon Tremblay, ed., *Les politiques publiques canadiennes* (Sainte-Foy: Les Presses de l'Université Laval, 1998), pp. 249–50 (their emphasis, our translation).
36 Kallen, 'Multiculturalism,' p. 54.
37 Canada, House of Commons Debates, statement of Prime Minister Trudeau, 8 October 1971.
38 Abu-Laban, 'Politics of Race,' p. 471.
39 Linda Cardinal and Claude Couture, 'L'immigration et le multicultural-isme,' p. 251.
40 Abu-Laban, 'Politics of Race,' p. 472.

41 Vince Seymour Wilson, 'The Tapestry Vision of Canadian Multicultural-
    ism,' *Canadian Journal of Political Science* 26, no. 4 (1993), p. 657.
42 Rainer Knopff and Fred L. Morton, *Charter Politics* (Scarborough: Nelson
    Canada, 1991), p. 88, quoted in ibid.
43 Joppke, 'Multiculturalism and Immigration,' p. 454. Joppke compares
    Germany, Great Britain, and the United States.
44 Since Quebec has negotiated bilateral agreements with Ottawa in matters
    of immigration, the central government has signed parallel agreements
    with all of the other member states of the federation except Ontario in order
    to offset the perception that Quebec has made asymmetrical gains. See
    Leslie Seidle and Gina Bishop, 'Public Opinion on Asymmetrical Federal-
    ism: Growing Openness or Continuing Ambiguity?' (Institute of Intergov-
    ernmental Relations, School of Policy Studies, Queen's University,
    Asymmetry Series, 2005), p. 11.
45 Morton Weinfeld, 'Myth and Reality in the Canadian Mosaic: "Affective
    Ethnicity",' *Canadian Ethnic Studies* 13 (1981), p. 94.
46 Yasmeen Abu-Laban and Christina Gabriel, *Selling Diversity: Immigration,
    Multiculturalism, Employment Equity and Globalization* (Peterborough: Broad-
    view Press, 2002), p. 124.
47 For more on these cutbacks, see Leslie Pal, *Interests of State: The Politics of
    Language, Multiculturalism and Feminism in Canada*, (Montreal and Kingston:
    McGill-Queen's University Press, 1993).
48 See Michael Mandel, *The Charter of Rights and the Legalization of Politics in
    Canada* (Toronto: Thompson Educational Publishing, 1989).
49 Gilles Bourque and Jules Duchastel, 'Multiculturalisme, pluralisme et com-
    munauté politique: le Canada et le Québec,' in Mikhaël Elbaz and Denise
    Helly, eds., *Mondialisation, citoyenneté et multiculturalisme* (Sainte-Foy: Les
    Presses de l'Université Laval, 2000), pp. 147–70.
50 Will Kymlicka, 'Ethnicity in the USA,' in Montserrat Guibernau and John
    Rex, eds., *The Ethnicity Reader: Nationalism, Multiculturalism and Migration*
    (Cambridge: Polity Press, 1997), p. 240. See also Bourque and Duchastel,
    'Multiculturalisme, pluralisme et communauté politique,' p. 159, where the
    authors argue that Canadian multiculturalism is in large part a product of a
    refusal to define the country in multinational terms. The Canadian political
    community is thus in itself constructed around the negation of multination-
    alism precisely because of the perceived imperative to undermine Quebec's
    place as a national minority.
51 For more on the distinction between national minorities and polyethnic
    communities in the framing of citizenship status, see Gilles Paquet, 'Politi-
    cal Philosophy of Multiculturalism,' in John W. Berry and Jean A. Laponce,

eds., *Ethnicity and Culture in Canada* (Toronto: University of Toronto Press, 1994), pp. 60–80.

52 For more on the argument that official multiculturalism represents a wholesale redefinition of Canada's constitutional order in terms of collective identity references, see Fernand Dumont, 'La fin d'un malentendu historique,' in *Raisons Communes* (Montreal: Éditions du Boréal, 1995), pp. 33–48; and Gilles Bourque and Jules Duchastel, 'La représentation de la communauté,' in *L'identité fragmentée* (Montreal: Éditions Fides, 1996), pp. 29–51.

53 Giroux, 'Le nouveau contrat,' p. 141 (our translation).

54 Gilles Bourque, Jules Duchastel and Victor Armony, 'De l'universalisme au particularisme: Droits et citoyenneté,' in Josiane Ayoub, Bjarne Melkevic, and Pierre Robert, eds., *L'Amour des lois* (Sainte-Foy/Paris: Les Presses de l'Université Laval/l'Harmattan, 1996), p. 240.

55 Kymlicka's work is mainly directed towards the contentions of Neil Bissoondath, who asserts that in the Canadian model minority cultures are recognized, *a priori*, in a vacuum of time and space, which tends towards ghettoization and fragmentation in terms of allegiance to a larger polity. Bissoondath argues this point forcefully, labelling the phenomenon 'cultural apartheid.' The contention here is that multiculturalism in effect defines culture provisionally – in a static sense – and prohibits full social interactivity. In other words, the dynamic nature of cultural sources of meaning are neglected, resulting in the stagnant 'folklorization' or 'commodification' of cultural production, reducing culture to 'a thing that can be displayed, performed, admired, bought, sold or forgotten ... [it is] a devaluation of culture, its reduction to bauble and kitsch.' As such, neither unity or citizen dignity accrued from cultural recognition is achieved in such a context. This is the result of recognizing cultures in juxtaposition without any expectation that such cultures may contribute to the overall direction of the larger society in an evolutionary interplay of ideas. The substantive elements of minority cultures, their bases of meaning, are virtually predetermined and unchanging, disregarding the very real effects of displacement into a new context. See Will Kymlicka, *Finding Our Way: Rethinking Ethnocultural Relations in Canada* (Toronto: Oxford University Press, 1998); and Neil Bissoondath, *Selling Illusions: The Cult of Multiculturalism in Canada* (Toronto: Penguin Books, 1994), p. 83.

56 Kymlicka, *Finding Our Way*, pp. 17–19.

57 Bhikhu Parekh, *Rethinking Multiculturalism: Cultural Diversity and Political Theory* (London: Macmillan, 2000).

58 Jeremy Webber, *Reimagining Canada: Language, Culture, Community and the*

Canadian Constitution (Montreal: McGill-Queen's University Press, 1994). See, in particular, ch. 6, 'Language, Culture and Political Community,' pp. 183–229.

59 Carens, *Culture, Citizenship and Community*, p. 133.

60 See Pierre Boyer, Linda Cardinal and David Headon, eds., *From Subjects to Citizens: A Hundred Years of Citizenship in Australia and in Canada* (Ottawa: University of Ottawa Press, 2004).

61 Labelle, *Immigration et diversité ethnoculturelle*, p. 14.

62 Christian Joppke and Ewa Morawska, in discussing the tendency of contemporary liberal states to converge in their discourse and treatment of immigrant integration, assume that Quebec is paying lip service to cultural pluralism while its nation-building efforts are necessarily monocultural. To quote them: 'Consider the case of Quebec, the secessionist French-speaking province of Canada, which shows that in a world of liberal states even an *extreme nation-building project* must bow to the dominant rhetoric of cultural pluralism. Because of its nation-building (*and thus monocultural*) ambition, Quebec has always rejected the official multiculturalism practiced since the early 1970's by the Canadian government' (our emphasis); see 'Integrating Immigrants in Liberal Nation-States: Policies and Practices,' in Joppke and Morawska, eds., *Toward Assimilation and Citizenship* (New York: Palgrave Macmillan, 2003), p. 9.

63 Kenneth McRoberts reminds us of this essential distinction between nation-states and internal nations. In his words, 'With the nation of the nation-state, the citizenship laws of the state provide clear answers as to who is a member of the nation and who is not. The internal nation may not have a central institution to perform this task'; McRoberts, 'Managing Cultural Differences in Multinational Democracies,' in Gagnon et al., eds., *The Conditions of Diversity in Multinational Democracies*, pp. iii–iv.

64 Daiva Stasiulis, in an introductory piece on the reconfiguration of Canadian citizenship, points out new developments in citizenship studies in Canada, and implicitly subsumes Quebec's societal project under the broad heading of an emerging 'multiplicity of citizenships': 'A feature ... of citizenship is the multiplicity of citizenships that currently exist in the geo-political territory of Canada ... Several of the contributions to this issue are informed by an understanding of the harsh reality of the inequality and the disempowering aspects of the current arrangements of power inscribed in contemporary Canadian citizenship – for communities such as First Nations, migrants, gays and lesbians, and children – yet several are also animated by a heady and impassioned sense of new boundary-challenging options and opportunities, under changed social conditions, deriving espe-

cially from the rich legacies of communities, and the creativity and culture-setting agendas of contemporary social movements (aboriginal, Québécois, diasporic, queer, children); Stasiulis, 'Introduction: Reconfiguring Canadian Citizenship,' *Citizenship Studies* 6, no. 4 (2002), p. 367.

65 Kymlicka's concern for liberalism has led him to discount any societal culture that places illiberal internal restrictions on its citizens as illegitimate. For Kymlicka, the Quebec model is very much in line with most liberal democracies in its commitment to liberal citizenship. See Kymlicka, *Multicultural Citizenship*, pp. 75–130. Joseph Carens agrees with this conclusion. See Carens, *Culture, Citizenship and Community*, pp. 107–39.

66 See Jocelyn Maclure, 'Narratives and Counter-Narratives of Identity in Quebec,' in Alain-G. Gagnon, ed., *Quebec: State and Society*, 3rd. ed. (Peterborough: Broadview Press, 2004), pp. 33–50. Maclure offers an excellent overview of the main tenets of thought on Quebec's self-interpretation, from 'melancholic nationalism' to anti-nationalist discourses, and their implications for political sovereignty that dominated the era of the Quiet Revolution. He then moves on to discuss more contemporary foundations of collective consciousness and their reconciliation with an increasingly pluralistic society. It is these latter debates that are addressed here.

67 See Michael Keating, *Plurinational Democracy: Stateless Nations in a Post-Sovereignty Era* (Oxford: Oxford University Press, 2001).

68 Fernand Dumont, *Raisons communes* (Montreal : Boréal, 1997), p. 66 (our translation).

69 Nicole Gagnon, 'Comment peut-on être Québécois? Note critique,' *Recherches sociologiques* 41, no. 3 (2000), p. 545, quoted in Maclure, 'Narratives and Counter-Naratives,' p. 50.

70 Michel Seymour, *La nation en question* (Montreal : Hexagone, 1999).

71 Conseil des relations interculturelles, *Un Québec pour tous ses citoyens: Les défis actuels d'une démocratie pluraliste* (Quebec City: Bibliothèque nationale du Québec, 1997); Ministère des Relations avec les citoyens et de l'Immigration, *Forum national sur la citoyennete et l'intégration* (Quebec City: Government of Quebec/MRCI, Publications officielles du Gouvernement, 2000).

72 In recent manifestations of Canadian policies on immigration, language, multiculturalism and citizenship, and in part as a response to criticisms related to the potential fragmentation of identity due to the active promotion of ancestral cultures, the central government has begun to elaborate a new discourse that emphasizes national unity and territorial integrity as a condition of belonging; that is, an active Canadianization of new immigrants. For Micheline Labelle and François Rocher, these effects of the ceremony of citizenship operate outside of any reference to

Quebec symbols of identity. See Micheline Labelle and François Rocher, 'De la politique québécoise de l'immigration au débat sur la citoyenneté: Regards critiques sur une gestion concurrentielle de la diversité,' paper presented at the conference 'Jornada immigració i autogovern: Perspectives teòriques i institucionals, Universitat Pompeu Fabra, Barcelona, 27 June 2005.

73 Danielle Juteau, 'The Citizen Makes an Entrée: Redefining the National Community in Quebec,' *Citizenship Studies* 6, no. 4 (2002), p. 441.

74 On 20 March 1985, the Parti Québécois government of René Lévesque officially recognized that Aboriginal Nations in Quebec constitute distinct nations with a right to autonomy, in a resolution that was unanimously approved in the National Assembly.

75 Dimitrios Karmis, 'Pluralism and National Identity(ies) in Contemporary Quebec,' in Alain-G. Gagnon, ed., *Quebec: State and Society*, 3rd. ed. (Peterborough: Broadview Press, 2004), p. 87.

76 See *Briller parmi les meilleurs. La vision et les priorités d'action du gouvernement du Québec* (Québec: Gouvernement du Québec, 2004); and Québec, ministère des Relations avec les citoyens et de l'Immigration (MRCI), *Des valeurs partagées, des intérêts communs: Pour assurer la pleine participation des Québécois des communautés culturelles au développement du Québec, Plan d'action 2004–2005* (Montreal: Direction des affaires publiques et des communications, 2004).

77 Micheline Labelle and François Rocher, 'De la politique québécoise,' pp. 13–15.

5. Citizenship and Democracy

1 For a good overview of debates surrounding the role of the nation-state as a sovereign actor, see Geneviève Nootens, *Désenclaver la démocratie: Des Huguenots à la paix des Braves* (Montreal: Québec Amérique, 2004).

2 For the classic account, see John Rawls, *A Theory of Justice* (Oxford: Oxford University Press, 1972).

3 Thomas H. Marshall, *Citizenship and Social Class* (Cambridge: Cambridge University Press, 1965).

4 David Miller, 'Citizenship and Pluralism,' *Political Studies*, 43 (1995), p. 435.

5 See Will Kymlicka and Wayne Norman, 'Return of the Citizen: A Survey of Recent Work on Citizenship Theory,' in Ronald Beiner, ed., *Theorizing Citizenship* (Albany: State University of New York Press, 1995).

6 See Charles Taylor, 'The Politics of Recognition,' in Amy Gutmann, ed., *Multiculturalism: Examining the Politics of Recognition* (Princeton, NJ: Prince-

ton University Press, 1994); and Michael Sandel, *Liberalism and the Limits of Justice* (Cambridge: Cambridge University Press, 1982) for communitarian contributions to the debate, while Kymlicka's *Multicultural Citizenship* brought such normative accounts into the liberal framework.

7 See Charles Taylor, 'Democratic Exclusion (and Its Remedies?),' in Alan C. Cairns et al., eds., *Citizenship, Diversity and Pluralism: Canadian and Comparative Perspectives* (Montreal and Kingston: McGill-Queen's University Press, 1999), pp. 265–87.

8 Alan Patten, 'Liberal Citizenship in Multinational Societies,' in Alain-G. Gagnon and James Tully, eds., *Multinational Democracies* (Cambridge: Cambridge University Press, 2001), pp. 279–98.

9 Note that this is not an appeal to traditional republicanism in which all particular identities are to be subject to the primacy of loyalty to the political unit. More robust versions of citizenship in the liberal tradition include a set of minimal safeguards against the incursion of the state as a representative of the larger society.

10 See, for example, Charles Taylor, 'Cross-purposes: The Liberal-Communitarian Debate,' in Nancy L. Rosenblum, ed., *Liberalism and the Moral Life* (Cambridge, Mass.: Harvard University Press, 1989), pp. 159–82; and Will Kymlicka and Wayne Norman, 'Return of the Citizen,' in Beiner, ed., *Theorizing Citizenship*, pp. 283–322.

11 Miller, 'Citizenship and Pluralism,' p. 435.

12 See Iris Marion Young, 'Polity and Group Difference: A Critique of the Ideal of Universal Citizenship,' *Ethics* 99 (1989), pp. 250–74.

13 This distinction is generally understood to form the liberal-communitarian debate. Postmodern perspectives are much more critical of the institution of citizenship, claiming that by definition citizenship creates categories of exclusion. This approach is largely relegated to deconstructionism and does not offer much in the way of reformulating the institution of citizenship itself as a unifying device, therefore it will not be pursued at length here.

14 John Rawls operates from the assumption that liberal democracies constitute a 'cooperative scheme in perpetuity.' The boundaries of the community are not in question when theorizing from a position of indifference. In classical liberal thought, justification for the existence of culturally based nation-states was somewhat neglected as well. The individuals in Locke's state of nature are homogeneous, while Kant's categorical imperative conceptualized individuals as having the same claims. Rational individuals in most liberal accounts are the same regardless of space and time. For more on this view, see Jeffrey Spinner, *The Boundaries of Citizenship: Race, Ethnicity*

and Nationality in the Liberal State (Baltimore: Johns Hopkins University Press, 1994), p. 2.

15 See Ulf Hedetoft and Mette Hjort, 'Introduction: Home and Belonging: Meanings, Images and Contexts,' in Hedetoft and Hjort, eds. *The Postnational Self: Belonging and Identity* (Minneapolis: University of Minnesota Press, 2002).

16 For further clarification of this conceptual category, see David Miller, 'Nationality in Divided Societies,' in Gagnon and Tully, *Multinational Democracies*, pp. 299–318. Miller distinguishes between 'rival' and 'nested' nationalities, with the former implying that the instruments of the state belong to one group at the expense of the other, and the latter implying some power-sharing formula.

17 James Tully, 'Introduction,' in ibid. pp. 2–3.

18 See Will Kymlicka, *Multicultural Citizenship: A Liberal Theory of Minority Rights* (Oxford, Clarendon Press, 1995), for further clarity on the distinction between various minority groups that challenge unitary liberal models of citizenship.

19 For more on the importance of social policy in engineering a sense of social citizenship in the context of competing national identities in Canada, see Keith G. Banting, 'Social Citizenship and the Multicultural Welfare State,' in Cairns et al. eds., *Citizenship, Diversity and Pluralism*, pp. 108–36.

20 Alan C. Cairns, 'The Fragmentation of Canadian Citizenship,' in William Kaplan, ed., *Belonging: Essays on the Meaning and Future of Canadian Citizenship* (Montreal and Kingston: McGill-Queen's University Press, 1993), pp. 181–220.

21 See, for example, Charles Taylor's assertion that citizenship should accommodate 'deep diversity' in defining citizenship, or Alan Patten's call for the promotion of an explicitly 'multinational' identity, or David Miller's conceptual category of 'nested nationalities,' where a political community includes dual allegiances and an overlap of national identities, and thus should strive to recognize each layer of identity in defining the whole. Charles Taylor, 'Shared and Divergent Values,' in Ronald L. Watts and Doug Brown, eds., *Options for a New Canada* (Toronto: University of Toronto Press, 1991), pp. 53–76; Alan Patten, 'Liberal Citizenship in Multinational Societies,' in Gagnon and Tully, eds., *Multinational Democracies*, pp. 279–98; and David Miller, 'Nationality in Divided Societies,' in ibid., pp. 299–318.

22 For a good sampling of arguments that generally advocate resistance towards the recognition of collective rights in a liberal polity, see Jeremy Waldron, 'Minority Cultures and the Cosmopolitan Alternative,' *University*

of Michigan Journal of Law Reform 25 (1992), pp. 751–93; Brian Barry, *Culture and Equality* (Cambridge: Polity Press, 2001); and Chandran Kukathas, 'Are There Any Cultural Rights?' *Political Theory* 20 (1992), pp. 105–39.

23 See Nootens, *Désenclaver la démocratie.*

24 Michael Keating, *Plurinational Democracy: Stateless Nations in a Post-Sovereignty Era* (Oxford: Oxford University Press, 2001).

25 Keating does not limit this approach to minority nations, but extends it to include various manifestations of post-sovereignty, including cities and regions. The key point is that these remain territorial conceptions of sovereignty, where communities coalesce around given spaces that need not be fixed in time. This is not an argument for radical post-territorial sovereignty of social identities to which the very concept of citizenship is not a useful organizing principle.

26 Michael Keating, *Beyond Sovereignty: Plurinational Democracy in a Post-Sovereign World* (The Desjardins Lecture), Quebec Studies Program, McGill University, 8 March 2001, p. 26.

27 Indeed, in November 2001, the United Nations Educational, Scientific and Cultural Organization (UNESCO) adopted a Universal Declaration on Cultural Diversity and its Action Plan. On 20 October 2005, a preliminary draft of a Convention on the Protection of the Diversity of Cultural Contents and Artistic Expressions was adopted. This charter aims to grant states the right to support their cultural industries as collective goods that ought not be subject to economic liberalization.

28 See Christian Joppke and Ewa Morawska, 'Integrating Immigrants in Liberal Nation-States: Policies and Practices,' in C. Joppke and E. Morawska, eds., *Toward Assimilation and Citizenship* (New York: Palgrave Macmillan, 2003).

29 Will Kymlicka has done pioneering work in this area. Kymlicka looks at the challenges that diversity poses for liberal citizenship and contends that the 'bundle of rights' for ethnocultural communities cannot be the same as those considered for national minorities. The former seek inclusion into a larger political community, or equalized conditions for integration, while the latter seek self-government rights that in many respects constitute a rejection of a citizenship as defined at the level of the multination. See Will Kymlicka, *Multicultural Citizenship: A Liberal Theory of Minority Rights* (Oxford: Clarendon Press, 1995), and *Finding Our Way: Rethinking Ethnocultural Relations in Canada* (Toronto: Oxford University Press, 1998).

30 Will Kymlicka, *Liberalism, Community and Culture* (Oxford: Clarendon Press, 1991), pp. 162–81.

31 For more on collective mobilization and nationalism, see Doug McAdam,

Sydney Tarrow, and Charles Tilly, *Dynamics of Contention* (New York: Cambridge University Press, 2001).

32 Ramon Maiz and Ferran Requejo, eds., *Democracy, Nationalism and Multiculturalism* (London and New York: Frank Cass, 2005), pp. 1–12.

33 Jane Jenson, 'Understanding Politics: Concepts of Identity in Political Science,' in James Bickerton and Alain-G. Gagnon, eds., *Canadian Politics*, 3rd. ed. (Peterborough: Broadview Press, 1999), p. 44.

34 See, for example, Wayne Norman, 'The Ideology of Shared Values: A Myopic Vision of Unity in a Multi-Nation State,' in Joseph Carens, ed., *Is Quebec Nationalism Just? Perspectives from English Canada* (Montreal and Kingston: McGill-Queen's University Press, 1995), pp. 137–59.

35 This term is generally attributed to Hans-Georg Gadamer.

36 Charles Taylor, 'Why Do Nations Have to Become States?,' in G. Laforest, ed., *Reconciling the Solitudes: Essays on Canadian Federalism and Nationalism* (Montreal and Kingston: McGill-Queen's University Press, 1993), p. 49.

37 Charles Taylor, 'Cross-Purposes: The Liberal-Communitarian Debate,' in Nancy Rosenblum, ed., *Liberalism and the Moral Life* (Cambridge: Cambridge University Press, 1991), p. 170.

38 See Michael Ignatieff, *The Rights Revolution* (Toronto: Anansi, 2000), particularly pp. 62–6, for a concise overview of Trudeau's approach to national unity.

39 For an overview of Trudeau's political philosophy, see J. Bickerton, S. Brooks, and A.-G. Gagnon, *Six penseurs en quête de liberté, d'égalité et de communauté: Grant, Innis, Laurendeau, Rioux, Taylor et Trudeau* (Quebec City: Les Presses de l'Université Laval, 2003), pp. 129–157.

40 Pierre Elliott Trudeau, 'The Multinational State in Canada: The Interaction of Nationalism in Canada,' *Canadian Forum*, June 1962.

41 Ignatieff, *The Rights Revolution*, p. 61.

42 See Nootens, *Désenclaver la démocratie*, particularly ch. 1, where she traces the emergence and consolidation of the nation-state.

43 In recent years, nationalism has also gained legitimacy as a complement to liberalism, with some observers highlighting its capacity to provide the solidarity and cohesion necessary for liberal values to take hold in any society. For example, Jeffrey Spinner notes that liberalism enhances the importance of language as a marker of identity. As such, the liberal ideal of equal opportunity could not be realized in Quebec unless language was institutionalized. By reducing the salience of ascriptive ethnic markers of identity, liberalism may increase the likelihood that people will attach themselves to national identities. For Spinner, nationalism is compatible with liberalism if two conditions are met. First, the nationalist movement should mobilize

around a speech community that is large enough to support the institutions of an industrial society. And second, the movement should be willing to construct a liberal, pluralistic public space. See Jeffrey Spinner, *The Boundaries of Citizenship: Race, Ethnicity and Nationality in the Liberal State* (Baltimore: Johns Hopkins University Press, 1994), p. 157. Conclusions commonly referring to postnational developments may be pointing to developments in liberal thought and practice that do not undermine the existence of the nation altogether, rather, they reinforce its relevance. Indeed, though diversity involves the acknowledgment of difference as a defining aspect of a particular political community, according to Yael Tamir, all liberal nations are nevertheless entitled to a public sphere in which they constitute a majority. See Yael Tamir, *Liberal Nationalism* (Princeton: Princeton University Press, 1993). The very logic of liberalism, by softening the edges of thick nationalism, is deemed by many to reflect a new phenomenon of postnationalism.

44 See Frédérick-Guillaume Dufour, *Patriotisme constitutionnel et nationalisme. Sur Jürgen Habermas* (Montreal: Éditions Liber, 2001), pp. 157–210.

45 Ignatieff, *The Rights Revolution*, p. 84.

46 'Universal' models of membership in a multinational context often exhibit strong majority nationalist pressures on the definition of the larger political community, in the sense that the will of the majority nation is reflected in public policy outcomes. See Alain-G. Gagnon, 'Undermining Federalism and Feeding Minority Nationalism: The Impact of Majority Nationalism in Canada,' in Alain-G. Gagnon, Montserrat Guibernau and François Rocher, eds., *The Conditions of Diversity in Multinational Democracies* (Montreal: Institute for Research on Public Policy, 2003), pp. 295–312.

47 See Kymlicka, *Multicultural Citizenship*.

48 See James Tully, 'Liberté et dévoilement dans les sociétés multinationales,' *Globe: Revue internationale d'études québécoises* 3, no. 1 (Autumn 1999), pp. 13–36.

49 See Martin Papillon and Luc Turgeon, 'Nationalism's Third Way? Comparing the Emergence of Citizenship Regimes in Quebec and Scotland,' in Gagnon, Guibernau and Rocher, eds., *The Condition of Diversity in Multinational Democracies*, pp. 315–45, for a good overview of the expanding citizenship regime in Quebec.

6. Contemporary Challenges and the Future of Canada

1 Michael Ignatieff, *The Rights Revolution* (Toronto: Anansi, 2000), p. 78.

2 See Alain-G. Gagnon, 'Everything Old Is New Again: Canada, Quebec and

208 Notes to pages 156–60

208   Notes to pages 156–60

208   Notes to pages 156–60

Constitutional Impasse,' in Frances Abele, ed., *How Ottawa Spends: The Politics of Fragmentation, 1991–92* (Ottawa: Carleton University Press, 1991), pp. 63–105.

3 Harvey Lazar, 'Non-Constitutional Renewal: Towards a New Equilibrium in the Federation,' in Harvey Lazar, ed., *Canada: The State of the Federation, 1997: Non-Constitutional Renewal* (Kingston: Institute of Intergovernmental Affairs, 1997), p. 5.

4 For more on the 'new public management' model in Canada, see Leslie A. Pal, 'New Public Management in Canada: New Whine in Old Battles?' in James Bickerton and Alain-G. Gagnon, eds., *Canadian Politics*, 4th ed. (Peterborough: Broadview Press, 2004), pp. 185–202.

5 Lazar, 'Non-Constitutional Renewal,' p. 7.

6 Thomas J. Courchene, 'The Changing Nature of Quebec-Canada Relations: From the 1980 Referendum to the Summit of the Canadas,' *Working Papers: Institute of Intergovernmental Relations* (Queen's University, 2004), p. 5.

7 Jennifer Smith, 'Informal Constitutional Development: Change by Other Means,' in Herman Bakvis and Grace Skogstad, eds., *Canadian Federalism: Performance, Effectiveness and Legitimacy* (Toronto: Oxford University Press, 2002), pp. 40–58.

8 Liberal Party of Canada, *Moving Canada Forward: The Paul Martin Plan for Getting Things Done* (Ottawa, 2004).

9 See the Report of the Commission on Fiscal Imbalance and Supporting Documents (Yves Séguin, Principal commissioner), http://www.desequilibrefiscal.gouv.qc.ca/en/document/publication.htm.

10 François Rocher, 'Les relations fédérales-provinciales à l'ère Martin,' in Michel Venne, ed., *L'annuaire du Québec, 2005* (Montreal: Fides, 2005), pp. 445–55.

11 See Alain-G. Gagnon and Joseph Garcea, 'Quebec and the Pursuit of Special Status,' in R.D. Olling and M.W. Westmacott, eds., *Perspectives on Canadian Federalism* (Scarborough: Prentice-Hall Canada, 1988), pp. 304–24.

12 Gérald Beaudoin, 'La philosophie constitutionnelle du rapport Pepin-Robarts,' in Jean-Pierre Wallot, ed., *Le débat qui n'a pas eu lieu: La commission Pepin-Robarts, quelque vingt ans après* (Ottawa: University of Ottawa Press, 2002), p. 86.

13 For a more detailed overview on the ruling, see Stephen Tierney, 'The Constitutional Accommodation of National Minorities in the UK and Canada: Judicial Approaches to Diversity,' in Alain-G. Gagnon, Montserrat Guibernau, and François Rocher, eds., *The Conditions of Diversity in Multinational Democracies* (Montreal: Institute for Research on Public Policy, 2003), pp. 169–206.

14 *Reference re Secession of Quebec*, [1998] 2 SCR.

15 James Tully, 'Liberté et dévoilement dans les sociétés plurinationales,' *Globe: Revue internationale d'études québécoises* 3, no. 1 (Autumn 1999), p. 30 (our translation).

16 Samuel V. LaSelva, 'Understanding Canada: Federalism, Multiculturalism, and the Will to Live Together,' in James Bickerton and Alain-G. Gagnon, eds., *Canadian Politics*, 4th ed. (Peterborough: Broadview Press, 2004), pp. 28–9.

17 See Andrée Lajoie, 'The Clarity Act and its Context,' in Alain-G. Gagnon, ed., *Quebec: State and Society*, 3rd ed. (Peterborough: Broadview Press, 2004), pp. 151–64.

18 For more on such spending practices, see the Commission of Inquiry into the Sponsorship Program and Advertising Activities (Justice John H. Gomery, Principal commissioner), http://www.gomery.ca.

19 François Rocher and Nadia Verrelli, 'Questioning Constitutional Democracy in Canada: From the Canadian Supreme Court Reference on Quebec Secession to the Clarity Act,' in Gagnon, Guibernau, and Rocher, eds., *The Conditions of Diversity in Multinational Democracies*, p. 218.

20 Rocher and Verrelli, 'Questioning Constitutional Democracy in Canada,' p. 217.

21 Roger Gibbins, 'Constitutional Politics,' in James Bickerton and Alain-G. Gagnon, eds., *Canadian Politics*, 4th ed. (Peterborough: Broadview Press, 2004), p. 141.

22 Michael Ignatieff identifies a prominent list of Canadian scholars who 'are making a theory out of the elemental experience of Canadian politics. The adjudication of rights claims between national minorities, aboriginal groups and individuals.' The list includes Will Kymlicka, Charles Taylor, James Tully, Peter Russell, and Guy Laforest. See Ignatieff, *The Rights Revolution*, p. 10. See also Kenneth McRoberts, *Misconceiving Canada: The Struggle for National Unity* (Toronto: Oxford University Press, 1997); Samuel LaSelva, *The Moral Foundations of Canadian Federalism: Paradoxes, Achievements and Tragedies of Nationhood* (Montreal and Kingston: McGill-Queen's University Press, 1996); Philip Resnick, 'Repenser le fédéralisme canadien: provinces, régions-provinces et nation-province,' in Alain-G. Gagnon and Jocelyn Maclure, eds., *Repères en mutation* (Montreal: Québec Amérique, 2001), pp. 377–91; and Simone Chambers, 'New Constitutionalism: Democracy, Habermas, and Canadian Exceptionalism,' in Ronald Beiner and Wayne Norman, eds., *Canadian Political Philosophy: Contemporary Reflections* (Toronto: Oxford University Press, 2001), pp. 63–77.

23 Ignatieff, *The Rights Revolution*, p. 120.

24 Indeed, René Lévesque had proposed a reciprocity arrangement in the application of language clauses at the Premier's Conference in St Andrews in 1978.

25 See Jeremy Webber, *Reimagining Canada: Language, Culture, Community and the Canadian Constitution* (Montreal and Kingston: McGill-Queen's University Press, 1994).

26 In 1978, the Parti Québécois adopted Quebec's law on popular consultation. For the first time in Canada, the door for popular sovereignty in constitutional matters had been opened. In a multinational federation, popular consultation cannot be conceived on a country-wide basis, since majority nationalism would prevail in most constitutional matters. Indeed, Pierre Trudeau's view of the Canadian Charter of Rights and Freedoms was that it would establish the sovereignty of a single people. We contend that exercises that draw upon popular sovereignty can only be legitimate if undertaken within constituent internal nations if the spirit of multinationalism is to be maintained in a federal setting. This spirit lies behind the approach advocated here.

27 For arguments against the legitimacy of mass participation in Canadian constitutionalism, see Janet Ajzenstat, 'Constitution Making and the Myth of the People,' in Curtis Cook, ed., *Constitutional Predicament: Canada and the Referendum of 1992* (Montreal and Kingston: McGill-Queen's University Press, 1994), pp. 112–26; and Michael Lusztig, 'Canada's Long Road to Nowhere: Why the Circle of Command Liberalism Cannot be Squared,' *Canadian Journal of Political Science* 32, no. 3 (September 1999), pp. 451–70.

28 See, for example, Jocelyn Maclure, 'The Politics of Recognition at an Impasse? Identity Politics and Democratic Citizenship,' *Canadian Journal of Political Science* 36, no. 1 (March 2003), pp. 3–21; Matthew Mendelsohn, 'Public Brokerage: Constitutional Reform, Public Participation and the Accommodation of Mass Publics,' ibid. 33, no. 2 (June 2000), pp. 245–73.

Index